Conquest to Dissolution 1067–1538

PER BELLVM PATRIA

The blazons on the front cover, left to right
Norman kings – the count of Eu – the Lusigan counts of Eu
Early dukes of Brittany – later dukes of Brittany – the Pelham family
Sir Thomas Hoo – Lord Hastings of Hastings – Angevin kings

The above blazons represent the Norman and Angevin royal arms and the blazons of most of the lords of the Rape of Hastings

The blazons on the back cover, left to right
Cinque Ports – early Sussex – the Laigle family – the de Luci family
Simon de Montfort – Abbot Hamo de Offyngton – John of Gaunt
Lancaster, York and early Tudor Royal kings – Sir Anthony Browne

These blazons relate more generally to the administrative links of eastern Sussex, and selected representatives of those who had major influence on the area

Conquest to Dissolution 1067–1538

A history of eastern Sussex, Battle, Bexhill, Hastings, Pevensey, Robertsbridge, Rye and Winchelsea

Keith Foord

Per Bellum Patria

Battle and District Historical Society Research Group 2019
Also published:
Keith Foord & Neil Clephane-Cameron: *1066 and the Battle of Hastings: Preludes, Events and Postscripts,* 2015, 2016, 2018 (revised)
George Kiloh: *The Brave Remembered: Battle at War 1914–1919,* 2015
Adrian and Sarah Hall: *Edmund Langdon and his World,* 2018

ISBN: 978-1-903099-04-9

Copyright © Battle and District Historical Society 2019

First published in the UK in 2019
by the Battle and District Historical Society
https://battlehistorysociety.com

All rights reserved. No part of this publication
may be reproduced, stored in a retrieval system,
or transmitted in any form or by any means,
electronic, mechanical, photocopying,
recording or otherwise, without
prior permission in writing from the Society

Typeset in Garamond by Helm Information
amandahelm@uwclub.net

Cover back ground illustration from a seal of Battle Abbey, front and back cover upper borders illustrate key blazons of persons or organisations of influence in eastern Sussex

Printed by Ingram's Lightning Source
Lightning Source states that it expects its paper suppliers to be environmentally responsible, and not use papers sourced from endangered old growth forests, forests of exceptional conservation value, or the Amazon Basin.

BDHS has no responsibility for the continuity or accuracy of URLs for external or third party websites, nor for the present or continuing accuracy or appropriateness of those websites referred to in this publication

Contents

Foreword		vii
A Timeline for eastern Sussex 1066 to 1538		ix
1.	Introduction	1
2.	Local influences of the Norman and Angevin Kings: 1067–1272	9
3.	Abbots of Battle Abbey 1070–1538	37
4.	A Critique of the Rolls of Battle Abbey	73
5.	Not just Battle Abbey: other religious houses in eastern Sussex to 1538	88
6.	The Great and Terrible King Edward I and his son: Battle and the Cinque Ports of eastern Sussex 1272–1327	113
7.	Warrior Abbots, Wars, Revolts and the Black Death: Edward III to Henry VI's usurpation 1327–1461	127
8.	Wars of the Roses, the rise of the Tudors and the Dissolution of the Monasteries 1461–1538	137
9.	Rapes of Sussex and Hundreds of the Rape of Hastings	141
10.	Lords and People of the Rape of Hastings to 1538	153
11.	The Lowey or Liberty of Pevensey to 1538	180
12.	Members of Parliament representing Sussex, Hastings, Rye and Winchelsea 1334 until 1538	185
13.	An End Piece	197
Appendices		200
Bibliography		201
Web Bibliography		209
Other recent books by members of BDHS		211
Index		212

The years that followed (1066) saw one of the most fundamental transformations in British History

Robert Bartlett (1950–)

Foreword

1066 remains a significant year, possibly the most significant year, in the history not only of England, but also of those many countries deeply influenced by British history. Famously it was not fought at Hastings but on a hillside in the countryside not far away, where an abbey was to be erected in penance for the deaths of those who died there and where a town to be named Battle grew up around it.

What is less well known is what happened after the battle – from 1067. The Norman conquerors imposed their own rule, but not without significant compromises with what their Saxon predecessors had left in place. This applies to both the organisation of how they ruled and influenced and to the structures they left for posterity. They built well, and not only castles but also Battle Abbey and many other religious foundations testify to their power base and deep sense of religion.

This book concerns the influences of kings, local lords and abbots in the area closest to the battlefield in Sussex, which is represented by the area now known as '1066 Country', or, as it is called here, eastern Sussex. Abbeys and their sister bodies such as priories were not just homes for praying monks and nuns but also centres of support for the local populations – they were in effect the precursors of the welfare state, though nothing as well organised, and after they disappeared, the English people suffered. The abbots were men of influence, and in Battle they reported directly to the king and not to a bishop; this status, known as a Peculiar, transferred to St Mary's Church after the Dissolution and lasted until the nineteenth century. The vicar is still known as a Dean.

This book is a sequel to that by Keith Foord and Neil Clephane-Cameron, *1066 and the Battle of Hastings – Preludes, Events and Postscripts,* which told in detail how the battle came to be fought, and what happened when it was being fought.

Keith Foord picks up the story of the Normanisation of eastern Sussex from 1067. The aftermath is described here from a local historical viewpoint, up to the point when Henry VIII dissolved the Abbeys in 1537–39. This is via periods of kingly rivalry, civil wars, the Black Death, rebellions, the creation of Parliament and the loss of almost all the parts of France that England had held. It was a time of constant change, with a major influence on how the now-United Kingdom behaves today.

George Kiloh
Chairman, Battle and District Historical Society,
2019

Time is like a river made up of things that happen, and its current is strong: no sooner does anything appear than it is carried away and another comes in its place, and will be carried away too.

Marcus Aurelius (AD 121–180)

A Timeline for Eastern Sussex 1066–1538

1066	Edward the Confessor dies Harold Godwinson crowned king William invades by sea, landing around Pevensey on morning of 28th or 29th September Battle of Hastings 14th October William crowned at Christmas
1067	William travels to Normandy via Pevensey, returns to Old Winchelsea
1069	Castelry of Hastings given to Count of Eu Rape of Pevensey given to Count of Mortain
1070	Ermenfrid's Penitentiary issued by this date. Building of Battle Abbey starts, led by Robert Blancard
1071	Initial post Conquest Rapes of Sussex all created by this date.
1072	Fifth Sussex Rape of William de Briouze, later called Rape of Bramber created
1076	Robert Blancard drowns in the Channel Gausbert appointed Abbot of Battle
1085	Charter by William I to the Abbey of Fécamp giving Steyning and the Manor of Bury in exchange for their possessions in Hastings William at Pevensey to embark for Normandy
1086	Domesday population of eastern Sussex estimated to have been about 3000
1087	William I dies William II (Rufus) becomes King of England and Robert Curthose Duke of Normandy
1088	Revolt against Rufus who besieges Pevensey Castle and captures Earl Odo and Robert de Mortain William de Warenne dies of wounds received at the siege De Mortain allowed to retain Pevensey
1090	Collegiate College of St Mary in the Castle founded within Hastings Castle by Robert d'Eu
1091	Rufus uses Hastings as a base
1093	Rufus again uses Hastings as a base from which to invade Normandy
1095	Rufus holds court at Hastings Consecration of first part of Battle Abbey Abbot Gausbert of Battle dies
1096	Henry appointed Abbot of Battle

1100	Rufus dies in a hunting accident. Younger brother Henry rapidly has himself crowned
1101	Henry I encamps at Wartling expecting Robert Curthose's army Curthose later landed at Portsmouth and was soon 'paid off' by Henry
1102	Death of Abbot Henry of Battle. No new abbot appointed In inter-abbacy a start is made on building St Marys Church in Battle William de Mortain forfeits Pevensey. Pevensey granted to Gilbert Laigle
1105	Henry I invades Normandy
1106	Henry invades Normandy again, wins the Battle of Tinchebrai and captures and imprisons Curthose
1107	Ralph of Caen appointed Abbot of Battle
1115	Possible consecration of St Mary's Church, Battle
1120	Henry I's son William drowns
1124	Abbot Ralph dies
1125	Abbot Warner of Canterbury appointed to Battle
1133	Last recorded notifications concerning Battle Abbey from Henry I, who had helped the Abbey since 1101
1135	Henry I died. Nephew Stephen crowned over Henry's daughter Matilda
1138	Abbot Warner induced to resign and abbacy of Battle given to Walter de Luci, brother of Richard de Luci, chief justiciar of England
1147	Pevensey Castle held by Gilbert de Clare, besieged by king Stephen. When taken given to Stephen's son, Eustace
1148	Dispute between Battle Abbey and the Bishop of Chichester about Battle's unique position as a Royal Peculiar Lands in Bexhill Hundred returned by Eu to Bishop of Chichester
1153	Henry, Matilda's son, invaded England Eustace died and Stephen recognised Henry as his heir. Al-Idrisi an Arabic geographer described Hastings in an atlas
1154	Stephen died and Henry of Anjou became King Henry II Bishop of Chichester and Pope Adrian IV try to excommunicate Abbot of Battle
1155	First three Cinque Ports established by Royal Charter Cinque Ports to provide 57 ships for 15 days each year Abbot Walter de Luci of Battle travels to Saumur on the Loire to meet king Henry II
1157	Pevensey Castle surrendered to the crown by King Stephen's second son William of Blois who had been set aside from the monarchy Legal case before the king involving Thomas à Becket and Richard de Luci re-states Battle Abbey's Royal Peculiar status

TIMELINE

1171	Abbot Walter de Luci died. Until 1175 his brother Richard de Luci 'presided' over the Abbey
1175	Odo of Canterbury appointed Abbot of Battle A new house for pilgrims was built outside Battle Abbey gate
1176	Abbey of Robertsbridge established at Salehurst. First Abbot called Denis
1180	Church at Brede founded by Fécamp Abbey Small abbey at Otham near Pevensey
1189	Henry II dies, Richard I (Lionheart) becomes king
1190	Approximate date of founding of the Augustinian Priory of the Holy Trinity at Hastings by Robert d'Eu
1191	Rye and Winchelsea become 'limbs' of Hastings and provide five times more ships for Cinque Ports than Hastings
1192	Abbot Denis of Robertsbridge sent with the Abbot of Boxley to find king Richard I
1195	First mention of St Michael's church in Hastings
1198	The same two Abbots as in 1192 acted as agents to the Pope for the Archbishop of Canterbury
1199	Richard I dies at Chinon John become king
1200	Odo dies. John of Dover elected Abbot of Battle
1201	King John deprives Ralph d'Eu of the Rape of Hastings Otham Abbey moves to Bayham to build a new abbey
1205	First mention of St Margaret's church in Hastings Otham and Brockley Abbeys combined at Bayham
1206	King John visits Battle Abbey
1207	Pevensey granted Royal Charter by King John
1208–11	Sometime between these years King John was bribed to confirm grants to Bayham Abbey
1209	Hospital of the Holy Cross established at Old Winchelsea
1211	John commissions new ships for the navy to be built at Winchelsea
1212	Abbot William of Robertsbridge acted as King's messenger
1213	John visits Battle Abbey twice whist preparing defences at the Cinque Ports
1214	Rape of Hastings restored to the Eu family
1215	1st Magna Carta. Richard of Horwode elected Abbot of Battle
1216	Civil war. Louis of France, married to Blanche, John's niece, invited by the barons to invade. King John orders Hastings and Pevensey Castles to be slighted John dies in October Henry III becomes king

1217	Civil war continues. Louis took refuge at Winchelsea but escapes via Rye as William Marshall closed in Peace treaty signed in September 3rd Magna Carta issued.
1219	A Hospital of St Bartholomew was established at Playden, just outside Rye by this date
1220	New settlement at Robertsbridge encouraged by the local Abbot
1222	The Abbot of Robertsbridge was sent as a messenger by the king, probably to the Pope
1225	Henry III visited the Cinque Ports New version of Magna Carta issued
1229	Michelham Priory founded as a daughter house of Hastings Priory
1233	First of a series of 'Great Storms' in English Channel recorded. Great floods on Romney Marsh
1235	Abbot Richard dies and Ralph of Coventry elected Abbot of Battle
1240	Abbot Ralph joins group protesting to the king about papal extortion First mention of St Peter's church in Hastings
1243	House of Eu forfeits the Rape of Hastings
1245	Foundation of Franciscan (Grey friars) Priory at Old Winchelsea before this date, possibly as early as 1224
1246	Peter of Savoy granted Pevensey Castle
1247	Henry III resumes ownership of Rye and Winchelsea from the Abbey of Fécamp for strategic defensive reasons. Fécamp retained manor of Brede
1250	About this time Robertsbridge Abbey moved from Salehurst to a new site just outside of Robertsbridge
1252	Last mention of Battle's Abbot Ralph of Coventry Old Winchelsea's sea walls breached (also in 1254)
1253	Weekly market granted at Robertsbridge
1257	Friary of the Sack established in Rye.
1258	Barons demanded sweeping reforms and 'Provisions of Oxford' agreed
1261	Henry III obtains papal bull proclaiming reforms unconstitutional De Montfort, Henry's brother in law, retires to France Reginald of Brecon appointed Abbot of Battle
1263	De Montfort returns
1264	Full civil war: Henry III moves aggressively through Ticehurst, Robertsbridge, Battle, Winchelsea and Herstmonceux on way to Battle of Lewes, which he loses on 14 May Henry III brought back to Battle Abbey by Simon de Montfort then taken to London Royalists holed up in Pevensey Castle besieged – held out until July 1265

TIMELINE

1265	Barons defeated at Battle of Evesham by Henry's son Edward Peter of Savoy receives Pevensey Castle
1266	Dictum of Kenilworth issued ending the Barons War. Cinque Ports had to send grovelling apologies for supporting the barons. Winchelsea refused to apologise and its leading citizens were executed in an assault led by prince Edward
1267	Hastings Collegiate Church of St Mary in the Castle becomes a royal free chapel after the death of Alix countess of Eu
1268	Rape of Hastings and the Earldom of Richmond granted to the Dukes of Brittany Pevensey resumed by the crown
1272	Henry II died and Edward I king – but away on the 8th Crusade
1274	Edward I crowned Old Winchelsea appeals for help as severely storm damaged Edward possibly visits Hastings, but there is no record of a visit to Winchelsea
1275	Rape of Arundel divided by this date into Rapes of Arundel and Chichester
1276	Edward I visits Battle Abbey then goes on to Winchelsea
1278	Edward I issued a Great Charter to the Cinque Ports
1280	Abbot Reginald resigns from Battle Abbey, Henry of Aylesford becomes Abbot Edward gave instructions to buy land on the hill of Iham for the purpose of building New Winchelsea Charter of land at Hastings identifies probable site of Haestingaceaster
1283	Edward instructs to start building New Winchelsea
1285	Winchelsea Franciscan friary rebuilt in New Winchelsea
1286	St Clement church, Hastings, destroyed by sea and rebuilt more inland
1287	Old Winchelsea's final destruction by storms The Hospitals of the Holy Cross and of St John moved to sites in New Winchelsea
1288	Freehold of New Winchelsea granted to the local burgesses by Edward I.
1290	Edward I grants an annual fair on St Bartholomew's Day for the hospital at Playden
1291	Churches of Saints Margaret, Michael, Peter, Leonard all recorded west of the Priory valley in Hastings
1292	Hospital of St Bartholomew created before this date at Winchelsea
1294	Hospital of St Mary Magdalene created before this date at Hastings Petronella de Cham gives 5 acres of land to support hospital
1295	Ship service demanded from the Cinque Ports Edward visits his fleet, lodging at Udimore, and visiting Winchelsea
1297–8	Edward returns, holding a court at Brede. Stays at Udimore, from where he summoned a Parliament that met in his absence in London He sailed with his fleet to Flanders
1300	Etchingham family construct Glottenham Castle at about this time

1302	Edward's final visit to eastern Sussex, visited mid Sussex in 1305 Hospital of St John the Baptist created before 1302 in Westham near Pevensey
1307	Death of Edward I. Edward II became king
1312	Edward II confirmed new charters for Battle Abbey which were of future legal value
1315	Edward II with Queen Isabella visited Hastings and Winchelsea; whilst at Winchelsea they bought 6000 litres of wine
1318	Edward II approved a Dominican priory at Winchelsea (Black friars)
1324	Edward II visited Battle Abbey, possibly also Robertsbridge Abbey Manor of Brede temporarily taken into the king's hands from Fécamp Abbey
1325	Queen Isabella sent to France to negotiate and refused to return
1326	Isabella and Roger Mortimer invade Edward's regime collapsed. He fled to Wales
1327	Edward II made to abdicate. Edward III became king
1330–40	Approximate date of the Auchinleck Roll of Battle Abbey
1337	Start of 100 Years War. King commanded Abbot Alan de Retlyng of Battle to defend the eastern Sussex coats and to fortify Battle Abbey
1338	Licence to crenelate Battle Abbey issued
1339	French raids on eastern Sussex. Rye and Hastings burnt Cinque Ports fleet burns Boulogne
1343	People of Hastings burgle Hastings College
1346–7	Siege of Calais. Hastings supplies five ships, Rye and Winchelsea more
1348	Outbreak of Black Death
1350	Local population and numbers of monks at Battle Abbey reduced by about 35% by the Black Death. Abbot Alan amongst dead monks Battle of Winchelsea – English Cinque Ports fleet beat the French
1358	Recorded that 94 properties abandoned and 90 derelict in Winchelse
1360	French seriously damage Rye and Winchelsea again. Abbot of Battle, Robert de Bello, chased French away from Winchelsea. Treaty of Bretigny gave a brief respite from 100 Years War until 1369. Approximate date of Robertsbridge Codex: a rare 14th century musical manuscript
1363	409 properties in Winchelsea now abandoned or derelict
1364	Augustinian Friary established at Rye
1366	People of Hastings burgle Hastings College again
1367	Economic stress causes Battle town to shrink
1369	War resumes. Coast remains under defended – all money being spent on war in France

TIMELINE

1372	French and their Castilian allies make lightning raids on the ports Pevensey Castle granted to John of Gaunt
1377	Edward II died and Richard II became king French capture Rye with 66 deaths and burn it. They also burn Hastings destroying St Clement church, which has to be re-built again, and ransack Hastings Castle and College Winchelsea defended by Abbot Hamo de Offyngton of Battle Bailiff of Rye cruelly ordered to hang and quarter those of Rye responsible for its failure to defend itself Poll tax imposed and repeated three times to 1380
1378	Augustinian Priory at Rye moved within town walls
1380	French severely damage Winchelsea again Poll tax of 12d per head financially cripples poor families Battle Abbey distributes food aid
1381	Peasants' Revolt Pevensey Castle ransacked
1382	Abbot Hamo de Offyngton died
1384	Winchelsea partially deserted.
1385	Richard II granted Sir Edward Dallingridge permission build a crenelated manor house (Bodiam Castle)
1386	French invasion fleet set out, defeated by 'England's friend' – a storm in the Channel. Some French ships driven ashore and captured
1399	Richard II deposed by Henry (Bolingbroke) IV Dukedom of Brittany forfeits the Rape of Hastings Sir John Pelham granted Pevensey Castle and later the Rape of Pevensey
1412	Pelhams receive the Rape of Hastings
1413	Hastings Priory removed to Warbleton because of sea damage. Henry IV died and Henry V crowned
1415	Agincourt: both Sir Roger Fiennes of Herstmonceux and Thomas Hoo, future lord of the Rape of Hastings involved Winchelsea and Rye mariners provide ships
1416	Henry V dissolved all alien priories and the manor of Brede was confiscated from Fécamp Abbey, passing eventually to the monastery of Syon
1417	All Saints church, Hastings re-built after this date
1419	Henry V wins Battle of Rouen
1421	St Elizabeth's Day floods in November
1422	Henry V died and Henry VI became king
1431	Henry VI crowned King of France
1440	Bishop of Chichester reports that the parishes of St Andrew, St Leonards, St Michael and St Margaret in Hastings no longer had any churches. St Peters not even mentioned

1440–1	Sir Roger Fiennes granted permission to build a crenelated castle at Herstmonceux
1443	House for pilgrims rebuilt outside Battle Abbey gate
1445	Rape of Hastings granted to Sir Thomas Hoo
1447	Hastings Collegiate College lost Royal Free chapel status. Granted to Sir Thomas Hoo, lord of the Rape of Hastings
1448	Possible burning by French of Rye and Winchelsea
1449	Robertsbridge Abbey fair attacked by early supporters of Cade
1450	Cade's rebellion
1451	Abbot Richard Dertmouth, monks and servants of Battle Abbey and many others in the Rape of Hastings and Lowey of Pevensey pardoned for supporting Cade
1453	Battle of Castillon lost by England. End of '100 Years' War', 116 years after it began
1455	Start of the 'Wars of the Roses'
1460	Cinque Ports support Yorkists. Help capture royal fleet at Sandwich Hastings Collegiate College becomes subject to the jurisdiction of the bishop of Chichester
1461–2	Edward IV visits Battle Rape of Hastings passed to William, Lord Hastings
1470	Edward IV visits Battle again, soon before his brief six month deposition
1471	Edward IV restored, issues general pardon to Abbot John Newton of Battle
1475	Inner port at Winchelsea no longer accessible to larger ships
1483	William, Lord Hastings summarily executed by Richard III
1485	Battle of Bosworth. Richard III killed and Henry (Tudor) VII king.
1487	Date of Le Talleur's Roll of Battle Abbey
1488	Henry VII visits Battle Abbey and Rye
1509	Henry VII dies, Henry VIII becomes king
1512–4	Construction of central round artillery tower to protect Rye Camber (first stage of Camber Castle). The second stage started in 1539 and the final outer walls in 1542
1513	Henry VIII meets with king of France at 'Field of Cloth of Gold' Winchelsea supplies four ships
1524	Lay Subsidy Roll of 1524/5 gives insight into the people of Battle Bayham Abbey dissolved by Cardinal Wolseley to help fund his new colleges at Oxford and Ipswich
1533	Approximate date of Leland's Roll of Battle Abbey
1538	Suppression of Battle Abbey, Robertsbridge Abbey, all remaining Priories, Friaries and some Hospitals

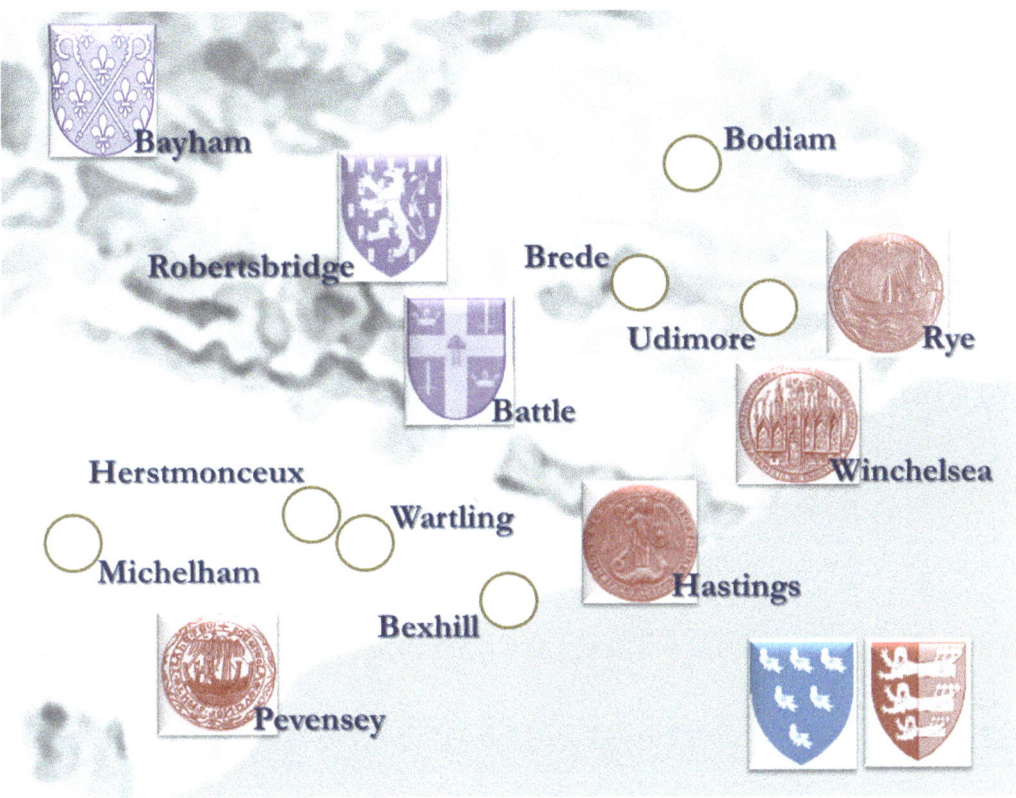

Eastern Sussex, its abbeys and ports, plus other locations in the text 1067–1538
Not to scale, nor fully inclusive of locations.

The blazons bottom right represent the old blazon of Sussex (left), and the arms of the Cinque Ports (right). The blazon associated with Bayham is of the Premonstratensian order and that of Robertsbridge of the Eu family, representing Alix d'Eu a co-founder of the abbey. The seals are derived from the ancient seals of the Cinque Port of Hastings and its 'limb', Pevensey, and the seals of the 'Ancient Towns' of Rye and Winchelsea.

The unofficial motto of the County of Sussex is 'We wun't be druv', reflecting the strong-willed nature of its people in past centuries. This can, with certainty, be applied in eastern Sussex, between 1067 and 1538, and still can be today.

With the English and Normans living side by side and the intermarrying, the peoples have become so mingled that nowadays one can scarcely tell – as far as free men are concerned – who is English and who of Norman descent

Richard fitzNeal, 1178

1
Introduction

Eastern Sussex will never escape its connection with one seminal event which influenced the English speaking world – the successful invasion of England by Duke William of Normandy in 1066. But how did he and his successors change eastern Sussex? The history is hidden away in ancient charters, writings, oral histories and state and local records. Their very nature is that they record only a tip of a huge iceberg of a story, and what is seen is mainly about the foibles and actions of kings, nobles, bishops and abbots, usually written by authors with vested or contractual interests in power and land, careful about what they wrote.

Occasionally an event occurred that gives us a glimpse of ordinary folk and these aspects of social history are sought out here. But this is limited and depends much on inference and interpretation. Such aspects were normally only recorded when orinary people paid taxes, infringed a law, wanted to become a tenant or their services were required in war – or they had the temerity to revolt, had differing religious thought, or suffered unspeakable natural disasters, diseases and plagues. War service was a particular manpower and financial burden in the case in eastern Sussex – where ships were built and portsmen, merchantmen and fishermen became pressed into naval service, abbots were warrior abbots and landsmen were mustered as a first line of defence of the realm.

At the heart of 1066 Country near the site of the Battle of Hastings is a place now called eponymously Battle. An historical issue which has always faced writers about the town of Battle is that it did not exist before 1066, in fact not before 1070. The site of present Battle town was a hilly scrubby place at the junction of ancient tracks where a ridge of sandstone starts to stretch from the High Weald towards the sea – where it ends in some rather spectacular cliffs between Hastings and Fairlight. Between Cooden at the western end of Bexhill and Pett Level east of Hastings is the only area where the Wealden sandstone and clay formations meet the sea.

On each side of the Battle ridge is a watershed – to one side westwards towards the small Combe Haven River which enters the sea at Bulverhythe, between St Leonards-on-Sea and Bexhill, where there was a small harbour. North-westwards the Ashburn stream feeds to the Wallers Haven River which flows across what was the Pevensey embayment, now drained marshland. On the eastern side of the ridge the flow is via tributaries to the River Brede and thence to the also once embayed waters of the Rye Camber around Old Winchelsea, Rye and Old Romney, now the Pett Level marshes and Dungeness. A narrow neck of high land connects the Battle ridge to the higher Weald, at the northern exit of what was essentially a Hastings peninsula. This neck was where the English and Norman armies clashed in 1066.

1066 Country is the part of East Sussex which was directly involved in the invasion of William of Normandy and the build up to the Battle of Hastings. This area stretches from just west of Pevensey to just east of Rye and from the English Channel coast in the south to the East Sussex–Kent border in the north and northeast. It virtually corresponds with the old Rape of Hastings and the south-easternmost Hundreds of the Rape of Pevensey and is the littoral and hinterland of Battle, Bexhill, Hastings, Pevensey, Robertsbridge, Rye and Winchelsea. The history of all these places cannot be ignored in the history of any of the local settlements. Geographically its best

Where the High Weald meets the English Channel – just east of Hastings
Photograph: © Keith Foord

description is eastern Sussex – that is the eastern part of present day East Sussex.

In historical geographic terms, it does appear to have been an entity somewhat separate from the Kingdom of Sussex, and many would say it still is. It must also be nearly coterminous with an ancient area called Hastingas – which may have been so called between the 6th to the early 11th centuries and been sociologically influenced more by the Kingdom of Kent to the east than the rather fragmented sub-kingdoms of Sussex to the west. Partially cut off in the past by the stretches of marsh and water on each side and the Andreadsweald to the north, eastern Sussex/Hastingas has been used by man from at least the Neolithic age and was well known to the Romans as a source

I INTRODUCTION

of iron ore – together with plenty of wood from which to make charcoal to smelt it.

As time went by, its small fishing ports developed. These became important for a while as part of the Cinque Ports, defending the developing English nation, providing ships and sailors for the royal fleets. Then Hastings was eroded away by the sea and the others gradually silted up one by one and faded. But it remained and remains front line Britain, always possible landing zone for unwanted intruders and invaders. It was dealt a very bad hand in feudal times, being expected to be the first line of defence using its own resources, with little support from the nation as a whole. It was also a potentially very dangerous place to be in both Napoleonic times and certainly in 1940–1, as we can see confirmed in German Operation Sealion plans. But this book focusses on the history of 1066 country until another major event – the dissolution of the monasteries in 1538.

The records of Battle Abbey give us a good view of how Battle developed as a town and interacted with the rest of eastern Sussex. Fortunately, we also have very good detail from Rye and Winchelsea, and some from Pevensey and Robertsbridge, but less from Bexhill and the villages. Sadly, there is not as much as one could wish for from Hastings' very early days, probably thanks to French raiders' pyrotechnics and the entrepreneurs of the 18th century who conveniently 'lost' many of the old charters in order to reduce their taxes and do deals – although fortunately much can still be inferred.

The first information about the Cinque Ports, whether they were termed as this at first or not, was given by King Edward the Confessor in 1050, when he proclaimed that the ports would provide ship service for 15 days each year. Henry I later confirmed their mercantile privileges as had his father and his brother. In the Domesday entry for Dover the arrangement is confirmed that Dover would supply 20 ships, manned by 21 men for 15 days each year and a similar demand was made of Hastings, about which there is surprisingly little in Domesday – but more of this later. Various charters and confirmations concerning the Cinque Ports were made down the years. In 1155–6 King Henry II granted a royal charter to the Cinque Ports, as long as they provided 57 ships for 15 days each year, and he confirmed that, of these, Dover and Hastings were each expected to provide 21 ships. Hastings was still a major provider of ships at that time, but only just, as by 1191 the struggle to maintain a good port at Hastings led to Rye and Winchelsea becoming limbs of Hastings, and the two limbs between them eventually provided five times more ships than their parent. In the charter of Edward I of 1278, the privileges granted to the barons of the Cinque Ports were detailed. There were also two letters patent of Edward I dated 1298. The first excused the portsmen of all taxes in respect of their ships and tackle. The second dealt with the contribution of members to ship duty. Edward II granted a confirmatory charter in 1313. A charter of Edward III in 1326–7 explained further the wording relating to the contribution of ships in Letters Patent of 1298. Further Letters Patent from him then updated the numbers of ships required from each port – this included three from Hastings, one from Pevensey, five from Rye and ten from Winchelsea – yet more indication of the relative changes concerning the wealth of the towns and condition of their harbours. He also granted a further confirmatory charter in 1364, and more confirmatory charters were made by Richard II in 1378, Edward IV in 1465 (as well as adding further privileges), Henry VII in 1487, and Henry VIII in 1510.

After 1066, Hastings had briefly continued to thrive as a significant port, to the extent that it appears between Shoreham and Dover on a world map made by the Arabic geographer al-Idrisi for King Roger II of Sicily (a Norman outpost) compiled in 1153–4. In its descriptive text, Hastings is described as 'a town of large extent and many inhabitants, flourishing and handsome, having markets, work people and rich merchants'. It was also used as a base by William I's son, William II Rufus. After that, Hastings continued its decline, accelerated by the great storms of the 13th century which also washed away Old Winchelsea, plus the most unwelcome attentions of the French particularly during the 100 Years' War. The French became enthusiastic pillagers and arsonists at that time, to the extent that they even attacked Hastings Castle which was already dilapidated and falling into the sea. They would not have got much from what was left of the College of St Mary in the Castle as apparently relations between town and gown were not good and the people of Hastings burgled it and imprisoned the clergy in both 1343 and 1366.

Battle Abbey was founded in 1070, and in Hastings the Priory of the Holy Trinity was established in the reign of Richard I (1189–1199). The latter was near the junction of Cambridge Road with Cambridge Gardens. Sometime later, 192 acres (78 ha.) of land were transferred to it from St Michael's parish. This land was all on the west side of the Priory valley, and some of it would have been the typical water meadow so beloved of monastic institutions. The sea encroached until the priory was in danger of being swept away, and in 1413 Sir John Pelham gave them a site at Warbleton, and Henry IV licensed them to remove to this inland site well away from Hastings. But this was not before they had become a mother priory to Michelham, aided by the lords of Pevensey. St Andrew sub Castro church on the eastern side of the Priory valley at Hastings was first mentioned in the return of 1291, and again in 1372. Probably plundered by the French, and also threatened by sea flooding, St Andrew sub Castro fell into disuse by 1440, although there is evidence that some ruins were still visible in 1610, and the graveyard was still in use after that time. Papal returns also give us more information about the early churches in Hastings.

St Michael's ruins were discovered when building Prospect Place in the 1820s. During the construction of an electricity sub-station in 1970 in St Michael's Place, bones from 22 to 35 bodies were found in a single grave. Hastings museum believed that they came from the original graveyard of St Michael's Church and had been re-buried after the cutting of a new road in 1834. Another church at Hastings, St

Margaret's, stood on top of the small cliff to the rear of 50 Eversfield Place behind which its ruins were found. Its name is preserved in the adjacent St Margaret's Road. Its parish was the same as the newer St Mary Magdalene. St Leonard's church was in the area of Norman Road, west of London Road, nowhere near the present St Leonard's church. St Leonard's was valued at £4.13.4d (£4.67) in 1291 and in 1334 belonged to the Abbey of St Katherine of Rouen. Old St Leonard's graveyard was disturbed when building the former Methodist Church there in 1834. The modern St Peter's church is at Bohemia, nowhere near the presumed location of the 1240 St Peter's which has disappeared, the suspicion being that, as its name suggests it might have been the fishermen's church, it would have stood nearest the sea, and thanks to sea erosion went over a cliff along with much of the earliest settlement of Hastings and later two-thirds of Hastings Castle. The cluster of four chapels west of Priory valley is not insignificant, and does suggest that they were serving a community of reasonable size which had not sprung up overnight. Of these only St Leonard is mentioned after 1372, although a parson for St Michael is named in 1404. The Bishop of Chichester, in 1440, reported that

> ... the parishes of St Andrew's, St Leonard's, St Michael's, and St Margaret's, had so suffered from the depredations of the sea in the last 100 years, that they had no longer any churches.

He could also have mentioned the unwelcome attentions of the French. He made no mention of St Peter's at all. The great storms of the 13th century, the continued erosion by the sea, shingle movements, inundations of the Priory valley and predations by the French through to the 15th century have hidden a lot of Hastings' history, just as in Winchelsea. The losses clearly finalised a wholesale population move eastwards into the Bourne valley, settlement of which had started with the small Hastings of Domesday. The areas described above appear to have depopulated well before 1440, perhaps by the mid-14th century in the wake of the French raids, the Black Death and incessant erosion.

There were extensive saltpans around the Pevensey embayment and also around the Rye Camber within Rameslie manor. At Rye there was probably a Saxon church before the Conquest, but after Abbot William of Fécamp visited in 1103, building started on a new church of St Mary. Down the years much repair and rebuilding work has taken place on this church, particularly after the severe damage by the French in the 14th century. Fécamp Abbey also founded St George's at Brede in 1190. By 1200 the management of the manors of Rameslie (held since before the Conquest) and Brede by the Abbey of Fécamp appears to have become less hands on and more commercial.

Bexhill, whose name may have been OE *byxe leah* (box tree clearing) had evolved since the end of the eight century to support a minster church which had an extensive estate. The minster was annexed to Hastings' St Mary in the Castle College before 1086 and the church rebuilt. There was probably a scattered population of 80 families by 1086, with a small focal village on a knoll around St Peter's church. The manor was seized by the Count of Eu after 1070, and only given back to the See of Chichester in 1148. There was slow growth over the next few centuries whilst it remained in the ownership of the Bishop of Chichester (until 1561): there were only 29 persons assessed for tax in 1296, 46 in 1327, 52 in 1352 and 98 in 1524.

To the west, the medieval borough of Pevensey originated as a quite late Anglo-Saxon settlement, but by the mid-11th century, Pevensey was established as a significant borough. It had grown quickly, for there was no significant population there around 800. Pevensey is referred to by name in a charter of 947, but the name is simply used to locate a saltpan. In 1054, a saltpan and 12 houses had formed part of a local grant to the Abbey of Fécamp. More significantly, Domesday records that Pevensey was a pre-Conquest town with 52 burgesses, with tolls to the value of 20s and port dues of 35s. When the Count of Mortain was given Pevensey as part of the Rape of Pevensey in about 1069, there were only 27 burgesses; but by 1086 there had been a rapid expansion to 110 burgesses and it was regarded as a large town. The late Saxon and Anglo-Norman development must have been influenced by the shallow harbour at Pevensey which developed into a port in the late 10th and 11th centuries. But this too gradually silted up as land was reclaimed and longshore drift of masses of shingle deviated the Pevensey Haven river outlet to the sea to the east. It also partially blocked it, with the town's subsequent decline.

Examples of use of the port at Pevensey include Earl Godwin's arrival from Sandwich with a fleet of 42 ships in 1049 and again arriving in 1052 from Bruges, when he added to his fleet by taking ships from Pevensey before sailing on to London. William I used the port for his first return to Normandy in 1067 and may also have used it in 1085. Later a small abbey was founded at nearby Otham, which later moved to Bayham, and an almshouse at Westham. A mint existed at Pevensey after the Conquest and coins minted there in the reigns of William I and II have been found but nothing after that. Another mint was founded at Rye before 1115 and was briefly active during the reign of Stephen and the pre-Conquest mint at Hastings also remained active until the end of Stephen's reign.

Prior to the mid-13th century the focus of activity near Robertsbridge had been at nearby Salehurst, where the parish church remains to this day and where Robertsbridge Abbey was founded. The Abbey moved from its founder site to a new site 1.4 km (1 mile) from the centre of Robertsbridge in 1250, barely nearer to the town. Robertsbridge township itself was developed after 1220 possibly as a new settlement encouraged by the Abbot, who in around 1250–60 developed his own Hundred of Robertsbridge and created the posts of constable, ale-conner and street-driver. The Abbey also had a private prison at Redland in 1279, this was moved into the town

I INTRODUCTION

around 1400 when the courthouse was constructed. This in turn probably became redundant by the mid-1500s. Robertsbridge market became a significant centre for trading and manufacturing by about 1300, possibly at the expense of nearby Salehurst market. Martin and Martin published an architectural history of the town in 1974.

The early development of Battle from 1070, dominated by its abbey, is extremely well covered in texts by Searle in her translation of the *Chronicle of Battle Abbey* and in her *Lordship and Community* and by Martin, Martin and Whittick in *Building Battle Town*. Rye is similarly well covered by Vidler's *A New History of Rye*, Mayhew's *Tudor Rye* and Draper's *Rye*. Lucey wrote an excellent summary of Sedlescombe in *Twenty Centuries in Sedlescombe*, and Pratt's histories of Winchelsea are very detailed.

Within the following chapters, the relationships of the post-Conquest kings of England to Battle, Rye, Winchelsea and all of eastern Sussex between 1087 and 1538 are explored. In addition, the book looks at the development of the local religious houses; the curiosity of the Rolls of Battle Abbey; the general status and associations of the Rape of Hastings and considers the area's representation at the parliaments called before 1538. The area eastern Sussex corresponds to that described as 1066 Country in modern tourism parlance and covers the area west to east from Pevensey to Kent and south to north from the English Channel coast to Kent.

Clearly the general histories of the monarchs and associated events must be severely truncated in such a wide-ranging local study. But hopefully, to maintain relevance, just enough information is given to link the key points of the local histories to the kings, and events surrounding the kings. Also in studies which have focal local interest there can inevitably be large time gaps between events, and some local events of really momentous concern can only be described from very little information. Other smaller events can be overwhelmed by detail, particularly later in the sequence, when more detailed records become available and when editing down is required to keep some basic perspective.

The work is drawn from the wide selection of sources given in the bibliography and, as much as possible, the events have been cross-referenced between different works. Throughout the texts, Winchelsea if seen without a prefix refers to New Winchelsea. This replaced the destroyed Old Winchelsea which may have only been a small fishing village in 1066, but which by the 1200s had become a sizeable and important, if somewhat independently minded and anarchic town. This stood on a large shingle bank east of the present Winchelsea, possibly just south of where Camber Castle still stands today. As noted above, Old Winchelsea was destroyed in the great storms of the late 13th century and has been completely lost to the sea.

Reference should also be made to Foord and Clephane-Cameron's book about 1066 and its preludes which synopsises (in rather more detail than can be included here) the coastal changes which occurred around the eastern Sussex coast between the Conquest and 16th centuries. These diminished the fortunes and strategic positions of Hastings, Pevensey and Winchelsea and, to some extent Rye, quite profoundly over the 1066 to 1538 period. It might have been tempting to retell this aspect in detail, but it would have been unnecessary duplication.

Throughout the book and its sections a time order from 1066 to 1538 is sought after, but because different topics often involve the same people an objective has been to explain issues in detail the first time they occur, or, if more appropriate, to refer forward. If and when an incident is once more relevant, a brief synopsis may be given followed by a reference to the detail in an attempt to avoid excess duplication.

This book cannot cover everything that has happened in or to eastern Sussex in a span of 471 years and can only be an in-depth overview. For more detail, the reader is directed to the bibliography, particularly to the major texts which are mentioned.

Some interpretations are the author's, and you may sometimes disagree. Any errors and spelling mistakes are also the author's. But spelling in the 'old days' was very variable, even within the same document and by the same hand – and these are often deliberately copied as spelt – so please forgive the old and odd rather weird spellings, which give a further flavour of the times. As always, if errors are spotted, or any copyright has been inadvertently bridged, or there is some glaring omission, please let the author know so that correction may be made in any future edition.

The author would like to thank George Kiloh, Neil Clephane-Cameron and Gina Doherty for adding to, editing and checking the punctuation, grammar and content, Amanda Helm for layout and typesetting and all members of the Committee of the Battle and District Historical Society for their pre-publication readings and support. And of course his wife, Paula, for many cups of tea and coffee and biscuits as well as much patience.

This book is part of a series of volumes covering various periods of local history, based on material from the writings and archives of Battle and District Historical Society, published on line on BDHS's website which will be supplemented by further research.

2
Local influences of the Norman and Angevin Kings: 1067–1272

1067–1087 William I after the Battle of Hastings

There is no evidence that William I ever revisited Hastings or came to Battle to review the progress of his abbey – although he clearly issued orders about its leuga or banlieu and received reports on its false start and then its progress, which are discussed in detail in the chapter concerning the Abbots of Battle.

The record of the itinerary of William the Conqueror is actually very sparse and it is hardly possible to know where he actually went, apart from the known headline events. So we cannot absolutely say he never returned to the scene of his triumph, although we do know that the English ports for his first return visit in 1067 to Normandy after being crowned king of England were on the eastern Sussex coast – from Pevensey in March with a return to Old Winchelsea in December. He may also have travelled via Pevensey to Normandy in 1085. There were no Abbey foundations to inspect in 1067 at Battle and his major attentions would surely have been elsewhere in England and later back in Normandy.

'Two Stars' coins were minted soon after the appearance of a bright comet in 1075. The stars, one on each side of William's head, represented the new comet and Halley's comet of 1066

A new stone castle at Hastings had been started soon after the Conquest on land exchanged with the Abbey of Fécamp, and William granted the Rape of Hastings and its new castle to a kinsman, Robert Count of Eu, in 1069–70. The mint at Hastings must have been reactivated soon after the Conquest. The names of two moneyers, Dunninc and Eadwine issuing 'Two Stars' coins of about 1075–77 are recorded on the Portable Antiquities Scheme (PAS) website. It is notable that these moneyers had English names.

The Conqueror died on 9th September 1087 following an accidental abdominal injury after being thrown against the pommel of his horse saddle. This event occurred near Mantes, in the Vexin, a troublesome 'buffer' county on the borders of the dukedom of Normandy and the kingdom of France. He was leading his forces against those of a combination of his problematic oldest son, Robert Curthose, and King Philip I of France. He was taken to Rouen where he died, following which his body was interred at the Abbaye aux Hommes in Caen. He never saw the consecration of his Abbey at Battle, built as a penance for the many deaths he had caused in England, during and after his victory over Harold Godwinson in 1066.

1087–1100 William II (Rufus)

Following the Conqueror's death his territories were split, with Normandy going to his surviving oldest son, Robert Curthose, and England to his second son, William, nicknamed William Rufus as he was described as having a ruddy complexion and light blond hair. Without going into detail here, the division between Normandy and England led to Curthose coveting England; William II defending his new kingdom; and the third brother, Henry, born in England, left as a rich young man who was later given holdings in the Cotentin and Avranchin, where he would create a small personal power base. The additional complication was that most of the powerful Norman landowners held lands on both sides of the English Channel and many were prepared, mainly for their own reasons, to back the less assertive Robert Curthose against the stronger and more ruthless William II, rather than serve two masters. We have an early indication of Rufus' strategic interest in eastern Sussex. Cole says in a statement which may have been somewhat exaggerated:

> William Rufus, on arriving in England in 1087, after the death of his father, made it his first care to secure the Castle of Hastings, where he often afterwards resided.

Unfortunately for William II, Robert de Mortain who held the Rape of Pevensey was a supporter of Curthose, as were many others across England. Most importantly, Earl Odo of Kent, Bishop of Bayeux, and the half-brother of the Conqueror, who controlled Duke Robert Curthose's council, schemed and revolted against Rufus. It has been suggested that many Norman lords, many of who were aggressive opportunists, considered Curthose a softer touch and that they were more likely to enhance their possessions under Curthose than Rufus.

Rufus rapidly needed to take full control of England and sent for Englishmen under the command of Norman sheriffs – and determinedly focussed his forces on the south-east. He was hunting Odo. He secured London and blockaded Rochester and Pevensey. After capturing Tonbridge Castle, he found that Odo was at Pevensey Castle which Rufus forced to submit after a six week siege. At about the same time an invading fleet from Normandy was routed by an English fleet, mainly made up of ships from Sussex and Kent. Odo then promised Rufus that he would persuade the defenders at Rochester to surrender, but he rejoined them, hoping for Robert Curthose's fleet to arrive. They did not, and in the end Rochester Castle also surrendered. Odo was banished. Gradually, other revolts around the country came to an end, and many major landholders subsequently lost some or all of their lands. The king pragmatically kept in place those he needed, and removed those who were a threat. Rufus was now in a very strong position, and after 1090 he took the dispute to Normandy. The brothers were in intermittent conflict, with periods of short-lived settlements, mainly broken by Robert, partially ended when Rufus re-unified England and Normandy in 1096 by bribing Curthose with a great fortune to go on the 1st crusade.

There were two views in England about Rufus, one ecclesiastical and deprecating, the other more secular and supportive. The former may have been important as far as Battle Abbey was concerned spiritually. However, in spite of William II's supposed indifference to religion, he was materially supportive of the Abbey as we shall see below. The latter view was somewhat more important to the rest of eastern Sussex. Clearly Rufus had become successful in war. Hastings and Pevensey at that time still had good harbours, plus new intact castles, and were on the route to Normandy. Given the above scenarios, they were clearly of great strategic importance to Rufus and this would have benefitted the area economically.

At his coronation in 1087 Rufus had given Battle Abbey a number of items, it is believed at William I's command 'for his soul'. These included his father's royal cloak trimmed with gold and jewels, 300 gold and silver amulets (small objects to ward off evil, harm, or illness or to bring good fortune), and a feretory (a portable shrine). The last, it has been reasonably conjectured, was one of the shrines pictured in the Bayeux tapestry on which Harold is reputed to have sworn fealty to Duke William (see illustration below, with feretories). He also gave the Abbey the large manor of Bromham in Wiltshire and acknowledged the Abbey's special liberties, granted by direct royal command from his father.

One moneyer at Hastings, Theodred, who was active about 1089–92 minted coins of William II (PAS). The College of St Mary in the Castle at Hastings was founded in about 1090 by Count Robert of Eu, holder of the Rape of Hastings. As a Collegiate

College, within the Castle itself, and with its own canons not from any specific religious order, it was independent and was outside of the See of Chichester's jurisdiction. It would pass into the hands of the crown in 1267 and this would later cause some of the same issues between crown and the Bishop of Chichester as Battle Abbey would later encounter. It did not prosper long term as the Castle itself deteriorated and with it the college, although somehow the college managed to survive to the dissolution and just beyond. Some detail of this will be covered in a later chapter.

Rufus clearly used Hastings Castle as a base as (again according to Cole):

> ... in 1091, before sailing to Normandy, he summoned his nobles to swear fealty. And again in 1093 his army mustered at Hastings to cross the Channel, but was detained by contrary winds a whole month, during which the king lodged in the Castle. In the following year, 20,000 men were encamped here preparatory to a war with France, but William, giving up his design, dismissed them, first of all, however, taking from them the ten shillings (50 pence) a head travelling money they had received from their counties.'

When at Battle for the dedication of Battle Abbey's church, Rufus was in a more generous mood, giving the Abbey the living of nine more churches. Added to the generous endowments already received from William the Conqueror after 1076, these made Battle Abbey a very wealthy abbey indeed. Still it seems without some of its roof leading, the Abbey was fully consecrated on 11 February 1095. The service of consecration was performed by Anselm, Archbishop of Canterbury, and was attended by King William II (Rufus), with Bishops Walchelin of Winchester, Ralph of Chichester, Osmund of Salisbury, John of Bath, William of Durham, Roger of Coutances and Gundalf of Rochester, as well as many earls, knights, clerics and laymen. The full dedication of the Abbey was to 'the Holy and indivisible Trinity and the blessed Mary, forever virgin also the blessed Martin, confessor of Christ'. Afterwards they all enjoyed an oblation of charity which would have been celebrated with a slap-up meal and all went joyously away. The reason that so many of the great magnates of the nation attended the consecration at Battle was that Rufus was yet again holding court at Hastings Castle, as he was contemplating a new campaign in Normandy against his brother, Robert Curthose. An Anglo-Norman army and a fleet to transport them to Normandy were being assembled near Hastings, but there had been considerable delays because of bad weather and winds (not very surprisingly in February). According to the *Anglo-Saxon Chronicle*, Rufus was:

> hated by almost all his people and abhorrent to God.

The *Chronicle of Battle Abbey* is one of few documents to praise Rufus. Rufus' relationship with the church hierarchy generally and Anselm in particular was frosty to say the least. Archbishop Lanfranc of Canterbury had died two years after William I, and Rufus took his time in agreeing the appointment of a new archbishop, meanwhile directly receiving rentals from the see of Canterbury, a manoeuvre which would not have endeared him to the Church. Anselm was not appointed Archbishop of Canterbury until 1092 and went into exile in France four years later – mainly it seems because he and Rufus were so incompatible. But for Battle Abbey Rufus was the tops:

> … the magnificent prince who endowed us with churches in Suffolk, Norfolk and Essex … So much did he love, cherish and defend our church, maintaining its dignity and royal customs, that no one would dare oppose it, just as no one had dared do so in his father's time. Whenever he was in the neighbourhood, he would often visit, support and encourage it, so great was his affection for it.

Although exaggerated, this suggests that he had indeed several times passed via Battle and Hastings in transit to and from Normandy, with or without an army. And maybe this was also because, following the directions of William the Conqueror's founding charter, Battle Abbey was free of dominance by the church establishment and was under his direct royal patronage.

In 1095 Abbot Gausbert of Battle died and due to the squabbling between Rufus and Anselm, no new abbot was appointed for nearly a year, meanwhile Rufus pocketed some extra income from the Abbey. Eventually Henry, a prior from Christ Church, Canterbury was appointed Abbot in 1096.

Also in 1095, Rufus once more saw off another but smaller rebellion in England, after which those who had rebelled twice were dealt with harshly. These included a William of Eu, probably not a son of Robert of Eu (although others have queried this, and the matter is discussed in more detail later in the chapter on the Rape of Hastings). This William of Eu was blinded and castrated and died soon afterwards.

After this England was relatively settled. Rufus stayed mostly in Normandy, consolidating affairs there. He still returned to England from time to time and died on English soil on 2 August 1100 after being shot, maybe accidentally, by an arrow through the chest when out hunting in the New Forest.

Detail from a miniature of the death of William Rufus. From the 'Grande Chronique de Normandie'
British Library: Yates Thompson 33 f. 186

1100–1135 Henry I (Beauclerc)

Rufus' younger brother Henry had been only peripherally involved in his brothers' squabbles in Normandy, but appears to have become an anglophile with a penchant for beautiful English women and, when in England, lived in a ménage with his concubines and children near Woodstock, where he is said to have had a zoo.

He had been with the Rufus's New Forest hunting party. He now rapidly stepped in, seizing the royal treasury at Winchester, burying his brother on Friday 3 August 1100, the day after his death, and succeeding Rufus as King of England, being crowned at Westminster on Sunday 5th by Maurice, Bishop of London, the only available senior prelate. He was a fast worker.

He also decided to marry formally Princess Edith of Scotland. Archbishop Anselm, now recalled from exile, performed the marriage ceremony and crowned Edith as Queen of England on 11 November 1100. She took the name Queen Mathilda. She was sister to King Edgar of Scotland and descended from King Aethelred II of England, as she was the daughter of Edgar Atheling's sister Margaret, who had married King Malcolm III of Scotland. This re-introduced the royal blood line of Wessex, a move which apparently was well received by the English.

Curthose was in Italy, on his way back from crusading. He returned to Normandy, built up his support again and decided to confront his younger brother. This led to the single occasion when Henry I definitely visited eastern Sussex. Later he may have passed through the ports on his voyages to and from Normandy, but evidence points to the fact that he normally made these voyages through Portsmouth … Although Cole says:

> Henry I used the (Hastings) Castle as a palace, finding Hastings a convenient haven for the passage from England to Normandy, and the fittest station for his royal yacht'

The author can find no evidence to corroborate that he used Hastings at that time. A considerable proportion of the navy was based by now at Old Winchelsea and Rye and this may have led some confusion as they were 'limbs' of Hastings. To reinforce them on 24 June 1101, Henry led a powerful army, largely of Englishmen and vassals of the bishops, towards Hastings, expecting Duke Robert to land in the area, as had their father, and encamped around Pevensey. Whilst in the vicinity at Wartling he signed edicts in favour of the monks of Battle:

> Notification by Henry I to all his barons, sheriffs, and officials: That he has granted St. Martin of Battle to have his court in all matters. Wherever the Abbot shall be present in the abbey's manors or lands, or another in his place, let him have the royal privilege that if anyone has a plea against his tenant the plaint shall be heard in his court. If the plea cannot be determined in the Abbot's court, let it be transferred by the Abbot to the royal court in order that it may be settled in the presence of the Abbot and the justiciar.

The second edict obviously refers to a local matter, but this shows how difficult it was in those times for the Abbey to hold on to its property:

> To restore to the Abbot of Battle, by sureties his swine herd. If Robert wishes to plead the Abbot he is to come to the court of St. Martin of Battle and have right. The King wishes all his barons and earls to know that he has confirmed to the church of St. Martin of Battle its court.

Robert Curthose failed to turn up at Pevensey. He eventually left Tréport with a fleet of 200 or so ships and landed at Portsmouth on 20 July. Once more, many of the English landholding Norman lords favoured Robert, and Robert's mainly Norman army moved on towards Winchester, but passed the city by. Robert's and Henry's forces eventually met near Alton in Hampshire and talks took place between the brothers. After several days of negotiations this ended in a treaty, with twelve high-ranking lords from each side ratifying it by oath. Robert had accepted a payoff from Henry of 3000 marks (£2000) per year and a pledge of joint government. There is some evidence that Henry played along with this for a while, meanwhile working on a strategy to recruit Norman landowners favourable to himself, and to isolate or convert those who were still a threat. When William de Mortain, lord of the Rape of Pevensey, turned back to Robert in 1104 he was promptly deprived of his English lands.

Henry in turn invaded Normandy in both 1105 and 1106, and captured Curthose at the Battle of Tinchebrai, which was fought on 28 September 1106, almost forty years after Hastings. England and Normandy were again reunited under one king. Curthose was imprisoned, but not ill-treated and died in Cardiff Castle in 1134.

As far as Battle Abbey was concerned, they received no further gifts from Henry, but he many times supported the Abbey in its legal fights with others, even if the results were difficult to enforce. He at one point exchanged land that the Abbey held in Reading for land at Appledram in western Sussex, as he wished to build a new monastery on the land at Reading:

> for the salvation of my soul, and the souls of King William, my father, and of King William, my brother, and Queen Maud, my wife, and all my ancestors and successors.

He exchanged more land at Appledram for the Abbey's holding in Carmarthen which he gave to Bishop Bernard and the church of St. David. He also granted the right to hold a three-day fair at Battle in July and later a second fair in winter. Rather more critically for the Abbey, Henry did not appoint a new Abbot after the death of Abbot Henry in 1102. It was not until 1107 that Ralph of Caen was appointed. During this time, as usual, the surplus income of the Abbey went to the king. However, once appointed, Ralph was able to confirm via Henry's court the precise holdings of the Abbey and the boundaries of its banlieu (or leuga). These had been encroached on by surrounding landowners – as the Abbey had been unable to protect their properties from its less scrupulous neighbours, who had probably been resentful that William I had taken some lands from them to create the Abbey banlieu in the first place.

Examples of more notifications and grants made by Henry are below. As will be noted, he may not have visited Battle, but he certainly stood up for the rights of the Abbey:

- [1102?] Westminster. Precept by Henry I to Rembert [of Hastings] and Robert [son of Ralf] of Hastings: To enjoin on all the barons of Hastings to make enclosures against the land of the Abbot of Battle, as they did in the time of William I and of Abbot Gausbert.
- [1102?] Henry I directs the men of Hastings to fence their lands bordering those of the Abbot of Battle
- [1103–1106, July 31.] Windsor. Notification by Henry I to Henry Count of Eu and generally: That he has granted to St. Martin's, Battle, the meadows of Bodiam which Geoffrey the monk bought up for the use of the said church at Pentecost in the chapter and that they may hold them as freely as under William I and II and the Counts of Eu.
- [1106, May?] Marlborough. Notification by Henry I to Rai[m]bert of Hastings, Robert fitz Ralf, and all of Hastings: That he has granted the monks of St.

Martin's, Battle, and their men the same customs within and without their market as the men of Hastings have, as granted by William I. And they shall make their purchases everywhere free of toll.

[1102–7.] Westminster. Notification by Henry I to H[enry] Count of Eu and R[obert] the son of R[alf] de Hastings and all the King's justiciars and officials of Sussex: That he has confirmed to the monks of St. Martin at Battle to have all their roads through the King's lands and especially the road which goes from Battle to Hastings, &c., and their rights of chase and hunting in the rape of Hastings as fully as they had them in the King's time or the time of his father and brother. The addressees are not to meddle in the leuga of Battle any more than they would in the King's own demesne.

[1102–16, Apr.] Windsor. Notification by Henry I to Ralph Bp. of Chichester and all the King's barons: That the King has confirmed to St. Martin of Battle all gifts and purchases of lands in the rape of Hastings (list given); Henry Count of Eu also confirms this.

[1114–16] Writ addressed to Ralph bishop of Chichester and the ministers of Sussex notifying them that the Abbot and monks of Battle have deraigned before the king that they have not certain lands which the said bishop alleged that they had, as belonging anciently to Alciston; and mandate that they be henceforth quit thereof, and that their manor of Alciston be quit of shires and hundreds, and particularly of work upon London bridge and the Castle of Pevensey

[Ante May 1116] Notification to Ralph bishop of Chichester and his barons of the confirmation to the monks of Battle of lands given, with the consent of Henry count of Eu, in the rape of Hastings.

[1121–2] Notification, addressed generally, that the monks of St. Martin's, Battle, shall hold in peace, with certain liberties, their lands, including Appledram, which they have received in exchange for Reading.

[1100] Writ addressed to the sheriffs, ministers, and barons of England and Wales notifying them of the grant of acquittance of toll to the men of the monks of Battle.

Notification to Ralph Bishop of Chichester, William Fitz-Auger, and the barons of Sussex of the grant to the monks of Battle of the manor of Appledram, in exchange for their possessions in Reading, with 40s. of yearly rent in Appledram which the king had previously retained.

[1125] Notification, addressed generally, of the foundation of, and gifts to, the monastery of Reading. The signatories are: the king and Queen Adelaide; ... Warner of St. Martin's, Battle, ...

[1126–33] Notification to Siefrid bishop of Chichester, Anselm de Rouen, the sheriff, barons, and lieges of Sussex, of the grant to the Abbot and monks of Battle of 40s. of yearly rent which the king has retained in the manor of Appledram with the farm of Bosham, for part of the exchange for their land of Carmarthen, which he has given to Bishop Bernard and the church of St. David.

[1100–30] Westminster. Notification by Henry I to R[obert] son of R[alf] de Hastinges, D[rew] de Pevenesel, and all justiciars, &c., of Sussex: That he confirms to the monks of St. Martin's, Battle, and their men, all their roads throughout his lands, particularly that from Battle to Hastings, the roads round Battle, the crossings over (ultra) Winchelsea, and their road over Ashdown (Essessdone), as in the reigns of William I, William II, and in his own. No one is to injure their men or goods within the borough of Hastings or without. The justiciars are not to interfere within the lowy any more than in the King's demesne.

[1100–33] Winchester. Notification by Henry I to all his officials and collectors of the rape of Hastings: That he has confirmed the gift which Wening the man of William of Hastings gave with his lord's consent to St. Martin of Battle, namely the church of Westfield [co. Sussex] *'cum una wista terre, liberam et quietam ab omni consuetudine terrene servitutis in perpetuum possidendam'*. No one is to molest the monks of Battle therein.

[1120, Nov.–Dec.] Portsmouth. Notification by Henry I to Ralph Bp. of Chichester and William fitz Ansger and the barons of Sussex: That he has given to St. Martin of Battle in exchange for Reading, the manor of Appledram [co. Sussex], also 40?. which formerly pertained to the said manor, with the ferm of Bosham ; and of feeding in the woods of ' Bocfalde' and ' Betlesparrioc', one pig for every three that the King has there; and the fourth penny of pannage, and the fourth of all the oaks that are felled and the fourth penny from the land pertaining to those woods, &c. The monks and their men of Appledram are to be quit of all custom with sac, soc, toll, team and infangthief, geld, scot, hidage, danegeld, work on bridges, castles, parks, and enclosures, host-service, aids, shires, hundreds, wardpenny, lastage, larceny, murder-fine, treasure-trove, warren, and all pleas and plaints.

In 1120, Henry's legitimate son William and his natural son Richard drowned in the White Ship, which sank in the English Channel off Barfleur. This posed a succession problem, as Henry had never allowed any of his many illegitimate children to expect succession to either England or Normandy. Henry had a legitimate daughter, Matilda (widow of Emperor Henry V, subsequently married to the Count of Anjou). However, it was his nephew Stephen (reigned 1135–54), son of William the Conqueror's daughter Adela, who stepped in and succeeded Henry after his death in 1135, the barons being opposed to the idea of a female monarch. Henry I was buried in his new Abbey at Reading.

1135–1154 Stephen of Blois / (Empress Matilda)

Henry had named his eldest daughter Matilda his heir, but before doing so, he had at least considered naming his nephew, Stephen of Blois. When Henry died, Stephen invaded England and had himself crowned instead of Matilda.

Matilda's claim was supported by her half-brother Robert of Gloucester and her uncle, King David I of Scotland. Matilda landed at Arundel in September 1139 and there followed the Anarchy, with supporters of the contenders fighting in both Britain and Normandy.

A significant event in the conflicts was the first Battle of Lincoln, which took place on 2 February 1141. Stephen had been besieging Lincoln Castle but was attacked by a force loyal to Matilda, commanded by Robert of Gloucester, Matilda's half-brother. Stephen was captured and imprisoned, and Empress Matilda ruled for a short time, although she was never crowned. Stephen was imprisoned at Bristol, but in the following September he was exchanged for Robert of Gloucester, who had been taken by forces loyal to Stephen in the Rout of Winchester. This ended Matilda's brief period of power, but not the intermittent flaring of local conflicts between supporters of both parties, although Stephen held onto the crown after this.

Pevensey Castle was involved in the conflict between Matilda and Stephen, with its owners often switching sides. In 1147, Richer de Laigle (or d'Aigle, sometimes L'Aigle but the author believes Laigle to be most correct), whose father had been a supporter of Robert Curthose, rebelled against King Stephen and was dispossessed of Pevensey Castle. It was given to Gilbert de Clare, who then changed sides and Stephen besieged and starved the occupants to take the Castle, and then gave it and its property to Eustace, his eldest son. Following this, Eustace made various grants of Pevensey's fiefs, chapelry and fishing rights to Richard de Luci (see below and the chapter on the Abbots of Battle), to the See of Chichester and to Lewes Priory. The details of events during the Anarchy are complex, but no other noted events took place in eastern Sussex.

The mint at Hastings, originally founded in the time of Aethelred II is not heard of after Stephen's reign. This is probably indicative of Hastings's decline, even though in the same reign an up-and-coming monk called Thomas à Becket had something to do with the college within Hastings Castle. He was not the dean as some have recorded, but the count of Eu gave the patronage of the prebends of Hastings to him.

By now the crown had less affinity with Battle Abbey, but the Abbey was still tied to the crown. However Stephen did issue a general confirmation of status quo for Battle Abbey in 1137, issued via and witnessed by Robert fitzRichard de Clare (a steward of King Stephen), at Hastings. Stephen also used Battle Abbey to advance the de Luci family. At Christmas 1138 Abbot Warner was induced to resign and Walter de Luci, the brother of one of Stephen's justiciars (the equivalent of a senior minister today), Richard de Luci, was named Abbot. This was a ploy to elevate the de Luci family, but Abbot Walter was soon summoned to Chichester, to be told that Bishop Hilary now expected Battle to be a fully under his jurisdiction.

Stephen wanted his son Eustace to inherit his throne. He tried to convince the church to agree to crown Eustace to reinforce this claim, but Pope Eugene III refused. Meanwhile in Anjou Mathilda's second husband, the Count of Anjou, died in 1151 and their son Henry became the new Count. In 1152 Henry married Eleanor of Aquitaine, who had divorced the French king, but held Aquitaine in her own right, and so between them they then held the vast territories of Anjou, Poitou and Aquitaine.

Henry's mother (called Empress Mathilda as her first husband was Holy Roman Emperor Henry V) was still in de facto dispute with Stephen over Normandy, Brittany and England. In 1153 Henry invaded England and built an alliance to support his mother's claim for the throne. Stephen and Henry's armies met at Wallingford, but neither was keen to have a battle. Then Stephen's son Eustace died in August 1153 and Stephen moved towards a negotiated peace. Later in the year Stephen and Henry agreed the Treaty of Winchester, in which Stephen recognised Henry as his heir, ignoring his own surviving son, William. Stephen died in 1154 and Henry succeeded as Henry II, now overlord of a vast territory that stretched from Northumbria to the Pyrenees.

As soon as Stephen died, and before Henry II was crowned, Bishop Hilary of Chichester, in cahoots with Pope Adrian IV (the only English pope), tried to excommunicate Battle's Abbot, Walter de Luci.

1154–1189 Henry II (Curtmantle)

It was now nearly 100 years since the Battle of Hastings. The royal affinity that William I, and to a degree William II, had had for Battle Abbey, and the support at distance given by Henry I, was becoming a faded memory. Henry II, the son of Geoffrey Plantagenet, Count of Anjou, and Henry I's daughter Mathilda, was of the Angevin house and became the first Plantagenet king of England.

Bishop Hilary of Chichester had not realised the power of Richard de Luci, Abbot Walter de Luci's brother, who was soon to be one of Henry II's chief justiciars, and who maintained the administration of the kingdom even during an interregnum. The threat to Walter was rapidly overturned.

Henry II was a vigorous monarch, constantly putting down revolts small and large, and dealing with the unwelcome attentions of French kings. His empire, which included the Duchy of Aquitaine after his marriage to Eleanor of Aquitaine was both huge and restless. Not only that, but later in his reign the jealousy and scheming of his sons and wife gave him immense problems. The essence of his story will be familiar to those acquainted with the film and play *The Lion in Winter* and with the 1978 BBC series and book *The Devil's Crown*. Henry's reign was to be the apogee of the Angevin empire.

Late in his reign he landed at Old Winchelsea after one of his last tours of empire in January 1188. Otherwise he hardly touched Sussex, although a Royal Charter of 1155–6 had established the first three Cinque Ports, which included Hastings, to maintain ships ready for the monarch. He issued a further more general charter to the ports in 1160.

It is also noted that Pevensey Castle was once more surrendered to the crown in 1157, this time from William de Blois, Earl Warenne, the son of King Stephen, overlooked for the monarchy. He had become Earl Warenne by marrying the Countess of Warenne, who had inherited as she had no brothers. Gervase of Canterbury says a plot against Henry's life was discovered in 1154 and allegedly William of Blois had some knowledge of this plot. Whatever the truth, William fled to Normandy, unchivalrously leaving the countess behind (or maybe she was glad to stay). Pevensey Castle would remain a royal castle until the early 13th century.

Although King Henry II may have never visited Battle, he was a key figure in settling Battle Abbey's future status and relationships with the Church. He also allowed the foundation of a new Cistercian abbey at Salehurst near Robertsbridge in 1176. The details of these events are described in later chapters.

Henry II died at Chinon on the Loire on 6 July 1189. Curiously, a charter in favour of the monks of Robertsbridge was signed in his name by Stephen de Turonis at Chinon on the day before Henry II died.

His family was in disputational chaos and the French had made great inroads into his empire. His body was escorted to Fontevrault for burial by his natural (bastard) son Geoffrey. His decorated tomb (along with those of Eleanor of Aquitaine, King Richard I and King John's Queen Isabella of Angoulême) can still be seen at Fontevrault Abbey – which has been superbly restored in recent years.

Tomb effigies of King Henry II and Eleanor d'Aquitaine at Fontevrault Abbey
Photographs © Keith Foord

1189–1199 Richard I (Lionheart)

Richard was born in England, but once he became king spent very little time there. He was the third son, but his older brothers had died.

The Treaty of Falaise made between his father and King William I of Scotland was annulled in 1189 when Richard effectively sold southern Scotland back to the Scottish king to help fund his crusade. This led to his legendary but tumultuous history, including a crusade for which he departed in 1190, finally returning in 1194 after being captured in Austria during his return, transferred to Bavaria and then ransomed by the German Emperor Henry VI. The local connection to this is that, in 1192 Abbot Denis of Robertsbridge was sent together with the Abbot of Boxley to search for King Richard. Having found him, the Abbots were sent back to England with the details of the deal which had been done with Richard's keeper, which was for a huge ransom of 150,000 marks (£100,000). In modern terms this may equate to 30 billion pounds.

After Richard initially returned to England he recrossed to France and never returned. When besieging the Castle of Châlus in central France he was fatally wounded by a crossbow bolt, and he died of gangrene on 6 April 1199. He too was interred at Fontevrault.

Sometime during Richard I's reign, Hastings Priory of the Holy Trinity was established by either Sir Walter Bricet or Walter de Scotney, and the priory later obtained the advowsons of more churches from Ralph Neville in 1237 and lands at Michelham in 1229 from Gilbert de Laigle.

He never visited Battle. But nevertheless he did find time to confirm Battle Abbey's charter, but not the sole right of the Abbot to dispense justice within the leuga, which now increasingly fell into the remit of the realm's itinerant justices.

Richard I's tomb effigy at Fontevrault Abbey
Photograph © Keith Foord

1199–1216 John (Lackland)

John was born around Christmas time in 1166 or 1167 in Oxford, the youngest son of Henry II. When his brother Richard became monarch, John had received titles, lands and money. But in October 1190, Richard recognised his nephew, Arthur, son of his deceased brother Geoffrey – who would have been older than John had he lived – as his heir. John was regent in England whilst Richard was on crusade and he tried to take over, unsuccessfully. Richard returned in early 1194, and when Arthur was captured by Philip II of France in 1196, Richard then named John his heir. Arthur later passed into the hands of John and was 'disappeared'. Strong rumour has it that after some prevarication John had Arthur murdered. After becoming king, John once more renewed Battle Abbey's charter, on the same terms as Richard.

War with France was renewed, triggered by John's probably strategic marriage to Isabella of Angoulême, who had been betrothed to Hugh de Lusignan. Somewhat surprisingly, this matter directly affected the Rape of Hastings, as we shall see later. Isabella became Countess of Angoulême in her own right on 16 June 1202, but by 1206, John had lost Normandy, Anjou, Maine and parts of Poitou. He wanted to win them back, but this required huge sums of money, so taxes were increased and he used his feudal rights in innovative ways to extract even more money from the barons. This bred much baronial discontent and eventually this led to his sealing of the Magna Carta in 1215, which was soon rendered impractical when, backed up by the Pope, John claimed that he had sealed the charter under duress.

The itinerary of King John was well researched by Hardy in 1835, but has recently been double-checked and updated in a project led by Crump of the University of Iowa – the 'Itinerary of King John Project' can be found on line. Combining the Hardy and Crump works with the histories of Battle Abbey, Hastings and Winchelsea, a good appreciation can be made of John's local visitations, and of other interactions with Battle Abbey and the towns and ports of eastern Sussex.

Some have suggested that John rather favoured Battle Abbey, but this really did not cost John much, just a few visits and gifts. During his rule Battle Abbey was visited by King John on a few occasions – his visits to Battle are noted to be 6 April 1206, 25 and 26 April 1213 and 13 June 1213. In 1206 he appears to have been on a general progress from London to Dorset, by way of the north and south coasts of Kent and the coasts of Sussex and Hampshire. Before Battle he had been at Romney in Kent, and was moving on to Malling near Lewes. He gave a fine cassock at the time of this visit to Battle Abbey.

In 1203 John had demanded a gift of 60 marks (£40) from Battle Abbey and in 1211 he sold to it his royal prerogative and confirmed its ancient liberties for 1500 marks (£1000), almost certainly because of his need for money for wars rather than from altruism or any thought of the potential consequences. No longer would the monarch take the Abbey's surpluses when there was an abbatial vacancy, and the lands would remain intact.

In 1212 the Abbot of Robertsbridge was again sent abroad as the king's messenger. John also issued edicts such as:

> The King to Ws beloved the Prior and Convent of Battle, greeting. Since the persons of your house are wholly unknown to us, we earnestly beg of you to choose by canonical election the best and most fit monk of your house as Abbot, and to present him to us, that to his election we may give our assent; and in testimony hereof, &c. Witness ourself at Guildford, on the 17th day of January, in the 16th year of our reign (1215)

> The King to the Convent of Battle, greeting. In our presence appeared Hugoline, the precentor of your church, and Julian and A. your monks, and presented to us the election of monk Richard, your confrère, according to canonical form, begging us to give the royal assent to such election. We, therefore, in giving our assent to the said election, command you to be obedient and intentive to the same elect henceforth as your Abbot ; and in testimony hereof, &c. Witness ourself at Knep, on the 23d of January, in the 16th year of our reign.

There is doubt about whether John may have visited Hastings on the 30 March 1201 after staying at Canterbury for Easter. There is a three-day gap in his itinerary between his leaving Canterbury and his being recorded to be in London. If so, this is reputed to been to issue, at Hastings, the Ordinance of the Sea which was later transcribed into the Black Book of the Admiralty which contains naval regulations, the Laws of Oléron (basic early seafaring rules), another three ordinances issued by King John, and other ordinances of Henry I, Richard I and Edward I. This was related to the sovereignty of the seas and demanded that if a king's ship is met, the second ship should strike its flag or lower its topsail or be regarded as an enemy. This was probably initially related to the fact that at that time he was nominally in possession of the land on each side of the English Channel (or seas), and therefore anyone else was crossing his waters. This was before he had to cede Normandy to Philip of France in 1205.

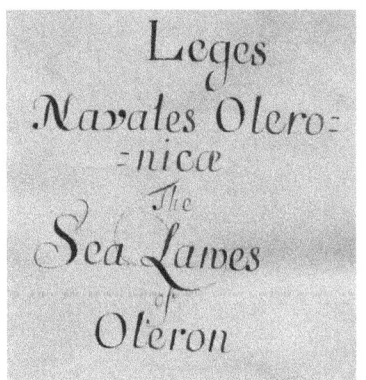

Title page detail from *The Sea Laws of Oleron*:
Undated and unknown author
University of Edinburgh

Around 1210–11 John had by various schemes and impositions raised huge sums of money, and commissioned new ships for the navy, ten galleys and another ten boats which were built at Old Winchelsea, where his own galley the *Deulabeneie* was also repaired. These ships were to be used in 1213 to raid the French coast, attacking Fécamp and Dieppe and destroying ships at the mouth of the Seine. Earlier he had issued orders to the Cinque Ports including Winchelsea, Rye, Hastings and Pevensey such as this of 1210:

> The King to his Barons of Sandwich, Dover, Hythe, Romney, Winchelsea, Rye, Hastings, Pevensey, and all his faithful men of the Cinque Ports, &c. We command you, as you regard your own safety and welfare and our honour and peace, to select immediately, on sight of these, the best and strongest men of your ports, and those who are well armed, to man our vessels, at our cost and for our service, and act in this as our beloved and faithful William de Wrotham, Archdeacon of Taunton, shall tell you on our part, that our affairs may not be impeded by your default. Witness Geoffrey Fitz Peter, at Marlborough, the 17th day of March, in the 9th year of our reign.

Similar writs were sent to Seaford, Shoreham, Chichester, Portsmouth, and Southampton. The visits of 1213 to Battle Abbey were brief and gift-less; but it was while there in 1213 that he

> annulled his previous sentences of outlawry against certain ecclesiastics and undertook never again to outlaw clerks.

The main purposes of the visits were related to the earlier threat from France, which had led to the above naval activities. On the first 1213 visit, he was moving from Arundel to the Cinque Ports – to Dover, then back to Rye and Winchelsea where he stayed two nights – after which he moved on to Rochester. The second visit of 1213 followed another naval success when the English fleet carrying an army to Flanders had come across the French fleet anchored off Zwin (near Zeebrugge) and inflicted severe damage on it. John was moving from Chilham near Canterbury to Aldingbourne near Chichester, then to Portsmouth (from whence he had intended to strike for Poitou, but he failed to get enough support) and so to Corfe, one of his favourite castles. Chilham Castle had been built for Henry II in 1174, and the Bishop of Chichester had his palace at Aldingbourne. Presumably John was using the coastal route to congratulate his navy once again, overnighting at Battle Abbey on the way to meet his hoped-for army.

Following on from John's repudiation of Magna Carta, a civil war erupted in 1216. In the end, the Dauphin, Prince Louis of France, married to Blanche, a niece of John via his sister Eleanor, was invited by dissident barons to invade England, with a view to taking the throne on behalf of his wife – who in modern primogeniture terms had the same right to the throne as her cousin Arthur, the deceased son of John's brother Geoffrey. He landed in England at Sandwich during late May 2016. John had been at Sandwich on 22 May but, as Gillingham says:

> rather than attack Louis's army as it came ashore, John decided to run for it. By the evening of the 23rd he was at Seaford, at least 60 miles away. If he had ridden through Battle that day, he cannot have stopped for long. Dover Castle held out for John, but Louis was soon in control of most of south-east England, and he had Alexander II, King of Scotland and the Welsh prince Llewelyn the Great on his side.

Louis and the barons made rapid and considerable progress and they captured the Cinque Ports. In 1215 John had given fruitless orders to the Cinque Ports to be defended. Also by early 1216 he had clearly feared that the Castles of Hastings and Pevensey would fall into French hands and ordered them slighted so as to be indefensible. At Hastings the damage was minor enough to be rectified when Henry III ordered the repair and re-fortification of the Castle in 1220. Pevensey Castle was rebuilt later, around 1250, under Peter of Savoy, the Earl of Richmond.

Louis reached London on 2 June 1216, and received the homage of the barons and the mayor. However the Castles at both Dover and Windsor remained held by those loyal to John. Louis was never crowned because the Archbishop of Canterbury was away at the papal court, and no bishop 'was available' to perform a coronation. John then died on 19 October 1216 at Newark, only in partial control of the western part of the country, with the war with the barons and Louis still in progress. His body was entombed in the choir of Worcester cathedral. But eastern Sussex had not yet seen the end of involvement in the war, which spilt over into the next reign.

There is no doubt that John was a very active and well-travelled king. Some have questioned the distances that he was able to travel in a day, but there is no doubting the detail of his itinerary which is very well recorded. He did no physical harm to Battle Abbey, and made it independent of himself and his successors, as well keeping it out of the hands of the bishops of Chichester. If he had not impecuniously 'sold' this right, the Abbey may have very soon lost its independence from Chichester.

1216–1272 Henry III:
the fourth longest reigning monarch of England

After the death of King John (18–19 October 1216), the supporters of his nine-year old son, the young Prince Henry, arranged his coronation as King Henry III (28 October 1216). His early coronation led to a long reign and he became the fourth longest reigning monarch of England (but not Scotland) after Queens Elizabeth II and Victoria and King George III.

Historians divide Henry's reign into four chronological periods and this division will also be followed here for clarity:

- The minority of Henry III and its aftermath, 1216–1234
- The personal rule of Henry III, 1234–1258
- The period of reform and rebellion, 1258–1267
- The final years, 1267–1272

1216–1234

Louis of France had continued to make progress after taking London and had moved on to take Hertford Castle and receive the surrender of Berkhamsted Castle by the end of 1216. Henry's followers, led by William Marshall, who was brother-in-law of King John and appointed protector of the young king, and regent of England in spite of his advanced years (he was then about 70), continued the fighting against Louis and his English baronial supporters.

Two weeks after the new king's coronation, Magna Carta was re-issued at Bristol in November 1216. The idea was to encourage the barons to abandon Louis. It was not identical to the charter of 1215, but it did retain the great bulk of the reform programme, and in some ways improved on it. The age of majority, for example, was for the first time set at twenty-one. The most important chapter of all, the one in which the king promised not to arrest or imprison anyone, or take their property, or outlaw them or exile them except by the lawful judgment of their peers or by the law of the land, was retained in full. The reissue of Magna Carta helped diffuse some of the hostility that existed between the government and the baronial insurgents.

Dauphin Louis continued to gain territory in the east and in January decided to go to France for more reinforcements. He had a slightly difficult trip, but by the end of February 1217 Louis had returned to the south coast and taken refuge at Winchelsea. Sensing an opportunity, William Marshall moved towards Winchelsea, but as he approached a French fleet arrived, and this allowed Louis to escape the short distance to Rye, which was rapidly captured from its inhabitants by the French – following which Louis escaped to France itself, then promptly returned to England once more. On the last day of February, Henry wrote to the men of Rye, saying that he had heard of the capture of their town by Louis, and bidding them to be of good cheer and not allow the enemy to take any hostage or pledge from them, as he would in a few days send an army under the Earl Marshal and other barons to drive out the French.

William Marshall did indeed detach Philip d'Aubigny to occupy Rye, but himself moved his army westwards to Shoreham, then on to Farnham, Knepp surrendering to him on the way. Chichester and Winchester were then retaken from Louis, and at Chichester a truce was made and the Earls of Arundel and Warenne re-joined the King.

Louis suffered a number of further reverses in 1217. There was a real turning point when Louis lost the second Battle of Lincoln on 20 May 1217. Equally important was his failure to take Dover Castle and not to have a clear passage to and from France. Lincoln was followed by further losses, including critically at the sea Battle of Sandwich on 24 August 1217 when a French fleet laden with reinforcements for a French army in London was destroyed. The English fleet had a strong core from the Cinque Ports, the men of which, including from the freed Rye and Winchelsea, had to be bribed to take part. However, the English proceeded to capture the French flagship and many supply vessels, forced the rest of the French fleet back to Calais and established full control of the English Channel. Negotiations then rapidly took place on 5 September 1217 near Kingston on Thames. On 11 September 1217 the Treaty of Lambeth was agreed and ratified nine days later, putting an end to Louis's pretensions.

Henry III's government struggled to rebuild authority and prevent a return to anarchy, and as part of the restabilisation process reissued a further modified Magna Carta late in 1217, with further revisions yet again in 1225. It was to be this last version, not the charters of 1215, 1216 or 1217, which entered the statute book as England's first and most fundamental statute.

Early in 1225 Henry visited the Cinque Ports, as a threat had been received that Louis was thinking of invading again. The 18-year-old Henry's visit was to view the naval defences and to ask for advice to be given to a great council which was convened for February. On the Patent Rolls are documents issued by Henry III to all the Cinque Ports when at Romney on 13 January 1225, and some more specific entries were made at Winchelsea on 19 January; at Rye on 20 January; Battle on 24 January; at Robertsbridge on 25 January; and one was issued to the Abbot of Battle just after this, from Westminster dated 7 February 1225.

In late 1222 the Abbot of Robertsbridge, who was clearly regarded with some respect, was once more sent as a messenger for the King overseas with a letter of protection, possibly to the Pope and once more concerning Magna Carta.

In 1225 the Abbot of Robertsbridge was granted a weekly Friday market and an annual three-day fair in August. Within three weeks the grant was cancelled, apparently due to the financial threat to existing markets in the area.

Louis did not reinvade and Sussex did not host any notable historical event for many years, although problems rumbled on in the background. Once Henry reached his majority he firmly held the throne.

1234–1258

In January 1237 Henry III married Eleanor of Provence, whose sister Margaret was married to King Louis IX of France (the son of the Prince Louis who had invaded England, and sometime later became King Louis VIII).

Following his marriage Henry started to grant what was perceived by the barons as excessive favours and appointments to foreigners. Peter des Roches, Bishop of Winchester and Henry's tutor, introduced Frenchmen from Poitou, and Italians followed through Henry's ties to the papacy. His reign coincided with an expansion of papal power and the Church was perceived as excessive in extorting money from England. As early as 1240, English churchmen were protesting to Henry about this and Abbot Ralph of Coventry, elected Abbot of Battle in 1235, was amongst the ecclesiastical spokesmen. So Henry was starting to upset both barons and clergy.

Lower records in his *Summary of the History of Battel Abbey*, which follows on from his translation of the *Chronicle of Battel Abbey*:

> A contemporary writer assures us that the large sum of 200 marks has been claimed and recovered from this convent' and '… notwithstanding the severe extractions they had suffered at the hands of his minions, who had, under various pretexts, levied unheard of contributions on the ecclesiastics of the kingdom'.

Eastern Sussex was involved to an extent in the King's policy of favouritism towards his foreign courtiers. The Castle and Manor of Pevensey were given firstly to the Poitevin Peter de Rivallis. Then, shortly after de Rivallis spectacularly fell from favour, to Henry's uncle Peter of Savoy, born in Susa, Italy. Savoy also received Hastings Castle.

1247 saw Henry III resuming ownership of Winchelsea and Rye from the Abbey of Fécamp which had held the manor of Rameslie, which included the two ports, since the time of King Cnut, i.e. from well before the Conquest. Fécamp was left with the manor of Brede (which included some rentals in Hastings) and with Steyning in West Sussex, but received other lands in Gloucestershire and Lincolnshire in exchange for the two strategically important Cinque Ports, which in defence of the realm terms clearly could no longer be owned by a French abbey.

Sometime, probably well before 1253, a Franciscan (Greyfriars) Priory was established at Old Winchelsea and in 1253, after waiting 28 years, the Abbot of

Robertsbridge was once again granted by the King a weekly Monday market and an annual fair on 14 September. William of Etchingham had been granted a Wednesday market at Salehurst five months earlier.

The rumbling national discontent rose to a head in 1258. Henry had levied extortionate taxes to pay for war with Wales, for failed campaigns in France, and for extensive ecclesiastical building, including the rebuilding of Westminster Abbey which had begun in 1245. The last straw was when he agreed to cover the debts of the papacy in a fruitless war with Sicily. The barons demanded sweeping reforms and Henry was in no position to resist. In 1258 he agreed to the Provisions of Oxford, an agreement placing the barons in virtual control of the realm through a council of 15 men, without whose consent Henry could do very little. The scene was being set for conflict, but also set a precedent which would curtail the authority of all subsequent English monarchs.

1258–1267

In 1258 the barons initiated a three-year period of reform, with new processes, which included sanctions against their default, covering justice, finance and the role of foreigners. Between 14 November 1259 and 21 April 1260 Henry was in France ratifying the Treaty of Paris by which he and his heirs formally renounced their claims to Normandy, Anjou and Poitou in return for Gascony, which was to be held as a fief from the King of France. This visit had enabled Henry to evade the reformers work and many of the reformers had become demoralised and support was evaporating.

As his father had done with the 1215 Magna Carta, Henry obtained a papal bull in 1261, proclaiming the 1225 and later reforms unconstitutional. Henry began to reassert his authority and by late 1261 the majority of reformers had acquiesced. The chief reformer, the Earl of Leicester (Simon de Montfort, married to Henry III's sister Eleanor, the youngest daughter of King John) returned to his native France.

Blazon of Simon de Montfort, Earl of Leicester

Various barons encouraged de Montfort to return to England in April 1263. He gathered supporters and began ravaging the estates of Henry's allies and generally being a thorough nuisance. In order to end the issues between them, Henry and de Montfort agreed to submit their arguments to King Louis IX of France for arbitration. Louis's verdict, known as the Mise of Amiens, was unsurprising as he declared in favour of his fellow monarch. One has to suspect de Montfort may have been using this as a delaying process to gain even more support rather than expecting a favourable result. Full civil war broke out and this led to the Battle of Lewes on 14 May 1264.

The leaders of the barons were Simon de Montfort and Gilbert de Clare, Earl of Gloucester. Each had some connection with Sussex, the former holding the manor of Sheffield near Fletching and the latter the manor of Rotherfield. London was held by the barons and strongly favourable to their cause. The barons, reinforced by a large contingent of Londoners, left London on 6 May and marched in the direction of Lewes.

Henry decided to focus his forces where they would have the support of the local lords. For this purpose Sussex appeared to him a good choice. Lewes Castle was in the hands of his brother-in-law, John de Warenne; Pevensey and Hastings were held by his uncle Peter of Savoy; and William de Braose of Bramber and John Fitz-Alan of Arundel had both proved their loyalty in the defence of Rochester Castle. In early May Henry's army moved southwards from Tonbridge, having taken Tonbridge Castle from the Earl of Gloucester on 30 April, with the aim of securing the Cinque Ports and south coast. En route they encountered an affray at Combwell near Ticehurst on 2 May and one of the king's cooks, Master Thomas, is reported to have been murdered. It may have been that the locals did not take kindly to the cook taking their produce to feed the army. John de la Haye, who was a member of the local gentry and would next be seen at Lewes and would become constable of Rye and Winchelsea, is said to have been involved in this affair, as were allegedly some of Battle Abbey's tenants. This is recorded in an original document thought to have been written by a contemporary monk at Battle Abbey, the manuscript of which is still held at the Bodleian library. The reprisal was an unusually severe act of terror even for its time. Carpenter says:

> 315 archers were beheaded in the Weald in the parish of St Mary, Ticehurst, in the place called Flimwell in the presence of the king, all of whom had been called deceitfully to the king's peace only to then incur that death through the counsel of Richard king of Germany.

Moving on to Robertsbridge Abbey, Henry, Edward and company were entertained, but the 'guests' were in an angry mood and obliged the monks to pay a heavy ransom of 500 marks (£333) to Prince Edward to spare their lives. The next day, Abbot Reginald of Brecknock and the brothers of Battle Abbey went out in procession, presumably in considerable trepidation, to meet the king and give him a loyal welcome. Henry was still angry and demanded 100 marks (£66.67) from the Abbey as he said that some of its tenants had been at Ticehurst – not that the Abbey was in a position to forbid them to go wherever they wished. Prince Edward demanded another 40 marks. In addition some damage was inflicted on the Abbey's goods, but compared to Robertsbridge they got off relatively lightly.

The King then went on to Winchelsea on 4 May, to ensure the support of the Cinque Ports. This was not forthcoming and Henry took hostages, who gave a grudging promise to obtain ships for the King's use. The army was let loose on Winchelsea's wine cellars, and worse. After four days Henry returned to Battle and there received the news that the barons were assembling near Lewes. He moved out westwards and lodged one night at Herstmonceux, where his army hunted and generally rampaged around the park, then moved on towards Lewes on 10–11 May. Henry lodged at Lewes Priory and Lewes Castle defences were bolstered with royalist troops.

The barons had encamped at Fletching, some 8 miles away. Some negotiations took place, but no accord was reached and on the 14 May the Battle of Lewes took place. The barons won and King Henry and Prince Edward were taken prisoner. On 15 May the Mise of Lewes was agreed and the Provisions of Oxford were enacted.

Prince Edward was initially sent to Dover Castle to be guarded by Henry de Montfort, a son of Simon de Montfort senior, whist King Henry was taken back to Battle Abbey by Simon de Montfort, 'no longer with power to extort money from his entertainers' as he had done on his last visit less than a fortnight before, and thence to London, but not before Henry signed royal orders at Battle for the appointment of Drogo de Baranton as governor of Windsor Castle and for the release of many prisoners, including another of de Montfort's sons, Simon junior. Blaauw says that 'the monks must have relished the spectacle of speedy retribution, which now brought the wrong-doer humiliated and harmless to their door'. Henry and his eldest son, Edward, along with his brother, Richard, Earl of Cornwall, were placed under house arrest.

In the aftermath of Lewes, the Cinque Ports ships, Winchelsea to the fore but also involving Rye and Hastings, joined a fleet off Sandwich to prevent foreign assistance being sent to Henry. 300 archers were stationed at Winchelsea whilst the fleet was away. The fleet also opportunistically pillaged Calais. After that things went further astray as Simon de Montfort junior allowed more naval anarchy. The Cinque Ports activity deteriorated into extensive piracy with ships of no nation, even English, being safe. The fleet even attacked Portsmouth in jealousy of its growing trade – they invaded and burned the town, murdered those who put up a defence and stole the ships in the harbour.

During the years before the Battle of Lewes, Pevensey Castle had been in the hands of the royalists. A number of prominent royalists fled from Lewes to Pevensey after the battle and then took ship to France. Soon afterwards the garrison at Pevensey were commanded not to leave the Castle. In July the occupiers were ordered to explain to the King, who was still under house arrest, their behaviour at Pevensey. Later in the month John d'Abernon was ordered to take over the Castle and to give the three principal defenders safe-conduct to either join the King under house arrest, or to go into exile. They refused to surrender and in September various baronial supporters joined Simon de Montfort junior in a siege of the Castle. As it was still possible at that time for the defenders to bring in reinforcements and provisions by sea, the siege failed. This was a microcosm of the problems still facing the barons.

De Montfort senior had taken control of the government in the name of the king but realised the need to obtain wide support. In 1264 he summoned barons from the whole country to an early pre-Parliament and in 1265 also invited burgesses from selected towns, with a representative parliament called in 1265. On 14 February 1265, during a parliament summoned in the name of King Henry III, an announcement was made that the King had promised to keep Magna Carta. This was the 1265 inspeximus (inspection) of Magna Carta 1225, which has been used to help inform the details of the attendance at that parliament.

Meanwhile Prince Edward had escaped from his confinement at Hereford, and rallied royalist forces. De Montfort had lost the support of the Earl of Gloucester, Gilbert de Clare, who had helped arrange Edward's escape and had guaranteed to him the military support of the Welsh Marcher lords.

In June 1265 de Montfort arranged for his wife Eleanor to move to the safety of Dover Castle from Odiham in Hampshire. She was met at Wilmington by her son Simon junior, taking a break from besieging Pevensey Castle, and they overnighted at Battle Abbey where the cost of their dinners and overnight stays (for which she paid, it seems) was detailed. This included the costs of pasture for 395 horses, which gives an idea of the size of her retinue. They went on to visit Winchelsea, holding a feast there with the burgesses, before reaching Dover Castle. The Countess of Leicester had with her at Dover a contingent of archers from Pevensey under John la Warre, a hundred sailors from Winchelsea under Richard de Montfort (another son of Simon senior), John de la Haye (who had been appointed constable of Rye and Winchelsea in August 1264), Waleran de Monceaux and Matthew de Hastings, the last of whom seems to have been instrumental in the final surrender of Dover Castle to Prince Edward in late 1265.

On 4 August 1265, Edward caught up with de Montfort at the Battle of Evesham. De Montfort and many of his supporters were killed. Inevitably the remaining reformers gradually capitulated. The Dictum of Kenilworth of 30 October 1266 was an accord with the rebels. The document marked the end of the reform movement and the restoration of royal power, although many of the reforms passed by Simon de Montfort's parliaments were accepted by the King. The Cinque Ports did not escape retribution for their support of the barons, although Rye and Hastings made 'grovelling apologies' in similar letters to the king. That from Hastings read:

> Most dear Lord, the most illustrious King of England, his liege and faithful barons of Hastings, greeting, in the Saviour of all, and prompt and ready willingness to obey in all things, even to the division of soul and body, with all subjection, reverence, and honour. We have thought it right to declare by these letters, to the excellence of your Royal Majesty, that extreme grief of heart, and anguish beyond measure, have now for a long time past affected all

and each of us, inasmuch as we have neither been able to approach the bodily presence of your loyal clemency during the delay of your long sojourn in remote parts, nor to direct sure messengers in order to ascertain the certainty of the good condition of your person, for the sake of both the love and honour of which we are ready to be crowned with a victorious death, if necessary. Moreover, let your Royal excellence take notice that we have, up to this time, guarded your town of Hastings for your use and that of your heirs, and at your good pleasure shall guard it for ever, although anything of the contrary may have been suggested to your pious ears by our enemies against us. To which enemies, indeed, do not give credence, since they are not to be believed in anything; and although some persons, without the assent of our community, may have offended your Royal Majesty, we have at no time adopted them nor their evil deeds, but, even in the presence of your Royal Majesty, have disapproved and disavowed them and their evil works, and have never ceased to disapprove them. Wherefore, we humbly implore the clemency of your Royal Majesty. May the excellence of your Royal Majesty be in health, and flourish to endless time.'

These apologies were successful in avoiding severe retribution but it is reported that Rye was sanctioned and its bailiff was replaced and all its ships were placed for the common good, forbidden to go venturing overseas without the king's permission. The barons of Rye were forgiven, just. But Old Winchelsea – at that time a town of possibly more than 700 houses, two churches and over 50 inns and taverns and a population of a few thousands did not apologise. In late 1265–early 1266 Prince Edward moved towards Winchelsea after taking Dover Castle, from which Simon de Montfort's wife had escaped to France never to be reconciled with her brother. Edward recruited ships from the east coast and Winchelsea was subjected to a combined attack from the sea and land with a force that contained 577 Welsh archers. The leading citizens were put to the sword, but the majority spared. Winchelsea rather foolishly revolted in a smaller way in 1267, the result was the same and more leaders disappeared into Rochester Castle dungeons never to reappear.

When Edward came to the throne a few years later he was to take a great interest in Winchelsea and its most useful port, and arranged the development of the planned New Winchelsea on the hill of Iham.

The final years 1267–1272

The King's authority was finally restored by the Statute of Marlborough (1267), in which the King also promised to uphold the latest version of Magna Carta and some of the Provisions of Westminster, evolved from the Provisions of Oxford. Eastern Sussex quietened after the excitements of the previous few years. Nothing of note is recorded for Battle and area for the last five years of Henry III's reign.

Henry had revered King Edward the Confessor, who had been canonised in 1161, even having a mural painted of him in his bedchamber. Henry III's life's major architectural work was the re-building of Westminster Abbey which had been founded by Edward. In 1269, the renovated Abbey was consecrated and Edward the Confessor's body reburied there with Henry III himself helping to carry the Confessor's coffin to its new resting place. The occasion was intended to show that rifts between the King and the barons had been overcome but, fearing violence, a planned crown-wearing was cancelled. Three years later Henry III himself died at his Palace of Westminster on 16 November, 1272, aged sixty-five. He became the first of the Plantagenets to be buried within the Abbey.

Effigy of King Henry III in Westminster Abbey
by Valerie McGlinchey [CC BY-SA 2.0 (http://creativecommons.org/licenses/by-sa/2.0)], via Wikimedia Commons

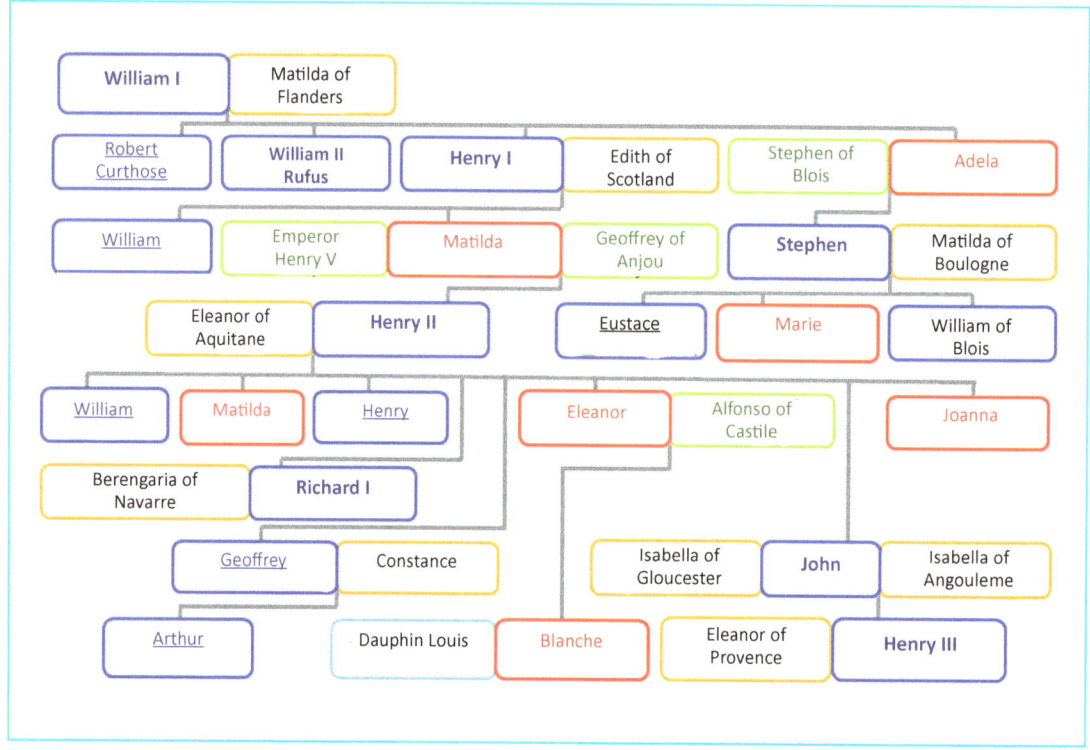

The English regal line from William I to Henry III

Males of English royal line in dark blue, females in red. Male spouses in green, female spouses in yellow. French royal in light blue. Those who died before they could be considered as possible inheritors have their names underlined. ©BDHS

3
Abbots of Battle Abbey
1070–1538

The new charter makes no specific mention of precedents, supercedes all previous ones and thus vitiates the risk of trouble if lost.
Henry II

Illuminated page from the frontispiece of Lower's *Chronicle of Battel Abbey*

Introduction

This chapter will cover the history of Battle Abbey with a focus on the lives and deeds of its Abbots and local events that occurred during their abbacies. Thanks to the books and researches of Searle, a great deal is known about Battle Abbey and its influence on its locality. The next chapter will then look at the influence of an artefact from the Abbey, followed by a chapter reviewing the histories of the other pre-Dissolution religious houses of the wider eastern Sussex.

There were 29, 30 or 31 Abbots of the Abbaye de Bello, depending on whether or not we count the very first, named Robert Blancard, who may not have been consecrated Abbot, and on whether there was an election or not covering the period 1529–31 before the abbacy of the final Abbot, John Hammond. Clearly not all the Abbots have memorable stories and many must have led relatively quiet lives leading the monks in their ecclesiastical duties and rubber-stamping various rentals and land deals – not that they were not busy supervising the life of the Abbey and leading the management of the wide-ranging Abbey estates and even acting as the local lord in legal matters.

We have reasonably good information about events in the lives of the first eleven Abbots, and these all have an entry in the text. After that those that have some recorded event or events of significance are selected. The complete list of the 31 possible Abbots and their dates of election or appointment, the reason why each ceased being Abbot, and some brief introductory notes to each is given directly below. Many but not all died in post.

1. **Robert Blancard,** ?designated 1070–1, appointed 1076, drowned same year. There is a mention in *Regesta Regnum Anglo-Normannorum* Vol.1 about an Abbot in 1070/1. Robert Blancard, one of the first monks, may have been designated by William I in 1070, not 1076, but maybe it was not possible to be formally appointed until the very first part of the Abbey church was consecrated in 1076.

2. **Gausbert**, a monk of Marmoutier, appointed 1076, died 1095. King William II Rufus then delayed appointing a new Abbot for a year in argument with Archbishop Anselm of Canterbury.

3. **Henry of Bec** (in Normandy), Prior of Christ Church Canterbury, appointed 1096, died 1102. The custody of the Abbey during the long vacancy which followed Abbot Henry's death was first held by one of the King's chaplains, named Vivian, then soon afterwards by a monk Gausfrid de Carileph (Calais). He was never Abbot, but under his watch the claims of Marmoutier that as the mother abbey it had jurisdiction and the right to appoint new Abbots of Battle were rejected. After Geoffrey's untimely death, the Abbot of Thorney 'had care' until Ralph of Caen became Abbot. The Abbot

of Thorney may have been Gunterus, an ex-monk of Battle, who had previously been Prior of St. Nicholas, Exeter (a cell of Battle).

4. **Ralph of Caen**, former monk of Bec, Prior of Rochester Priory, appointed 1107, died 1124.

5. **Warner of Canterbury**, appointed 1125, resigned 1138.

6. **Walter de Luci** (a monk from Lonlé, near Domfront in Normandy), appointed 1139, died 1171. In the four-year period from 1171 to the next Abbot's election, Richard de Luci, who was chief justiciar of England and Walter's brother, 'presided' over the Abbey which was de facto run by Sir Peter Criel and Hugh de Beche.

7. **Odo of Canterbury**, Prior of Christ Church, Canterbury, appointed 1175, died 1200.

8. **John de Dubra** (Dover), appointed 1200, died 1211–4 (see text for discussion). A person called Hugh was then elected according to 'Monasticon' and 'Willis Mitred Abbeys' but left to become Bishop of Carlisle. This information has been copied into later texts, but must be erroneous and a misperception of old texts where '*de Bello*' (of Battle) and '*Bello Loco*' (of Beaulieu) can be easily confused. British History Online has a record stating that the Bishop of Carlisle was the ex-Abbot Hugh of Beaulieu. Hugh of Beaulieu (Cistercian, Hampshire), who had been deposed (Ann. *Waverley* p. 291). He was made a bishop by the papal legate Guala before 1 August 1218, when royal assent given. Ref: *Fasti Ecclesiae Anglicanae 1066–1300: Volume 2, Monastic Cathedrals (Northern and Southern Provinces)*, ed. Diana E Greenway (London, 1971), pp. 19–21.

9. **Richard of Horwode** (possibly originally from Horwood, Buckinghamshire or Devon), a monk of Battle, elected 1215, died 1235. John assented to his election on 22 January. The 1215 sealing of Magna Carta was witnessed by the Abbot of Battle, who must have been Richard. Royal nomination had ceased and from now onwards the monks of the Abbey elected its Abbot, submitting his name for formal royal approval. John was not averse to allowing abbeys to remain without an Abbot as he then received the abbey profits. This is presumably what happened after the death of Abbot John de Dubra.

10. **Ralph de Covintre** (Coventry) elected 1235, last mentioned in 1252.

11. **Reginald of Brecon**, elected 1261, resigned 1281. Abbot at the time of the Battle of Lewes (1264) and host to Henry III before and after the battle.

12. **Henry de Aylesford**, elected 1281, died 1297.

13. **John de Taneto** (Thanet), elected 1298, resigned 1307.

14. **John de Whatlington**, elected 1308, died 1311.

15. **John de Nortburne** (probably Northbourne, near Deal, Kent), elected 1311, resigned 1318.

16. **John de Pevense** (Pevensey), elected 1318, died 1324.

17. **Alan de Retlyng** (now called Ratling. Retling was a manor near Aylesford, Kent), elected 1324, died 1350 (of the Black Death). A royal licence to fortify the Abbey was received in 1338 and the building of the great gatehouse and walls was begun. In 1340 he complained to the king about papal extortion.

18. **Robert de Bello** (of Battle), elected 1351, died 1364. In 1360 the Abbot was one of the landowners made responsible for the defence of the coast. In the Cartulary is a papal bull of 1355, commanding the Prior of Brecon, 'to conduct himself conformably to the accustomed rules of submission to the Abbot of the monastery of St. Martin, in Battel.'

19. **Hamo de Offynton** (of Offington, Worthing), elected 1364, died 1383. In 1371 the Abbot was again one of the landowners made responsible for the defence of the coast. See his account later for details of a defence of Winchelsea in 1377.

20. **John Crane,** elected 1383.

21. **John Lydbury,** elected 1398, died 1404.

22. **William Merssh**, monk of Battle, Prior of St. Nicholas, Exeter, elected 1405, died 1417.

23. **Thomas de Ludlowe** (Ludlow, Shropshire), elected 1417, resigned 1434–5. It was in this Abbot's time that a new Sword of Battle Abbey was made. His initials 't l' can be seen on each side of the coat of arms embossed on its hilt. He may have become Abbot of Shrewsbury. Died 1459.

24. **William Waller,** elected 1435, died 1437.

25. **Richard Dertmouth**, elected 1437, last mentioned 1461. Richard Dertmouth, the Abbey and all its servants were pardoned in 1450 for supporting the Cade Rebellion.

26. **John Newton**, also a Prior of St. Nicholas, Exeter, elected 1463, died 1490.

27. **Richard Tovy**, elected 1490, died 1503. Richard issued a 'passport' to the people of Battle, which confirmed their rights

28. **William Westfield**, another Prior of St. Nicholas, Exeter, elected 1503, died 1508.

29. **Lawrence Champion**, elected 1508, died 1529.

30. Questionable. There was a possible further Abbot 1529–31 as it is recorded that on the Thursday after the feast of St. Laurence in 1529, a proxy from the Prior of Brecon (a cell of Battle) was present in the Chapter House in Battle, to elect a new Abbot. This Abbot may not have been John Hammond for reasons discussed in the section about his abbacy.

31. **John Hammond**, elected 1529 or 1531, pensioned off 1538. The final act of surrender was signed by him and all his monks. The Abbey seal was applied in white wax to the front and the Abbot's seal in red wax to the reverse of this document. This was the final act of the Abbey. The Abbot and the monks all received pensions, apart from the novice. The lay staff lost their jobs but also received small pensions.

3 ABBOTS OF BATTLE ABBEY 1070–1538

Coats of arms of Abbots of Battle

Ecclesiastical coats of arms were probably not formalised until sometime after the 13th century, maybe later. Distinctive coats of arms or blazons had first appeared in the 12th century, being worn by nobles in battle to help distinguish friend from foe and to rally their supporters, later as colours in jousting and for just plain egotism. Before this, military shields might have carried some patterns as seen in the Bayeux tapestry, but this does not appear to have been heraldically formalised. The heraldic arms of the Abbots of Battle varied from their first introduction, and rather than being arms of the Abbey itself, they were the personal arms of the Abbot. Throughout, these arms have used combinations of red (gules), yellow (or) and white (argent). All have carried a large cross, smaller crowns and swords (usually or and in the quarters), and some had mitres in argent, or, or a combination of these, or blue (azure), and occasionally other embellishments, often in azure.

English Heritage have quoted that Abbot Hamo of Offyngton (1364–83) was granted papal permission to use the mitre and additional ornaments normally reserved for bishops, and after this time the mitre appeared on the Abbey's coat of arms. But the mitres may have appeared before that because Battle was a mitred abbey, with the Abbot being summoned to Parliament from time to time. This was covered in the directive by William I dated 1070–1, when he mentions an Abbot of Battle. When the Abbot was called to attend the King's court he had an allowance of food, wine, and wax candles for himself and two monks. From 1295 he was granted a residence in both London, the Inne of Bataille in Southwark near the present Hays Wharf, and also in Winchester, but perhaps the clearest privilege was that the Abbot, when passing through the king's forests, might hunt one or two game animals with his hounds.

Below are artistic interpretations of twelve coats of arms from illustrations and descriptions that can be unearthed .

The illustrations are: from some stained glass in the Burrell Collection, Glasgow; from the British Library's Lansdown Collection MS255; and from the final seal of the Abbey and the hilt of the Sword of Battle. In the last case there is no evidence of the colours, so possible alternatives are shown – although the field, argent and cross, gules are most likely if we believe Paton – who thought the cross had been filled with red enamel.

Solely descriptive evidence comes from: Fuller's *Church History of Britain*; *Monasticon*; Tanner's *Notitia Monastica*; *Gleanings, by a Native,* ascribed to Vidler; part of the original Cole Collection at the BL now indexed under Additional MS60513; and finally from texts describing the final seal of Battle Abbey, and a variant of this by Walcott.

Only three designs can be definitely ascribed: to one of the Thomas Ludlowe alternatives (f), 1417–34; to Lawrence Champion, 1515 (j); and Hammond as

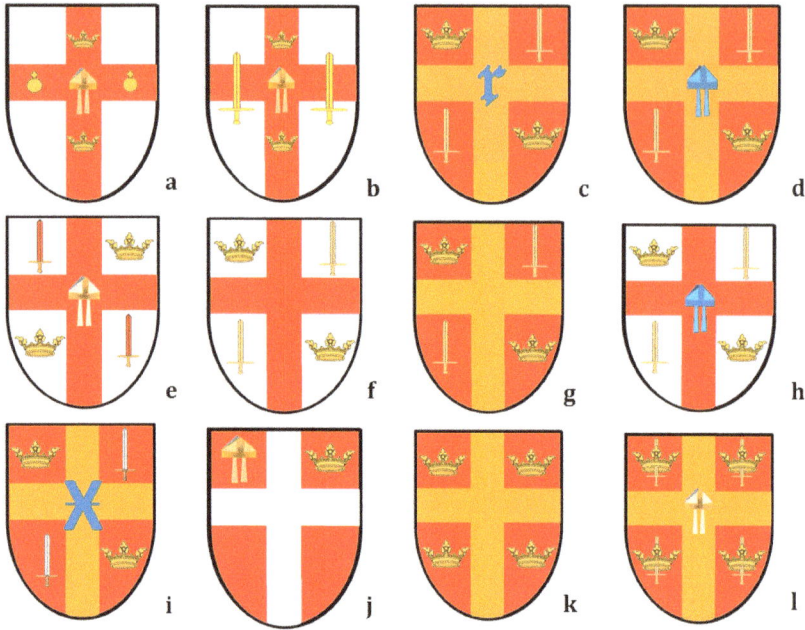

a,b,c,d from Tanner – b as modified by Anstis, d also in Fuller. All undatable : e Burrell c1380 : f,g Ludlowe's sword hilt variants c1417: h BL Lansdowne, undated : i Gleanings, undated, copied from Fuller : j House of Lord 1515s : k,l Final seal 1538, l as modified by Walcott

All arms images © K Foord

illustrated on the seal of 1538 (k). Walcott describes a variation of the last (l), with swords piercing the crowns and a mitre in fess, but this is rather over-complex and he cannot be describing it from the image of the seal, does not state the colour of the mitre or his source.

The stained glass in the Burrell Collections may probably be ascribed to Hamo de Offynton (e) – the fact that the blades of the swords are gules may also be bloody evidence that this shield belongs to Hamo as he was a warrior abbot. The mitres may have first appeared on Hamo's, but one cannot be certain. A mitre also appears on Champion's shield of 1515. Mitres also appear on a,b,d and h but these cannot be ascribed. The coat of arms (a), described by Tanner was the one used on Goss memento ceramics of Battle made between 1858 and 1939. The shield with the central letter 'r' (c) may be a misinterpreted Greek lower-case letter chi χ or X as in (i), which is found in Fuller and copied into Gleanings.

The first designated Abbot, Robert Blancard (1070–76*)

In the winter of 1069–70 William led the terrible rapine and reprisals of the Harrying of the North, which created famine and widespread death in Northumbria. Some rebellion leaders submitted or fled to Scotland. William spent Christmas at York, and in early 1070 he crossed the Pennines from York to Chester in appalling weather. He then returned south, relieving a siege at Shrewsbury, and for the third and final time subduing troublesome Mercia.

Meanwhile the local population of eastern Sussex would have slowly rebuilt their lives, much of the local area having been 'wasted' around the time of the invasion of 1066. It may be noted however that the lands belonging to the Abbey of Fécamp were little affected.

A papal delegation led by Cardinal Bishop Ermenfrid of Sion (in modern Switzerland), with Peter a cardinal priest and John a cardinal deacon, symbolically recrowned William and Queen Matilda at Easter 1070 at Winchester. This was not before imposing a rare Penitential Ordinance or Penitentiary on the Normans who had taken part in the Conquest of England, in atonement for the bloodshed and other sins at the Battle of Hastings and afterwards. The English were exempt from this edict 'as they had suffered enough'.

It is probable that part of the papal legation's conditions was that William should commence the building of Battle Abbey, as he had promised in 1066, as a penance and memorial to the dead of both sides, as per the third paragraph of the Ordinance, which undoubtedly applied to him.

> Anyone who does not know the number of those he wounded or killed must, at the discretion of his bishop, do penance for one day in each week for the remainder of his life, or, if he can, let him redeem his sin by a perpetual alms, either by building or by endowing a church.

To fulfil this papal penance William sent William Faber 'the Smith', a monk in his service, as a messenger to Marmoutier. The Benedictine Monastery of Marmoutier, near Tours in the Loire region of France, was the most important abbey in western France at the time. In the message it was asked to send monks to join Faber in starting to build Battle Abbey. We even know the names of the additional four monks sent – Theobald Vetulum, William Coche, Robert de Bologna, and Robert Blancard.

When the five arrived they found the cairn marking the place at which Harold had been killed and which was to be the site of the high altar, but tried to build the Abbey further down the hill to the west nearer water, at a place called Herste. This same location is mentioned later in the *Chronicle of Battle Abbey* which places two

Date ranges in this section refer to the dates of an abbacy.

Extract from Battle Community Tapestry
This scene shows the papal legates, with their rolled vellum penitentiary, re-crowning
King William I and his Queen Matilda at Winchester in 1070
©Tina Greene   Photography Peter Greene

acres in Herste next to the orchard adjoining the hostel (the hostel was on the site of the present Pilgrim's Rest) and would have been at most one league (2.4km, 1.5 miles) away, probably much less, lying north-west of the Abbey along the road that formed the north border of what became the Abbey's Great Park. Even in this better position they had few resources and probably little lay help, so progress would have been minimal. William eventually received news of this. Led by Robert Blancard the monks explained that:

> the place where he had decided to build the abbey was located upon a hill with parched soil, dry and lacking springs ... the ground forested for some distance around.'

But William angrily told the monks to build the Abbey where he had commanded, famously saying;

> If God spare my life I will so amply provide for this place that wine shall be more abundant than water.

Extract from Battle Community Tapestry
In this scene William is imagined telling the monks to build the abbey on top of the hill as he had commanded (there is no evidence that he actually visited the site, but this picture tells a better story)
©Tina Greene
Photography Peter Greene

The Abbey was to be 'mitred' which meant that the Abbot was required to attend the King's court and parliament when summoned. This is covered in the directive by William I dated 1070–1, when he mentions the Abbot of Battle, from this it is assumed that Blancard was designated to be Abbot.

A mitred abbot's mitre was silver gilt and gold, not all gold like a bishop's. An archbishop's was gold and red. See illustration below. A mitred abbot's crozier had to be held with the crook inward signifying only local influence, whereas a bishop held his crozier's crook outward showing a wider influence over a diocese. Early mitres were quite simple caps, perhaps embroidered but not bejewelled.

Mitres in about 1170
Left: mitred abbot; centre: bishop; right: archbishop after an example in the V&A ascribed to Thomas à Becket
© Keith Foord

Even after 1070 when resources were found, the building progressed slowly and it may not have been until 1076 that the first Abbot could be consecrated. Robert Blancard, one of the four monks who had first come over, was formally elected, and went to Marmoutier to inform his superiors of his elevation and of progress, and to possibly be consecrated. Crossing the English Channel was vary hazardous at that time, and not to be undertaken lightly. Unfortunately he was drowned in the Channel coming back from Marmoutier. So although we are to a degree uncertain, it does seem correct that we should call Robert Blancard the first Abbot of Battle.

Second or possibly the first consecrated Abbot, Gausbert de Marmoutier (1076–95)

When Blanchard died William sent to the Abbey of Marmoutier for another monk capable of taking the abbacy, and Gausbert was despatched with four more monks to join the original brothers. As Graham has pointed out all the monks were sent to oversee the building work '*qui operi preessen*', and would not be expected to build a great church without lay help. De Lasteyrie has clearly stated there were a fair number of monks practising architecture … many bishops and abbots were sufficiently instructed to supervise the skilled craftsmen whom they engaged, but the work was executed by laymen. Gausbert must have had these skills.

Gausbert visited Marmoutier and, when pressed, he refused consecration there. After this attempt by Marmoutier to regard Battle as a daughter house, King William disabused the Abbey of Marmoutier of any thoughts that it had any possible residual control over Battle. He declared that the Church of St Martin of Battle was to be free and exempted from all episcopal jurisdiction, in the same way as the Church of Canterbury. The charter was witnessed by the Archbishops of Canterbury and York, and several other prelates, earls, and barons. But Stigand, the Bishop of Chichester, in whose diocese the Abbey was located, was not a witness and he objected to the grant.

When Gausbert sought consecration from the Archbishop of Canterbury he was refused unless the Abbot-elect went to Chichester to receive the benediction. Gausbert appealed to William, who ordered that the Archbishop should perform the ceremony in the monastery, but the benediction was to be given to him by Stigand of Chichester, before the altar of St Martin of Battle. To remove all pretence of episcopal jurisdiction, William also ordered that the Bishop and his train should neither lodge in the monastery nor take a meal there. To put the matter beyond doubt, William also issued a writ addressed to Lanfranc, Archbishop of Canterbury, and to Stigand, enacting that all future Abbots should be consecrated at Battle, like Gausbert. This was the first time that such an issue was raised and the outcome created a precedent of a 'Royal Peculiar', by royal command, not by charter. As we shall see later, the Church would come back to this time and time again over the centuries to try to wrest control of the royal abbey fully back to Chichester.

Gausbert and his monks were now able to draw on the royal treasury for building costs and maintenance. William also endowed the Abbey with six manors: Wye in Kent, Alciston in Sussex, Limpsfield in Surrey, Brightwalton in Berkshire, Crowmarsh in Oxfordshire, and Hou in Essex and a wealthy church at Collumpton, Devon, with its dependent church at Exeter, all from his own holdings. William also gave considerable rights to the Abbey such as freedom from tolls during their travels. Importantly, for its upkeep in the future, the Abbey had also been granted the banlieu of all lands within a 1½ mile (2.4 km, one league) radius of the Abbey, allowing for slight irregularities at the boundaries where lands of neighbours abutted. This land was carved out of land previously granted to the count of Eu and others, with no compensation. William said that they should give up the land for the love of him, but of course they had no choice and this led to grumbling and later difficulties. So, not only did Gausbert need to be of architectural mind, but also a firm neighbour and land manager. He was starting from virtual scratch on almost undeveloped land that he found was capable of quite rapid development.

The Conqueror died in 1087 and during his son William II Rufus's reign the royal status was retained. Rufus seems to have been surprisingly fond of Battle Abbey, mainly as it had little to do with the mainstream Church, for which he apparently had little time. The port at Hastings was still in a good state at that time and was a staging post for his several visits to Normandy. He is said to have visited the Abbey regularly, possibly to irritate the new Archbishop of Canterbury, Anselm, with whom he constantly quarrelled and who tried to weaken Battle's immunities. When

Extract from the Battle Community Tapestry

Here is Gausbert as the first consecrated abbot, the first part of the abbey is completed and construction of the rest is proceeding. In the lower border we see the drowning Robert Blancard and an illustration of the fox and the crow fable. Likewise at the top there is an illustration of the bat and the weasel fable. These illustrations follow a theme in the original Bayeux Tapestry where additional parts of the story and relevant fables are illustrated in the borders.

©Tina Greene Photography Peter Greene

staying at Hastings in February 1094, Rufus and his court attended the dedication of the Abbey by Archbishop Anselm. William II gave it yet more property, this time the income of nine more churches, and gifts of his father's cloak and a feretory (portable altar), the last believed to have been the feretory on which Harold Godwinson was reputed to have sworn his oath of allegiance to Duke William of Normandy. Gausbert died in 1095 and the monks asked the king to appoint a successor. Rufus was still quarrelling with Anselm and the *Chronicle of Battle Abbey* (*CBA*) blames this for the delay of a year before a new Abbot was appointed. Eventually, and it would seem reluctantly, he took Anselm's advice and appointed Henry of Bec, the Prior of Christ Church, Canterbury as Abbot.

Henry of Bec, the third Abbot (1096–1102) and the five-year vacancy (1102–07)

The monks of Battle were not best pleased with the appointment of Henry, a monk originally from Bec in Normandy but a Prior of Canterbury. He was a disciple of Archbishop Anselm of Canterbury, former Abbot of Bec, who was campaigning for clear lines of authority within the Church from the pope downwards, and for the elimination of any role for laymen over the Church hierarchy. He brought in numbers of monks from Canterbury who, along with Anselm, advised Henry to go to Chichester to be consecrated, as Bishop Reginald was stalling about coming to Battle. This was an early case of gerrymandering and the Battle monks were outvoted. As the *CBA* says, this subtlety exposed the Abbey's status. Never again would an Abbot be consecrated at Battle. But they did maintain their royal rights, in spite of the lack of written proof, tending to reject what bishops demanded by right but giving in when requested nicely.

In short, according to the *CBA*, Henry seems to have been a bit of a disaster. Internal strife appears to have led to some neglect and ill fortune for the Abbey, as well as some dismemberment of the large and valuable manor of Wye in Kent by rapacious neighbours. He was only in post for six years, eventually and fortunately to be followed by a most able man. There was also a new king after 1100 when Rufus died in the New Forest pierced by a hunting arrow, being succeeded by his younger brother Henry I.

The five-year vacancy (1102–07)

When Henry of Bec died the abbatial custody of the Abbey was in abeyance for no less than five years. The vacancy which followed Abbot Henry's death was first managed by one of the king's chaplains, named Vivian, then by a monk called Geoffrey or Gausfrid of Carileph (Calais). The latter does not appear to have been appointed Abbot. Under his watch, a case was taken before the king's court to recover the large manor of Wye in Kent. Also some resurrected claims of the Abbot of Marmoutier, that Marmoutier as the mother abbey had jurisdiction over and the right to appoint new Abbots at Battle, were finally dismissed by Henry I. After Geoffrey of Carileph's untimely death at Battle, the Abbot of Thorney then had a rather unsatisfactory 'care of' the monastery from a distance until Ralph of Caen became Abbot – even though the Abbot of Thorney may have been Gunterus, an ex-monk of Battle, who had previously been Prior of St. Nicholas, Exeter, which was a cell of Battle.

From the *CBA* it appears that it was during the period 1102–7 that the monks commissioned the building of the first part of St Mary's Church, across the road from the Abbey. Also from the rental of Battle Abbey taken sometime between 1102–15 we see the parish church paying rent to the Abbey. The population of Battle had increased; the people were crowding the Abbey church and interfering with the ability of the monks to undertake their religious duties, so the monks determined to build a church outside of the Abbey precincts for the masses. If the monks had not done this and retained the Abbey church as the parish church the great Abbey church would not have been demolished at the dissolution of the monasteries.

The fourth Abbot, Ralph of Caen (1107–24)

Once Ralph was appointed by King Henry I he hurried to Battle. He had first come to England with Archbishop Lanfranc, Anselm's predecessor. Under Ralph, the Abbey recovered from their inter-abbacy both spiritually and in prosperity and looked to buy more lands and to recover those which had been lost. The many deals are listed in the *CBA*. Henry I himself exchanged land and a church near Reading belonging to Battle Abbey for lands near Chichester so that he could build a new abbey at Reading. Below is his notification of this:

> [1120, Nov.–Dec] Portsmouth. Notification by Henry I to Ralph Bp. of Chichester and William fitz Ansger and the barons of Sussex: That he has given to St. Martin of Battle in exchange for Reading, the manor of Appledram [co. Sussex], also 40?. which formerly pertained to the said manor, with the ferm of Bosham; and of feeding in the woods of 'Bocfalde' and 'Betlesparrioc', one pig for every three that the King has there; and the fourth penny of pannage, and the fourth of all the oaks that are felled and the fourth penny from the land pertaining to those woods, &c. The monks and their men of Appledram are to be quit of all custom with sac, soc, toll, team and infangthief, geld, scot, hidage, danegeld, work on bridges, castles, parks, and enclosures, host-service, aids, shires, hundreds, wardpenny, lastage, larceny, murder-fine, treasure-trove, warren, and all pleas and plaints.'

Henry also gave the Abbey several churches in Wales, which by now was under his overlordship. Henry may not have visited Battle, but he certainly stood up for its rights. Abbot Ralph also got on well with the Bishop of Chichester (an old friend also called Ralph), and Ralph, Bishop of Chichester, came to Battle and advised and preached. When the relics of the Abbey were rehoused in a fine gold and silver feretory set with jewels, Bishop Ralph came and blessed it. Boundary disputes with neighbours were settled via the King and the local barons were ordered to fence the lands adjacent to the banlieu to fix the boundaries. The leadwork and the encircling wall of the Abbey were finished off and the courtyard extended. His spiritual work appears also to have been of the highest quality as the words of the *CBA* bear witness.

Ralph died at the age of 84 having been a monk for just over 60 years. He was possibly the last of the community of Battle to have some experience of the Norman Conquest. His death, according to van Houts, could have been what soon spurred the writing in the Battle Abbey scriptorium of a copy of William the Conqueror's Ship List, a copy of the *Brevis Relatio* (a short Latin prose history of Normandy and England from about 1035 to the battle of Tinchebrai in 1106) and the first version of the Abbey's foundation history.

Warner of Canterbury, fifth Abbot (1125–38, when he was induced to resign)

Between the death of Ralph and the appointment of Warner, again of Canterbury, there was a short period of royal administration as Henry I was overseas. On his return Henry published an edict that all churches with no leaders should send a delegation to come to meet him and Battle sent a monk called Hildegard and three other monks. Taking the advice of Archbishop William of Canterbury and Seffrid the new Bishop of Chichester, Henry chose Warner who was obviously supported by the Archbishop to be Abbot of Battle – but Warner was out of England until after Easter 1125, when the Archbishop consecrated him. He arrived in Battle on 24 April and started to sort things out.

Seffrid then summoned Warner to a synod at Chichester and Warner asked the Battle chapter what he should do. They explained the custom that by royal authority he should not be summoned, but that if he wished to go anywhere he had a right to do so. So he went voluntarily and explained Battle's position which the Bishop understood, and the matter went no further.

Soon afterwards, Battle's church at Carmarthen, which was coveted by the local bishop, was exchanged by the King for some land at Langrish in Hampshire, near the Sussex border. However, also at about this time (1125), a founding community of monks from Battle Abbey arrived at Brecon led by a monk called Walter, who became its first prior. Bernard de Neufmarché, a Norman knight, had given the early church at Brecon to one of his followers, Roger, a monk from Battle Abbey, which then founded Brecon Priory as a daughter house of Battle. In the future Brecon would provide abbots for the mother abbey at Battle, as would the other daughter priory of

St. Nicholas, Exeter, which was founded a little earlier in about 1089.

The *CBA* asserts that Warner became somewhat dazzled by his efforts at furnishing the church with new ornaments and vessels for the altar, etc. and at the winter feast of St Martin, after whom Battle Abbey was named, Walter would often summon the Bishop of Chichester. Things got a little out of hand on one occasion and the Bishop's retinue got bolshie and started demanding things of the Abbey. The Abbot spoke with the Bishop, but things got further out of hand to the point where the Bishop and his retinue were denied food. The Bishop then declared that he would exercise lordship over the Abbey, with Warner retorting that he governed the Abbey as freely as the Bishop his diocese.

Henry I died on 2 December 1135 and his nephew Stephen succeeded. King Stephen did issue a general confirmation of status quo for Battle Abbey in 1137, issued via and witnessed by King Stephen's steward, Robert fitzRichard de Clare, at Hastings, but at the Christmas court in 1138, political disputations arose somehow involving Warner and one of the king's justiciars, Richard de Luci. Abbot Warner was induced to resign and Walter de Luci, a monk from Lonlé in Normandy and Richard's brother, was consecrated Abbot, at court.

So Battle Abbey, having sent Warner off to court for Christmas 1138, received a new Abbot, in the company of Seffrid, Bishop of Chichester, in the New Year 1139. Warner retired to the Cluniac Priory of St. Pancras at Lewes and lived there until his death.

Sixth Abbot, Walter de Luci (1139–71) and (1171–75); the 'presidency' of Richard de Luci

Walter de Luci had been staying with a kinsman who was Abbot of St. Albans, but had met the King and other powerful magnates through his brother, Richard. The de Lucis were from a not particularly wealthy but ambitious and able minor Norman family with strong loyalties to each other (West). The appointment of Walter was a ploy by King Stephen to elevate the de Luci family, but in the end a useful move which protected the Abbey from both the worst effects of the Anarchy and the Bishop of Chichester.

The relationship between Battle and Chichester appeared to be on even keel and remained undefined until 1148 when a new bishop was appointed. The relationship between Walter and the new Bishop Hilary, who had spent years in the curia at Rome, was clearly going to be difficult. Hilary was appointed by a pope who was trying to establish canonical reform in England. Things boiled rapidly to a head when Abbot Walter was summoned to Chichester, to be told that Bishop Hilary now expected Battle to be fully under his jurisdiction and pay episcopal dues. Abbot Walter reiterated the Abbey's position as a Royal Peculiar and Stephen's reaffirmation of that, referring to the written confirmation of this witnessed by Archbishop Lanfranc and Stigand of Chichester at the time of Abbot Gausbert. Hilary still tried to insist saying. with papal support, that unless Walter submitted he would place him under an interdict to attend synod and that if he did not he would be excommunicated. He soon tried this and Walter went straight to the royal court. After the case had been heard, Stephen commanded that the Abbey should remain free of subjection in accordance with previous charters. The matter then rested as such until Stephen's death. As soon as Stephen died, in November 1154, and before Henry II was crowned, Hilary of Chichester, in cahoots with the new Pope Adrian IV, the only English pope, tried to excommunicate Battle's Abbot.

It was now nearly 100 years since Hastings. The royal affinity that William I, and to a degree William II had had for Battle Abbey, and the support at distance given by Henry I, were becoming a faded memories. The new King Henry II, the son of Geoffrey Plantagenet, Count of Anjou, and Henry I's daughter Matilda, was of the Angevin house. He was the first Plantagenet king of England.

On the other hand, Bishop Hilary had not fully realised the power of Richard de Luci, Abbot Walter de Luci's brother, who was soon to be one of Henry II's chief justiciars and who could hold the power to maintain the administration of the kingdom even during an interregnum. Richard had words in the ear of Archbishop Theobald of Canterbury and the threat to Walter was rapidly overturned. The events which then followed are essentially a story of the de Lucis versus Bishop Hilary, about the continuing rights of Battle Abbey as a Royal Peculiar, or perhaps more cynically as a temporarily De Luci Peculiar.

In Lent 1155 Henry II held a council to confirm the grants and customs of his predecessors. Abbot Walter attended, taking with him some charters. The ecclesiastics were against confirmation, but the barons persuaded the king to accept them. First round to the de Lucis, said Searle. However the Abbey badly needed to sort out the conflict with Hilary of Chichester. In order to meet Henry II, the Abbot of Battle first travelled to the Loire, finding him at Saumur Castle on 29 August 1156. This raised the suspicions of other churchmen who had started to think he might not speak well of them and he was soon followed by Hilary, who stayed with the king until his return to England. This was followed up by Pope Adrian sending Walter a bull to hear his commands at Chichester in mid-Lent, which Walter duly did and attended a court presided over by the Dean of Chichester. The case opened with Walter giving an opening speech. After this the Sean asked him to produce the Pope's Bull, which Walter did not have with him, but the Dean clearly had a copy which was read out. As expected, it required the Abbot of Battle to offer subjection to the Bishop of Chichester and was followed up by a request that Walter should write a 'very little' schedule containing his profession of obedience. The Abbot then replied with the usual mantra about the Abbey's position as a Royal Peculiar and the written confirmation of this witnessed by Archbishop Lanfranc and Stigand of Chichester at the time of Abbot Gausbert. He then asked for an adjournment to consult with the King. This was refused and he was asked once more to sign the schedule. He again refused and the Dean dissolved the court saying that his refusal would be reported to the Bishop. The Abbot told his brother what had happened, who told the King, who ordered the Bishop of Chichester to leave Walter in peace until he returned to England.

Henry II came back to England just after Easter 1157. He and Walter met at Richard de Luci's castle at Ongar, followed by all attending Henry's court, firstly at Bury St Edmunds on 19 May, but because of lack of time it was deferred to Colchester on 23 May 1157. The king asked a council to join him. This contained amongst a number of others the Archbishops of Canterbury and York, Chancellor Thomas à Becket and Richard de Luci, Chief Justiciar.

The case heard on 23 May 1157 is transcribed in detail in Latin, with English notes, over no fewer than 20 pages in Palgrave's *The Rise and Progress of the English Commonwealth*. The details of the case are also given, from the perspective of Battle Abbey of course, at considerable length in the *CBA*. The preludes dating from 1148 onwards are also described by Palgrave. The English notes (very slightly updated to modern English, but still with the mixed tenses and spellings etc. of the original) are given below as they give a fascinating insight into the modus operandi of a medieval king's court.

> Richard de Luci on behalf of the Abbot offers the charters, which are read out by Thomas a Beckett. In turn they are inspected by the king who orders them deposited with those of William Rufus, Henry I and his own. The Chancellor says that Walter must reply to the objections made by the Bishop of Chichester who says that he has made this statement in the cathedral. The king asks for information about this profession. Richard de Luci then opens in favour of Battle Abbey, saying that it should be protected by the king and all Normans as the place where William the Conqueror gained victory, which is why the king wears the crown and we have all been enriched. He is backed up by Robert, Earl of Leicester. There is then a break whilst the king adjudicates on another case, then Richard de Luci resumes, insisting on the nobility of the Abbey. He urges the king, on behalf of the Norman nobility to defend Battle Abbey against its adversaries and particularly against the wiles of the English. The Abbot then requests that the Conqueror's charter be read. The charter having been read by a clerk, Thomas à Beckett tells the bishop that the reply lies with him.
>
> The bishop replies intimating a wish for an amicable compromise, which proposal is dismissed by the court. He therefore proceeds. He starts by maintaining the supremacy of the pope and that no bishop or other ecclesiastic can be deposed without the permission of the papal see. The king interrupts

joking that a bishop could be removed by force. The bishop continues that no layman, not even a king can confer any ecclesiastical dignity or liberty without the pope's consent. The king asks him to desist from attacks on royal authority and other members of the court join in to express their disapprobation. Hilary explains he did not wish to diminish the king's authority, but this is not accepted by the king.

Hilary states how the Abbot attended his consecration and how he had been received by the Abbey whilst visiting his diocese, to which Henry of Essex says that he makes a bad return for the hospitality he has received. The bishop continues to state that the Abbot had not attended his synod and sent his prior and other monks instead, and imputes ill will between him and the Abbot over the wish of the Abbot to be made bishop of London, as the Abbot believed he had been thwarted by Hilary's influence. Henry of Essex and Richard de Luci justify the Abbot's position. Hilary continues to say how he had published the conditional sentence of excommunication and that when he had appeared before King Stephen the Abbot had defaulted, so he went home and in due course pronounced the sentence of excommunication which he afterwards released at the insistence of the archbishop who also held up the renewal of the Battle charters. He added that all matters contained in the charters contrary to the privileges of the churches of Canterbury and Chichester had been declared to be void.

The king indignantly denied the right therefore assumed by the ecclesiastics of annulling the royal charters, or that decrees made by the king with the advice of his archbishops, bishops and barons should be repealed by the bishops.

The Abbot replied that the question of exemption having been disputed between Stigand and Gausbert, the charter of William the Conqueror had been granted to confirm the privileges of the Abbey. The charter containing the clause of exemption was produced and read out by a clerk. The bishop protested that he had never been able to obtain a sight of this charter. The Abbot attempted to reply but the Abbot and bishop were silenced by the king who declares that the determination of the question belongs entirely to him. Richard de Luci asks that his brother may be allowed to take counsel with his friends and this is allowed.

Following this Richard de Luci replies that the voluntary tokens of respect and submission by the Abbot did not prejudice the rights granted by the charter. Thomas à Beckett adds that the reception of the bishop was merely an act of hospitality such as might have been shown to a foreign prelate. The Abbot disclaims all ill arising from his supposed wish to obtain the see of London. As to the proceedings before King Stephen the Abbot asserts that they were mis-stated by the bishop and that the Abbot appeared before the king, obtained declaration in his favour and returned home by the king's command, not by default and that any attendance at the synod of Chichester was voluntary.

With respect to the excommunication the Chancellor argues as if he doubted the fact, quoting the occasion when the bishop gave the kiss of peace to the Abbot when he did not treat him as an excommunicated person, but as a brother. The bishop seems to confess he did so without consideration.

Thomas à Beckett resumes and argues that the charters do not infringe the dignity either of the archbishop of Canterbury or the see of Chichester, as they have been confirmed by the king, his prelates and barons. This justifies the conduct of the Abbot when called before the chapter. He also accuses the bishop of having attempted to infringe the royal authority by his application to the Pope,

The king expresses great indignation at the conduct of the bishop in procuring the papal bull. The bishop denied that the bull was procured with his knowledge or assent and insinuates that it was obtained at the instance of the Abbot. The king says that he does not believe this statement to be true. Thomas a Beckett then desires that the bull is read in order to understand its purpose and the Archbishop of Canterbury expresses his astonishment at the bishop's assertion.

Thomas a Beckett inquires in the king's name whether the bishop has obtained any other bulls which were injurious to the Abbot. The bishop denies this. At this point the Archbishop of Canterbury requests the king to allow the business to be ended according to canon law, but the king refuses to allow the clergy to determine the case.

The king then withdraws with the court and leaves the bishop and Abbot by themselves. The bishop, then the Abbot, are admitted to conference with the king. Before the king the bishop renounces all jurisdiction over the Abbot and the king demands the bishop acknowledges that his submission was voluntary and not enforced. The archbishop asks the king to pardon any imprudent expressions used by the bishop.'

The case was clearly ended. To Bishop Hilary's chagrin he had to write an apology to Battle's Abbot. The foundation charters presented at the court were dubious, even if they did describe the situation the Conqueror intended. This left the Abbey securely in the power of the monarchy and the king's favourites and virtually cut off from Rome and the English church hierarchy.

Walter de Luci was a man of considerable talent and in his brother had the backing of one of the most powerful men in the country. In the second half of his abbacy, the Abbey was able to use the law to recover lost estates and churches and also further expand its estates and income. One particular case has been described in that one Gilbert de Balliol had twenty years before taken over some land at Barnhorn, a little west of Bexhill, during the Anarchy. Walter took the case to the king's court and won, regaining the land.

Late in his abbacy Walter pulled down the humble cloister built by Abbot

Gausbert and replaced it with a fine cloister with marble slabs. It was finished before his death and some (vertical) remains of this cloister can still be seen at the base of the Tudor manor house built after the reformation.

Thomas à Beckett had become Archbishop of Canterbury after the death of Theobald in 1161. The tale of Henry II and the murder of Beckett on 29 December 1170 is well known. In the tail winds of this there was no Archbishop of Canterbury appointed until 1174 when Richard of Dover became archbishop. During this time many clerical vacancies occurred and Battle's abbacy was one of them.

The west walls of Abbot Walter's cloister can be clearly seen forming the lower part of the east wall of the post-dissolution manor house at Battle Abbey.
Photo: © Keith Foord

The 'presidency' of Richard de Luci (1171–75)

The blazon of de Luci.
The fish displayed are pike, also known as lucys

Walter died in 1171 and the Abbey was formally in the king's hands, but the monks knew that they remained in the hands of a de Luci – Richard, Walter's brother. Richard was custodian until 1175 when a new Abbot was appointed. He placed local Battle knight Peter de Criel and burgess Hugh de Beche, who were well known to the monks, as secular custodians. Richard had no hesitation in detaching what was left of the Abbey's manor of Wye and giving it to his son, and operated more openly in his own interests. Little profit found its way into the royal treasury.

Odo of Canterbury (1175–1200), seventh Abbot

The first job of Richard of Dover, the new Archbishop of Canterbury, together with the King, was to appoint to bishopric vacancies; then they moved on to the vacant abbacies. They wrote to every vacant abbey ordering their priors and some monks to Woodstock where abbots would be elected. Battle was specifically asked to take with them the charters of privileges and exemptions granted by William I. The monks of Battle were concerned about the potential implications of this, but also selected two of those going to Woodstock to be proposed as a home-grown abbot – two were selected in case one was unacceptable.

Battle's prior and four monks arrived at Woodstock, met up with all the other deputations and found that they were called first. At first they met Gilbert the Bishop of London and others for an exploratory meeting. There were no problems apart from the fact that they were informed that the king would not accept either of Battle's nominees and asked the monks to name another from a list of many possible ones that were offered. The monks were in a cleft stick. They did not know anyone on the bishop's list and had been instructed by their chapter to elect one of their two nominees. By all accounts things got a little heated and the King came in angrily, asking why they were holding things up.

By chance Prior Odo of Canterbury was there on another matter – concerning the charters of Canterbury which had been lost in a fire – and he wished to model new charters on Battle's (which was why Battle had been asked to bring its charters – this must have come as a relief to the Battle deputation – they were not being challenged again). The monks of Battle, knowing of Odo's fine reputation, said that they would accept him as their Abbot, as they knew something of him, which was more than could be said of anyone else on the proffered list of names. The Bishop of London informed the King and Archbishop of this and Odo was sent for, as were the monks of Battle, who made a long speech choosing Odo. Odo then refused, indicating that should he be forced, he would appeal to the Pope. He was argued with for a long time to make him change his mind and in the end he agreed. The reason Odo gave for accepting was that he had brought to mind the story of Theophilus who had denied Christ, and had realised that the election was the will of God. But he still wished to consult with his brothers at Canterbury. They basically blessed the appointment saying that they would still wish to receive his counsel and aid. Afterwards he clearly always held his mother church close to his heart.

Odo arrived in Battle on 4 August 1175. Something more needs to be said about Odo's background before he became Abbot of Battle. For this, reference has been made to the *Catholic Encyclopaedia* and its article on Odo by Parker. Odo had become a monk at Christ Church, Canterbury and a sub prior in 1163. After this he was sent by Archbishop Thomas à Becket to Pope Alexander III as his representative to attend an appeal, fixed for 18 October 1163, against the Archbishop of York who was continuing to act in the southern province of England, the province of Canterbury. In 1167 he became prior and wavered in his allegiance between King and Archbishop until the murder of Becket at the end of 1170, after which he favoured the Church. As we have seen above. there was no archbishop appointed after Becket's death, and in September 1172 the monks of Christ Church had put Odo forward for the archbishopric. The King had procrastinated, and there was no decision. Odo and others followed Henry II to Normandy and urged that a monk should be chosen as archbishop. After long negotiations Richard, Prior of Dover, formerly a monk of Canterbury was chosen and Odo wrote to Alexander III on his behalf.

At Battle, Odo was received with some apparent rapture by both the monks and people. But he needed to be consecrated Abbot and John, Bishop of Chichester was soon on the scene, sending his dean to Battle to discuss the matter. Odo had been well briefed and reiterated the detail of the charters. He sent the clerics away and went to see the King and Archbishop. It was suggested that another bishop should bless Odo in the presence of the King, but Archbishop Richard obtained royal permission to bless the Abbot-elect, which he duly did at his manor of Malling, near Lewes, which as a peculiar lay outside of the jurisdiction of Chichester.

The *CBA* records that Odo lived and worked amongst the monks. He was charming and eloquent and fluent in Latin, French and English. He was also a very able administrator. He appears to have had the ear of the king for, on his advice, Henry appointed an Abbot of St. Augustine's, Canterbury, and also after the new Prior of Canterbury had upset the King, Odo had mediated; in due course the same prior was made Abbot of Peterborough. He also showed the King one of the charters of William I that had deteriorated with age and the King agreed that it needed renewing, but would not agree to have it done except by judgement of his court. He took advice from Richard de Luci, who assured him that there would be no problem with this. In due course the court agreed.

It was normal for such charters, on being copied, to insert something to just refer back to the earlier copy, but in this instance to avoid future challenge, the king wished the wording to be:

> Since I have inspected the charter of William my ancestor, in which were contained the aforesaid liberties and exemptions and free customs given the church by him.

The King explained that if the normal phrase had been used the later charter would confer little without the presence of the earlier, but now this charter alone would be enough even if all the other charters of Battle were lost. The Abbot asked for and received three copies of this new charter, each with the King's seal attached to ensure at least one copy was always at the Abbey.

Odo tried to retrieve the manor of Wye from the de Lucis. He had great problems in finding an advocate as many were fearful of the powerful de Luci family. Even his old friends refused to help. When an advocate was at last found the case was brought before a legatine court, that is one presided over by a legate of the pope, not a royal court. It ended in compromise with Richard de Luci's son left as vicar of Wye church.

In Abbot Odo's time a new house or hospital was built for pilgrims and other travellers, just outside the Abbey gate. It stood behind a courtyard, itself behind some dwellings with a gateway onto Abbey Green. These other dwellings were once lived in by Brihtwin the town Beadle and Reinbald de Beche, the Abbot's lawyer.

At this point the *Chronicle of Battle Abbey* ceases and from now onwards, finer details of the Abbots of Battle become harder to find.

In 1184 Odo was put forward for the vacant primacy of Canterbury, but was rejected by the King, who preferred Bishop Baldwin of Worcester, who had a Cistercian background. After this, during a difficult struggle between Archbishop Baldwin and the almost self-governing monks of Canterbury, Odo played a prominent part, acting on the Pope's behalf against the primate. Odo was known as an ardent lover of books and a great theologian. There is some uncertainty as to his writings, owing to confusions with both Odo of Cheriton and Odo of Murimund, but a list of thirteen works, chiefly writings on the Old Testament and on sermons can be ascribed to him. Two of his books still remained in the library of Battle Abbey over 300 years later, at the dissolution in 1538. The Abbot of Battle at the time of Leland's visit just before the dissolution told him that there was a 'Life of Odo' in the library, if so, it has not survived.

Henry II died at Chinon on the Loire on 6 July 1189. He was succeeded by King Richard I, who never visited Battle. Nevertheless he did find time to confirm Battle Abbey's charter, but not the sole right of the Abbot to dispense justice within the leuga, which now increasingly fell into a shared remit with the realm's itinerant justices. When Richard I died in 1199 King John once more renewed Battle Abbey's charter, on the same terms as Richard.

Odo died on 20 January 1200, and was buried in the lower part of the church at Battle Abbey, under a slab of black Lydian marble. He was later venerated at Battle as a saint, and the relic list at Canterbury Cathedral mentions 'a tooth of the Venerable Odo, Abbot of Battle'.

The eighth Abbot, John de Dubra (1200–1211/14)

John of Dover succeeded Odo on 1 May 1200. He was a monk from Canterbury.

He had problems with King John as did many others. It has been suggested that King John rather favoured Battle Abbey, but this is debatable and, if so, it really did not cost John much, just a few visits and gifts. In fact he gained financially in no small way from other fees that he raised from the Abbey, which was undoubtedly his intent. Visits by John were in fact very few. His first visit to Battle was noted to be 6 April 1206. He was on a general progress from London to Dorset. He gave a fine cassock at the time of this visit. His further visits in 2013, as we saw in the last chapter, were stopovers as he moved from place to place at a time of war.

On 23 March 1208 English bishops were ordered by Pope Innocent III to lay a general interdict on England and Wales, as King John would not accept the papal appointment of Stephen Langton as Archbishop of Canterbury. Although Langton

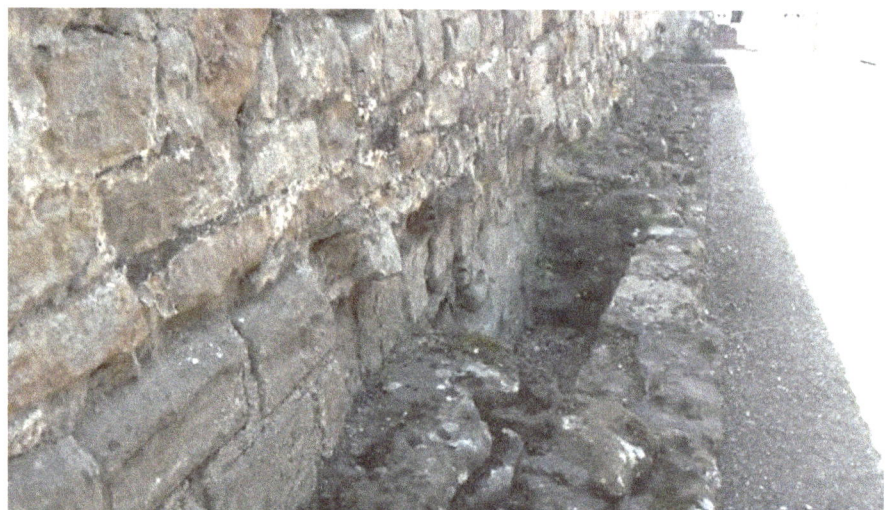

Odo's tomb?
Photo: © K Foord

was English, he had served at the French court for many years and John would have been extremely suspicious of him. The sacraments were forbidden; no one was allowed to attend Mass, receive extreme unction or bury their deceased relatives in consecrated ground. Only the baptism of infants and the confession of the dying were permitted. This state lasted for over six years until the interdict was lifted. Among other results of the interdict were that many ecclesiastical bodies refused to perform divine services and the dead were buried in unconsecrated graves. Battle Abbey was one of these refusing bodies and John took the property and the income of Battle Abbey and other refusers into his hands. On 9 April 1208 he appointed the Sheriff of Kent, Reginald de Cornhill, to take care of the Abbey and to give Battle Abbey reasonable sustenance.

Considerable detail of various transactions involving King John can be found in the Pipe Rolls, which are being published by the Pipe Roll Society, but unfortunately some of the Close and Fine rolls from this period have been lost. In 1211, during the interdict, John sold to the Abbey his royal prerogative and confirmed the ancient liberties for 1500 marks (£1000), to be paid over three years, a massive sum at that time. This was almost certainly because of his need of money for wars, rather than from altruism or any thought of the longer term potential consequences. He issued a charter to Battle Abbey which allowed the monks to run the Abbey and appoint their own Abbot from amongst themselves if there was a vacancy (which suggests that John de Dubra was still alive and Abbot at that time). But, curiously, in 1212 we still find that there is an account of the revenue of Battle Abbey in the King's hands. This shows that the monks are still being looked after, with £146 extracted for the Exchequer funds and another £100 going directly to the King. The full term of the custody is difficult to determine, but from exchequer accounts Searle suggests that control of their lands returned to the Abbey sometime late in 1212. It may be that the deal for the purchase of the royal prerogative was not final until the last instalment had been paid and that it also included an element of a bribe to allow services to be restored.

Although John submitted to Stephen Langton and had his own excommunication lifted in mid-1213, the papal interdict was not finally and fully lifted until 2 July 1214. It was reckoned that John had gained over £100,000, an enormous amount of money if converted to present day values, at the expense of the church over this period. Many abbeys had bribed him, some by as much as £1000, to allow them to perform services, and he also took all the profits from their lands and property over the whole period, only ever repaying about half of the money he had received as part of the final negotiations in 1213–14.

King John's visits to Battle in 1213 on 25–26 April and 13 June were gift-less, but it was while there that he annulled his previous sentences of outlawry against certain ecclesiastics and undertook never again to outlaw clerks. On the first 1213 visit he was moving from Arundel to to Dover, then back to Rye and Winchelsea where he stayed two nights – after which he moved north to Rochester. The second visit of 1213 followed a naval success against the French fleet anchored off Zwin. He was moving from near Canterbury to Portsmouth. He had intended to strike for Poitou, but failed to get enough support, and so he went to Corfe, one of his favourite castles. Presumably he was overnighting at Battle Abbey on the way to meet his hoped-for army.

John of Dover clearly had a very difficult abbacy. The date of his death is a somewhat obscure. It was most likely in 1213. Others have suggested 1211 or 1212, and it may have been as late as 1214, as the next Abbot would not be elected until January 1215. Whenever he died there must have been some delay in appointing the next Abbot, possibly because of the residuum of the interdict still hanging over England until mid-1214. But we can be certain that the impecunious King John continued to benefit.

The ninth Abbot, Richard de Horwode (1215–35) – The first Abbot to be elected by the monks of Battle from amongst their own brethren

Eventually, in January 1215, the King allowed an Abbot to be appointed. Under their expensive charter of 1211, the monks had requested to appoint a new Abbot from amongst their own, to which John agreed. They chose Richard, the almoner of the Abbey. King John as was his wont tried to micromanage the election process. He also sent William Brewer – an ex-sheriff of many counties, some of whose folk had bribed John to remove him as he was so unpleasant – to supervise the election 'to speak for the King and preserve the King's honour'. Abbot Richard was soon elected, so the monks did not have to put up with Brewer for very long and John confirmed Richard's election by letter. The new Abbot was sent to see the Archbishop of Canterbury, by now the in situ Stephen Langton, by whom he would have been blessed as Abbot of Battle.

The first Magna Carta was sealed on 12 June 1215. Amongst many other clauses this allowed free elections in the Church. But the position of the Abbey inevitably changed once John had sold off the rights of kings over it. Even towards the end of Odo's abbacy, the Abbey had been fishing for the Pope to confirm its founding charter and Pope Alexander III (1159–81) had half done so, studiously ignoring the bit about the interference of bishops. Once John had sold his rights to the Abbey, Pope Innocent III (1198–1216) again vaguely confirmed the liberties and Pope Honorius III (1216–27) referred to the liberties of 'William and Stigand', but not to what they were. Eventually Pope Gregory IX (1227–41) made some attempt to grasp the nettle of the anomalous Battle Abbey as part of general Church reforms. With a slightly false start, he mandated Chichester to appoint delegates for visitations to Battle, to check on how things were run. The Bishop of Chichester controversially, and probably deliberately, appointed the Abbot of Robertsbridge and an archdeacon of Lewes Priory. Not only were these both Cistercians, and Battle was a Benedictine abbey, but also Battle had had a long-running legal battle over properties with Robertsbridge so these appointments were not well received and the monks of Battle refused their visitation – at which point the visitors laid an interdict on the Abbey.

The monks of Battle Abbey immediately appealed to the Pope. Gregory IX then proceeded to a series of confirmations, starting at the end of 1233 with a woolly confirmation of the liberties of Battle, much like that of Honorius III, then rapidly confirming the previous agreement of Bishop Hilary of Chichester and Abbot Walter de Luci concerning protection from outsiders. He also very sensibly removed the appointed Cistercian visitors and replaced them with Benedictines who rapidly lifted the interdict. By 1235 Pope Gregory had finally set up a court of arbitration and this determined how things would work in the future. The final settlement, termed a Composition, drawn up by an Archdeacon of Norwich, magister Gentilis, and a Canon of Chichester and then agreed by both the Chichester See and Battle Abbey, kept Chichester at arm's length. The Composition said: Chichester would confirm that any abbatial election had been properly performed, and would bless the new Abbot anywhere but Battle. The Abbot would be installed by the prior of the Abbey. The Bishop of Chichester could request to visit every three years, but have no rights of visitation, i.e. he should be invited. Every three years the Abbey was bound to request the Bishop to appoint one Benedictine monk from within the diocese of Chichester and one chosen by the monks of Battle from another abbey to be visitors – they would report to the bishop who could order any necessary corrections. If this agreement was contravened by either party a fine of 50 marks (£33.33) would be levied by the Archbishop of Canterbury.

Hence the substantial rights of the Royal Peculiar were established and maintained and these persisted for very many years, translating after the dissolution, to the Deanery of Battle. St. Mary's Church kept some special rights and privileges stemming from this time. Even today the incumbent remains a dean, rather than a vicar.

The tenth Abbot – Ralph of Coventry (1235–61)

It must have been under the above papal rules that Abbot Ralph of Coventry was elected in 1235.

After Henry's marriage to Eleanor of Provence in 1237, whose sister Margaret was married to King Louis IX of France, the Pope gained influence over Henry III. Henry started to grant what was perceived by the barons as excessive favours and appointments to foreigners. Peter des Roches, Bishop of Winchester, introduced Frenchmen from Poitou, and Italians followed through Henry's ties to the papacy. His reign coincided with an expansion of papal power and the church was perceived as excessive in extorting money from England. The English prelates made a protest to the king against the extortion of the pope in 1240. Ralph was one of their spokesmen alongside the Abbot of Bury St. Edmunds.

Ralph of Coventry was clearly a moderniser and moved to run the Abbey and its banlieu's business more as a collaboration between the Abbey and the town, but still orientated towards keeping the Abbey's control over tenancies and land deals, with an associated court and charters. This would evolve with time and survived the ravages of the Black Death, when the Abbey community was reduced from 52 to 34 monks with Abbot Alan de Retlyng amongst the deaths. The control of lands and tenancies would later drift towards a system of oligarchy with much influence in the hands of powerful servants of the Abbey. Searle has described how this all worked in great detail and it is impossible to cover the voluminous subject here or to compete with her scholarship, so the interested reader is directed to her book *Lordship and Community: Battle Abbey and its Banlieu, 1066–1538*.

Reginald of Brecon, eleventh Abbot (1261–81)

Abbot Reginald, who from at least 1248 was Prior of Brecon, one of Battle Abbey's cells, was elected Abbot in 1261.

Only three years later in 1264 he was to find the Abbey to be in the path of King Henry III's army on the way to the Battle of Lewes. At Lewes Henry faced the barons and the Battle of Lewes took place on 14 May. The barons won the battle and Henry and Edward were taken prisoners. Henry was brought back to Battle Abbey by Simon de Montfort, and thence to London. Reginald would have been pleased to see him gone. Details of this are covered in the previous chapter.

Reginald died or resigned in 1281 after 20 years as Abbot. If he resigned the reason for this is unknown.

After 1281

At this point, as we can see from the list in the introduction, 17 or so more Abbots were still to be elected after Reginald, until the last Abbot, John Hammond, who was pensioned off at the dissolution of the Abbey in 1538.

It is difficult to say much about many of the Abbots after 1281. Their names appear on charters and elsewhere and for their effects on the general business of the Abbey great detail can be found in Searle's book. From this point forward many must have lived relatively untroubled lives, although things became rather difficult during the Hundred Years' War, as noted in a previous chapter. They administered the Abbey and its properties without apparent controversy. But some abbots come to our attention due to various events that occurred during their abbacies and these will be discussed below.

John of Whatlington, fourteenth Abbot (1308–11)

John of Whatlington is an interesting Abbot, not so much for his short three-year abbacy, but for his long service and his influences on the 12th and 13th Abbots within the Abbey before that. The reigns of Edward I (1272–1307) and Edward II (1307–27) were a time of crossover between the role of the Abbey and the role of the itinerant king's justiciars in the administration of justice. The justiciars, who were experienced in legal technicalities and litigation precedents travelled between areas holding eyre courts (circuit assizes). When sitting at Battle they also had to take into account the local charters, particularly Henry III's of 1271 which as a precedent had allowed a special eyre (assize) session to the Abbey, and so they would sit alongside the Abbey's lawyer-monks in special sessions at Battle. Interestingly, Edward I had never reconfirmed Battle Abbey's charters although he did uphold the legal franchise, but Edward II did reconfirm the full charters later, in 1312. The 15th Abbot, John of Northbourne, would pay him £50 for doing so. Later Edward II would issue some specifically detailed confirmations covering various issues.

John of Whatlington was probably of the Harmer family of Whatlington and is first recorded at the Abbey in the visitation record of 1283. At this visitation some other monks complained about him as he was the chaplain to 12th Abbot Henry of Aylesford (1281–97) and was felt to be influencing the Abbot into starting to oppress poor tenants. Searle has perceived him to be an able, unlovable, ruthless and ambitious man. John became steward of the Abbey by 1290 – a lawyer-monk – and was very active in the Abbey's court and elsewhere on behalf of the Abbey. He held this post until 1304, when he became sacristan, handing over the stewardship to his pupil, Henry of Rye.

Abbot John of Thanet, the 13th Abbot (1298–1307) issued a charter in 1304 passing management of tithes, rents and rent-charges to the sacristan. This gave John of Whatlington direct access to the management of Battle town and the banlieu holdings and in 1305 he drew up a new Battle rental, the first for 60 years. Such a move was probably long overdue, but, as ever, the idea of such change went down like the proverbial lead balloon. For some reason connected with this, he tried to use the local court to reduce the status of the poorer town and country folk to villeinage. Villeinage refers to the legal condition of servitude and the tenure by which a villein held land and tenements from a lord. John of Whatlington was clearly trying to increase the efficiency and value of the Abbey's holdings, by reducing tenants' rights. He justifiably lost the case, which he should not have brought in the first case. He also probably interfered with the traditional borough customs and increased the fees paid by the burgesses for the rights that they held.

Abbot John of Thanet resigned in 1307; the reason for this is unknown. John of Whatlington then consolidated his hold on the banlieu being elected 14th Abbot in 1308. Following this, the burgesses at first refused to pay their dues or perform the duties that they normally performed for the Abbey. However, by 1310, the new manor of Marley had been created and some of his measures managed to increase the productivity of local farmland. Also the value of services was for the first time accounted for in monetary values, rather than by amounts of work or produce, etc. due to the Abbey.

John of Whatlington died in 1311 leaving his successor to sort out some of the turmoil he had created. After the stewardship of John's protégé, Henry of Rye, the legal role in the eyre courts of the monk-steward/lawyer ended and the royal justices and sheriffs had full charge.

In retrospect the period of John of Whatlington had been one of significant transition. As with all such periods it left behind in its wake a local storm which presumably took a few years to settle.

Seventeenth Abbot – Alan de Retlyng (1324, died of the Black Death in 1350, which had also killed another 17 of the 52 monks and many in the town of Battle)

In 1337 the King commanded the Abbot, along with other local landowners, that they defend the coast of Sussex. This burden was placed on the Abbey for a long time during the Hundred Years' War, and the Abbots helped to organise local defences and to provide food and clothing for refugees fleeing the coastal towns. Subsequent to this order a royal licence to fortify the Abbey was received just after the start of the long war, and the building of the great gatehouse and the defensive walls that we still see today was begun during Alan's abbacy.

In 1338 Alan was excused from finding men from the Abbey's manor of Wye to guard the coastline because he had already sent all his available men to patrol the coast near Winchelsea. In 1340 he complained to the King about papal extortions and several times he petitioned the royal court over usurpations of the manor of Wye in Kent.

There is some confusion in some texts which suggest that there may have been another Abbot called John de Retlying until 1329. The name was also spelled Ketlying. This is unlikely as in the Patent Roll of 7 March 1323, Edward II signifies his assent to the election of Alan de Retlyng. The muddle must be due to errors in reading or transcribing old documents or simple mistakes, easily done it seems – as we shall see in the next chapter.

Robert de Bello, eighteenth Abbot (1351–64)

Clearly from his name, Robert must have been a local man who had joined the Abbey. In 1360 the Abbot was one of the landowners again made officially responsible for the defence of the coast.

He also had to deal with some disobedience to the mother house by the Prior of Brecon. Brecon, it will be remembered, was the cell from which Reginald was appointed to the abbacy back in 1261. In the cartulary is a bull of Pope Innocent VI, dated 9 June, 1355, commanding John Jose (or Lose), Prior of Brecon, 'to conduct himself conformably to the accustomed rules of submission to the Abbot of the monastery of St. Martin, in Battel.' Apparently he had written abusive letters and refused to come to Battle every three years as was required. After this the Priors of Brecon were required to swear a very long and specific oath of allegiance to Battle.

Hamo de Offynton: nineteenth Abbot (1364–82)

Offington is an area in north central Worthing, but members of his family lived in the area of Battle. As agreed, Hamo's election was confirmed by the parsons of Lancing and Selsey deputising for the Bishop of Chichester who was overseas, but he was consecrated by Archbishop Islip of Canterbury at his manor of Charing in Kent. Seemingly one of his first acts with reference to his privileges under Battle Abbey's charter was, on a journey to London, to free a man condemned to death. The King and nobles were apparently not amused.

He was also another major reformer of the Abbey's management – cutting its legal expenses and overheads and was soon able to undertake some major repairs to the Abbey fabric. But he was also nepotistic, his brother Edmund was his chaplain, a John de Offygton was sacrist and another Offygton, Walter was town beadle

By 1375 he was appointed visitor of the Benedictine monasteries in the dioceses of Canterbury and Rochester, much as others from elsewhere were appointed to the same role at Battle, but he was foiled in his attempt to visit the Cathedral Priory of Canterbury. The prior had appealed to the archbishop, who forbade anyone to make any visitation of the cathedral priory except himself. This appears to have been a matter of ecclesiastical pride, but it was supported by Edward III.

In 1371 the Abbot was still one of the landowners responsible for the defence of the coast. This became acutely necessary in 1377 when he took up arms and he and others successfully defended Winchelsea against the French. This is for what he is usually remembered. Unfortunately the French just turned their attentions elsewhere and burnt Hastings and Rye. In 1380 a Castilian fleet with a French escort turned up and fired Winchelsea. They were turbulent times. In 1368–73 and 1380–4 the almoner of Battle was purchasing extra food to distribute among the large numbers of war-affected needy who had come to the Abbey. The income to the Abbey also fell and its debt burden increased once again.

Sometime the Pope bestowed on Hamo the right to wear a mitre. English Heritage record that the papal grant to Abbot Hamo of the mitre and other pontificalia is discussed in various antiquarian sources, though the original document cannot be traced. A late 14th-century stained-glass panel of the Abbey's coat of arms, now at the Burrell Collection, Glasgow, is charged with the mitre (Eden). An interpretation of these arms is seen above.

Hamo died suddenly whilst administering mass in 1382. The notice of his death in the Westminster Chronicle stated that beneath his monkish habit he was a soldier of mark and a stout defender of home, neighbours, and coast against the attacks of pirates.

Twenty-second Abbot, William Mersshe (1405–1417)

Mersshe is not an uncommon name as it is derived from marsh, but it appears that the family of William had lived in Battle, owning a cottage in Middleborough since at least the mid-14th century. The unusual thing about William is that, when a monk, he had absconded from the Abbey and lived locally as an apostate, the evidence for which is in the Calendar of Patent Rolls 1396–9. On 16 February 1398 Richard II issued from Westminster:

> Appointment of Tomas Edemer, Stephen Shareshell and William Cordelay to arrest William Beket and William Mersshe, apostate monks of the Benedictine monastery at Battle whilst it was lately void and to deliver them to John, prior thereof to be dealt with according to the rule of the order.

Stephen Shareshell was the town beadle and it is presumed Edemer and Cordelay were constables. The two Williams were not the first monks to run away, for three others had done so earlier and one of those, John Lose, after his return was sent off to be Prior of Brecon. This time, after a couple of years back in the Abbey, William Mersshe would be sent off to be Prior of Exeter St. Nicholas in 1400 and was called to be Abbot of Battle in 1405. His fellow escapee William Becket would then take over his role at Exeter which priorship he held until his death in 1414.

Thomas de Ludlowe, twenty-third Abbot (1417–1434/5)

Thomas was previously cellarer and prior of the Abbey. During his abbacy, in 1420, the present Pilgrims Rest replaced the earlier pilgrims' hostel built in Odo's time. It is a Grade II* listed example of a timber framed Wealden house. It was originally tucked away behind other houses and its front courtyard was accessed through passages.

During Thomas's time a new ceremonial sword was made. This was described in detail by Paton who noted that the fashion of the sword is of a date before the period of Abbot Lodelowe, and suggested that it may have been copied from an earlier sword, implying that this earlier weapon may have been the original sword said to have been given to the Abbey by William I.

Swords were clearly an important part of the Abbey's regalia, and bear witness to its origins. Swords appear on most of the coats of arms that have at some time been ascribed to the Abbey.

This sword has passed through various hands but is now in the National Museum of Scotland. The sword from which it may have been copied has been lost. English Heritage commissioned a replica of Ludlowe's sword, which is now on display at the Abbey.

Thomas Ludlowe resigned in 1434–5 and we find his name in 1435 as the new Abbot of Shrewsbury, whose records show that he may have been there previously as prior, presumably before moving to Battle. He may have been going home as Ludlow is near Shrewsbury.

The Sword of Battle Abbey and a magnified view of centre of its pommel
Paton suggests that the cross on the coat of arms was once filled with red enamel. Note the lowercase initials t and l for Thomas Ludlowe. Both images above are from Paton's paper.

Richard Dertmouth, the twenty-fifth Abbot (1437, last mentioned in 1461 but the next Abbot was not elected until 1463)

Battle Abbey, Lewes Priory and many local landowners became implicated in supporting Jack Cade's rebellion in June 1450. King Henry VI was unpopular and generally believed to be surrounded by corrupt advisors. The country was in serious debt after the Hundred Years' War which was grinding to a close, and Sussex and Kent were being constantly raided by the French, with an invasion feared. Grievances were sent to the King, but in the absence of any action, the rebellion took place based in Kent and Sussex, with a confrontation in London. It failed, but so many were involved in supporting the cause that a general pardon was issued in July. This included Richard, Abbot of St. Martin's Monastery, of Battle, in the county of Sussex, and the Convent of the same place, and the servants of the said Abbot and Convent.

Cade was hunted down and is reputed to have been mortally wounded at the place now called Cade Street, near Heathfield. In the online appendices will be found a list of those from Hastings Rape who supported Cade. A wider list from across Sussex is given by Durrant-Cooper. Numbers of whole communities were involved.

Doherty has written a summary of Battle in the late fifteenth century. It still had its administrative centre based at the Market Place, a square which was situated between the end of Mount Street and Shitbourne Lane (now called Western Avenue), not on the Abbey Green outside the Abbey gates. This extended into an area now covered by buildings in the High Street and bounded on one side by what is now the end of Mount Street. The Court House, at which justice was administered and, in effect, local government carried out, was situated here, towards the right-hand end of the present Mount Street. Some foundations associated with this were found at the time of redevelopment of Jenner's mill, where Old Ladies Lane is now situated. Throughout the fifteenth and into the sixteenth century the Market Place gradually changed, with shops being merged and re-divided, providing larger, but fewer, shops. More shops also appeared on the High Street. The number of traders in the market gradually diminished. The addition of a smithy built on the Market Place in 1442 could indicate that the space was by that time already too large for the number of traders. The town underwent a contraction between the mid-fifteenth mid-sixteenth century at its outer borders, with fewer houses in these areas. By contrast, the town centre appears to have remained static in terms of house numbers, with some additions such as the Quarry Rents in Upper Lake, which were built in the 1470s.

Twenty-seventh Abbot, Richard Tovey or Tovy (1490–1503)

The Tovys were an influential Battle family, with Tovys serving on inquest juries from the early 15th century. A John Tovy was an inquest juror maybe at the same time that Richard was Abbot. We know little about Richard, but in 1493, he issued a remarkable passport to the citizens of Battle. What is even more extraordinary is that we knew nothing about this document until it suddenly turned up in 2018. It appears to have been seen by Dr Alan Moore of Whatlington near Battle in 1938–40, before ending up unnoticed in a pile of old papers in the BDHS archive. Some additional marks on the parchment suggest that it was once part of the Dering collection, which was sold in the 1850s and dispersed nationwide. Sir Edward Dering (1598–1644) was an antiquarian collector whose second wife was Anne, daughter of Sir John Ashburnham – maybe it was via this connection that the document came to be in the hands of the Derings. The Latin transcription's attribution to Dr Moore is backed by a reference in his diaries, showing that he had access to the document 'to try and decipher' on 11th November 1938. BDHS contacted East Sussex Record Office (ESRO) about the document and their chief archivist, Christopher Whittick, confirmed its authenticity as a 'pass' entitling the carrier to travel freely in England and quoting the old charter rights of the Abbey. Doherty has produced an excellent summary of this find which can be accessed in Section A3.4 of BDHS Collectanea. BDHS has lodged the parchment with ESRO and has also given a facsimile copy to Battle Abbey for future display. In summary the document says:

> 1. The Abbey and monastery had the power to hold its own courts for business and justice.
> 2. The Abbey and men of Battle were: free from various taxes and obligation to repair castles, bridges and fencing; not answerable to the shire

and hundred courts; granted the right to their own coroner; granted freedom from paying tolls anywhere in the country.

3.   The Abbey could impose its own fines and was also entitled to any fines imposed on its men and tenants by any justices, sheriffs and bailiffs.

4.   The Abbey could claim the chatells of felons, fugitives and outlaws and those hanged and of whomsoever condemned as well as the belongings found in the liberty of any wrongdoers. In addition it could claim any monies following a murder.

5.   No persons could enter the lands or property of the Abbot and monastery to make any distraint, summons or other business.

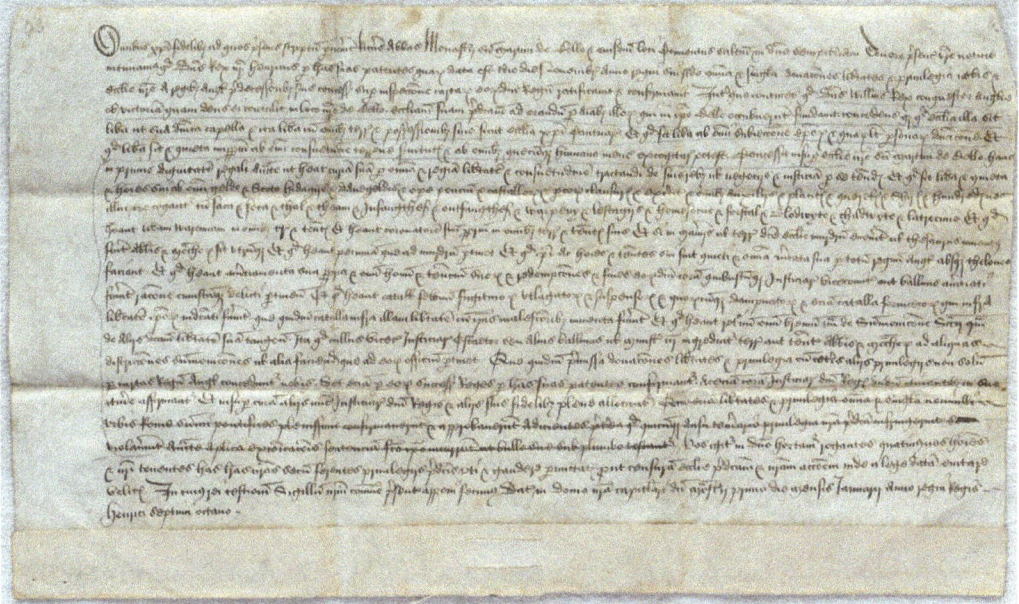

The 1493 Passport, written in Latin on Parchment
©BDHS   Photograph Peter Greene

Twenty-ninth Abbot, Lawrence Champion (1508–29)

The coat of arms of 1515 which was paraded at the House of Lords can probably be ascribed to Champion.

It is often overlooked that Battle Abbey church had what appears to have been a detached round bell tower or campanile south east of its crypt chapels. It may have had this tower before 1367 and in this respect would have been akin to that of Tewkesbury Abbey. It was reckoned to be 28 feet (8.5 m) in diameter and in the Duchess of Cleveland's guide is described as a grassy mound. In the sacristy accounts for 1516 there are mentioned two bells named 'Mary' and 'Gabriel'. In 1519 is mentioned a further bell called 'le Whyppe', and in 1523 one called 'Jesus'. These mentions may be of new bells or repaired bells but presumably all four would have hung in the campanile.

The thirtieth or thirty-first Abbot – John Hammond (1529/31, pensioned off 1538)

John was previously sacristan of the Abbey. It is possible that another Abbot was elected for 1529–31 as there is a record stating that on the Thursday after the feast of St. Laurence in 1529, a proxy from the Prior of Brecon (a cell of Battle) was present in the Chapter House in Battle, to elect a new Abbot. This may not have been John Hammond, as confusingly he was also still recorded as sacristan 'before 1531' – but it may be that he had retained these duties as well as the abbacy as there were so few monks in the Abbey by this time.

Abbot Hammond had only a few years in post before the dissolution of the monasteries caught up with Battle. It has been suggested that he may have prepared the Abbey for the end. But in the roll of accounts of John Hammond, sacristan, for 1512, the Abbey was still being cared for as there is a statement of expenses for repairs of the Abbey church, new vestments for the priest, two new silver candlesticks, two glass lamps to hang before the altars, and for repairs to the clock in the sacristy chamber. Copies of other sacristy accounts are held at ESRO.

The act for dissolving the great monasteries was passed in 1537–8. John Hammond continued to live in Battle across the road from the Abbey at 4, Upper Lake until his death in 1546, the same year as King Henry VIII's death. He bequeathed the few items that he had retained from the Abbey to St Mary's Church, to be used 'in the 'chappell of saynt Kateryn'. These included two chasubles (liturgical overgarments); a gilded chalice with a paten (goblet and plate for Holy Communion); and a scochyn (a depiction of a coat of arms) in silver. He left £6 13s 4d (£6.67) for a priest to sing in the Chapel of St Katherine on 23 July for the next six years from 1547, for his soul and all Christian souls. There was also £40 for requiem masses a month after his death and yearly for six years, with the balance going to the poor and charitable works, and rather curiously 10 shillings (50 pence) each to the next 13 poor maidens to be married.

There is some discussion of the development of the Abbey church and of its offspring Church of St Mary at Battle in Foord.

4
A Critique of the Rolls of Battle Abbey

We cannot all be of Norman descent.
J Horace Round (1854–1928)

The Battle Abbey Roll is one of the lost parchments or tapestries of Battle Abbey, one that used to hang in the Abbot's hall from some unknown time before about 1300 until it was presumably removed to Cowdray House in West Sussex by the Browne/Montague family sometime after the Dissolution. Cowdray House and many of its priceless artefacts, including the Roll was destroyed by fire on 24 September 1793.

The initial Roll was said to be a 'Companion Roll' for William the Conqueror and as such has fascinated historians, heralds, designers of heraldic blazons and genealogists since first produced. Compilers of family histories use derivatives of this roll to try to find the elusive ancestor who fought with William at the Battle of Hastings. Ever since 1066 families have been proud to boast, often on very flimsy evidence, that that their ancestors came over with the Conqueror. The lists have taken on mythical proportions, possibly encouraged by the event descriptively imagined by Lower:

> The Conqueror, having called to his presence a clerk who, previously to the departure of the armament from St. Valery, had written down the names of the chief men of the army, he caused him to read the roll to ascertain who had fallen, and who had survived; and Bishop Odo sang mass for the souls that were departed.

If that parchment ever existed and the original or a tapestry copy of the original pre-departure roll had been held at Battle Abbey, it would have been a true roll – but the various lists now available are of subsequent date, the earliest from about 1330, and have suffered from much repetition, errors of transcription, duplication of names and are accused of egotistical insertions and monkish manipulation. So just who did fight side by side with William? The definitive list of those who can be absolutely proved to be on the field of Hastings is painfully short. The list below comes from White:

Robert de Beaumont, later 1st Earl of Leicester
Eustace, Count of Boulogne, (aka Eustace II)
William, Count of Évreux
Geoffrey, Count of Mortagne & Lord of Nogent, later Count of Perche
William fitz Osbern, later 1st Earl of Hereford
Aimeri, Viscount of Thouars (aka Aimery IV)
Walter Giffard, Lord of Longueville
Hugh de Montfort, Lord of Montfort-sur-Risle
Ralph de Tosny, Lord of Conches (aka Raoul II)
Hugh de Grandmesnil
William de Warenne, later 1st Earl of Surrey
William Malet, Lord of Graville Odo, Bishop of Bayeux, later Earl of Kent
Turstin fitz Rolf (aka Turstin fitz Rou and Turstin le Blanc)
Engenulf de Laigle

Five additional names were agreed upon by Douglas and White:

Geoffrey de Mowbray, Bishop of Coutances
Robert, Count of Mortain
Wadard, believed to be a follower of the Bishop of Bayeux
Vital, believed to be a follower of the Bishop of Bayeux
Goubert d'Auffay, Seigneur of Auffay

Mason adds one additional name:

Humphrey of Tilleul-en-Auge

Douglas also published six more names but from comments elsewhere he clearly had some differences with Mason and White about these:

Robert de Vitot.
Gerelmus de Panileuse.
Robert fitz Ernis.
Roger, son of Turold.
Turstin, son of Rou.
Erchembald, son of Erchembald the Vicomte.

Douglas still later added a list of those witnessing Norman charters under circumstances which Douglas considered rendered them most probable that they accompanied the expedition (Author note: this of course do not make them definite companions even if they were closely involved with its planning or aftermath):

Gerald the Seneschal (grandfather of William de Roumare).
Rodulf the Chamberlain (? de Tancarville).
Hugh d'Ivry, the Pincerna.
Richard fitz Gilbert (de Clare)
Pons

He then added four more names – of those who witnessed Duke William's charter made at Caen on 17 June 1066 (Gall. Christ. XI, Instr. col. 59), who were, Douglas thought, most probably at Hastings. *Gallia Christiana*, is a listing and collection of brief histories related to all the Catholic dioceses and abbeys of France from early times (*Author note: this of course also does not make them definite companions either as the invasion took place three months after the date of the charter*):

> Richard the Vicomte of the Avranchin (father of Hugh Lupus).
> Ranulf the Vicomte of the Bessin.
> Ralf Tesson.
> Fulk d'Aunou.

It can only be commented that such differences between modern historians are not so surprising given the vigorous debates that have taken place in academic circles about the events surrounding the Conquest.

But what of the older Rolls which exist? These are lists of named families with single family names or names derived from places and descriptions rather than of individuals (with the exception of the more modern rolls of Dives and Falaise that do name individuals, so there can be multiple names from the same family). All these ancient rolls are very much larger than the definitive lists above.

The Rolls to be considered here are one derived by the author from a translation of the pages/verses of the *Roman de Rou* which describe the actual events of the Battle of Hastings, plus those called 'Auchinleck', 'Le Talleur', 'Leland' (two lists, called here I and II), 'Holinshed' and 'Duchesne'. The newer lists are those of 'Dives', to be found on a plaque over the main door of the church of Dives sur Mer, Dives added to by De Magny, and 'Falaise' (a list on a bronze plaque at Falaise, plus later additions made after the plaque was cast). It is not intended here to go deeply into the details of the provenance of these lists, which in themselves can become very debatable and can in any case be read about via the references, but to merely give the approximate date(s) of publication and to add a few notes, and maybe to attempt some conclusions.

Clearly down the years of copying and fancification, not to mention additions, considerable variations of spelling have arisen in old hand scripted lists. Also additional errors can easily be made when reading these old scripts particularly in differentiation of lower case letters: m, n, r, u, v, w; of y, g and I; f and s; also k and q can be interchanged; and v was often written as u. Some names have clearly been copied from list to list almost phonetically, and phonetically using a French accent. Indeed it is probable that the scribes may sometimes have had apprentice or novice assistants who read the names to them and the scribes then wrote the names as heard, without checking back to the assistant's script. Having copied and tried to cross-reference accurately over 3000 names, including slightly dissimilar names with various spellings, learning to see the common irregularities and using 'Soundex' like technique the author appreciates the tediousness of this task, and with some sympathy notes that the Duchess of Cleveland in her voluminous study comments about Duchesne (or his scribe) in particular appearing to miss chunks out of his Roll. She says he becomes 'puzzled as well as weary, and now and again helplessly loses his way in the entangling labyrinth of names'. At least today we have computers and spreadsheets to help.

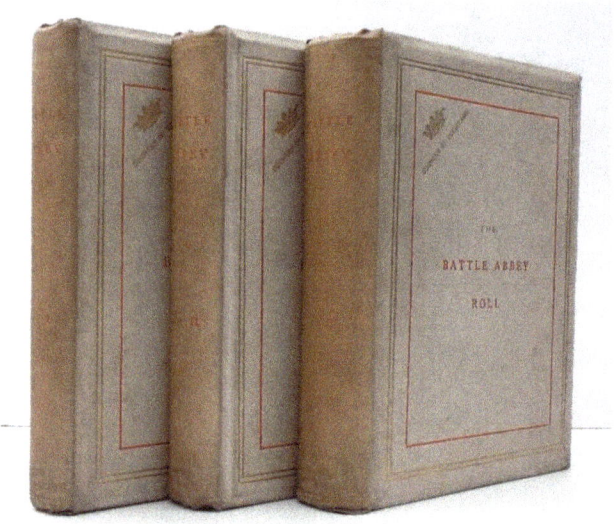

The three volumes of the Duchess of Cleveland's study.
Most of the volumes is taken up with the genealogies of the families

What us truly amazing is the number of papers that have been published on this subject which vary from the sycophantic and ridiculous to truly erudite ones and also the number of manuscripts that abound. Bliss made an exhaustive study of the manuscripts and listed 55 manuscripts and books in his paper 'Companions of the Conqueror' and produced a genealogical type comparison of each showing how they 'fed' on each other. And there are almost certainly more than 55.

It is no wonder there is such a myriad of variations of some of the names and inadvertent losses and apparent neologisms to confuse the historian. If only a true original Roll was to be found confusion would have a weaker reign.

As the documents stand one does wonder what true value they have – and this study (and its accompanying alphabetically-sorted by family name lists in the appendices) tries to place in context their value so that readers can make up their own minds about this. Hey gives short shrift to the genealogical value of the Rolls and Round in his somewhat excoriating paper of 1901 concerning the Rolls said, 'We cannot all be of Norman descent.'

Roman de Rou (about 1160)

The *Roman de Rou* was, according to its author (Robert?) Wace, commissioned by King Henry II, and was started in the 1160s, 90 years after the Battle of Hastings. Wace informs the reader of the *Roman de Rou* that he was born in Jersey. It mainly covers events from the foundation myth of Normandy up until the Battle of Tinchebrai of 1106 but mentions further events up until 1174. It uses extensive oral and written sources, giving rise to the normal doubts about verity and accuracy. But it may be the first partially useful Roll of those who actually fought at Hastings. The list of family/place names in the appendixes is taken directly from those found in the pages of Burgess' translation which cover the direct events of the Battle of Hastings.

Auchinleck (1330–1340)

The Roll of names forms one section of the whole Auchinleck manuscript. This is the oldest of the surviving rolls and provides, after sorting into alphabetical order, the key column of names listed in the appendices. This alpha-sorted list can then be used to compare across the various Rolls to check for the appearance, or not, of the name in the later Rolls. This is because as the oldest manuscript it is the most likely to have been copied from a pre-cursor, maybe even an original, but it still post-dates the Conquest by some 260 years. This baseline deletes obvious duplicates, but where any doubt persists names are retained.

The Auchinleck Manuscript is one of the National Library of Scotland's (NLS) great treasures. Produced in London in the 1330s, it gives a unique insight into the English language and literature of its time. It is named from its first known owner, Lord Auchinleck, a Scottish High Court justice and father of James Boswell, who discovered it in 1740 and donated it to the precursor of the NLS four years later. It is unknown who owned the Roll before this. The Roll's existence does not appear to have been widely known in Victorian times and it is not included in the Duchess of Cleveland's tomes. Transcription and editing of the manuscript was performed between September 2000 and August 2001 at the University of Sheffield by Burnley and Wiggins with the assistance of Sakemi of the University of Hiroshima.

The study amongst other conclusions deduced that the Auchinleck Manuscript provided the earliest example of book production in England which was both lay and commercial. Many books were produced in abbeys or by individuals for their own use or for family or community use, but Auchinleck provided evidence of four or five professional scribes collaborating on an essentially commercial venture.

In this context another conclusion was that the nature of the Battle Abbey Rolls and their lists of names has been misunderstood. They are not lists solely of individuals who were 'companions in battle' with William but seem intended to show which Norman, and other, families had origins as supporters, administrators, even fortune-seeking immigrants who came over with or to join the Conqueror, not necessarily in 1066 but in subsequent years.

Auchinleck's Roll was compiled in the early 14th century. It is a list of family surnames, many based on place-names, but clearly influenced by French sounding names, and includes many families of later settlement. It could be called a high value vanity list.

Deayuile.	Dyne.	Delamare.	Vaynse.
pygot.	limesy.	Courtruple.	Beke.
Vurnay.	Boys.	Saunz auer.	Desse.
Tregoz.	feries.	Mountagu.	Gangi.
Camoys.	fiz Roger.	fourneus.	Ravin.
hautayn.	Muse.	Valence.	payner.
Warayne	Quincy	Cleruaus.	fiz anger.

An sample extract from the Roll in the Auchinleck Manuscript.
Names are listed in four columns in no alphabetical order

Le Talleur (1487)

The origin of the names in this list has some commonality with the *Roman de Rou*, but this is not universal. What is perhaps more extraordinary is that only eleven names match to Auchinleck. One important name, FitzOsberne, who is a named and definite companion, only appears in this roll and that of the very much later Dives Roll. A few other names such as Avranches and Mandeville are also only in Talleur and Dives. So when and where did le Talleur find access to information that had eluded the others, and what were his criteria for inclusion?

Overall of the relatively short list of 143 unduplicated names there is a match somewhere across the other lists of 86 names, with no match at all for 57.

Leland (1533–1536) – There are two Leland lists, from his *Collectanea*.

In 1533, King Henry VIII authorized John Leland (1503–1552) to examine and use the libraries of all religious houses in England. Leland then spent the next few years travelling and visiting the majority of monasteries and abbeys shortly before they were dissolved, compiling lists of significant or unusual books in their libraries. This work also continued beyond the dissolution into the early 1540s and he appears to have rescued many books that might have been dispersed. During this time he must have visited Battle Abbey and noted the Roll, inscribed on a roll of parchment or as a tapestry and believed to have been hung up in the Abbey. He will also have visited Jervaulx Abbey and may have seen Brompton's Chronicle, the relevance of which comment will be seen later.

But as the Duchess of Cleveland writes, 'As time went on, it became more and more an object of ambition to own an ancestor that had come over with the Conqueror; and the monks were always found willing to oblige a liberal patron by inserting his name.' So its value as a potential true record was slowly lost.

Leland's *Collectanea* contains Leland's many notes and transcripts from his visits to monastic libraries, including most of his lists, mostly compiled 1533–6. This is therefore the likely dating for what is called here the Leland I Roll. Leland I is a list of names as couplets but these have been separated and all the names alpha-sorted and duplicates deleted for comparison purposes in the appendixes.

The Leland I listing contains quite a few names that also appear in Auchinleck, but do not copy through to the later Holingshed or Duchesne rolls, which suggests that Leland may have had access to an earlier version, also seen by the compiler of Auchinleck, than the later compilers may have had.

Leland II is entitled 'Un role de ceux queux veignont in Angleterre ovesque roy William le Conquerour' and gives only fifty-eight names, declaring 'Tous ycels seigners desus nome estoient a la retenaunce Monseir de Moion.' So II is a list of those in the retinue of William I de Moyon of the Cotentin. Planché proposed that it is simply a partial transcript of the names given in the *Roman de Rou*. The *Roman de Rou* and Leland 2 lists may be compared side to side in the appendices and the reader may make their own judgement about Planché's conclusion.

Holinshed (1577)

Raphael Holinshed (*c.*1525–1580) not only produced a Battle Abbey Roll but was used by Shakespeare as a source for some of his plays. His *Chronicles* were first published in 1577 and printed by Wolfe who had obtained some of Leland's papers and presumably would have shared them with Holinshed.

Holinshed's Roll is the largest of the group, but it contains a fair number of duplicates and many additional names not in any other list. Simply eliminating duplicates reduces the list by just under 20%. Name endings often differ, but this is probably due to naming conventions at different times. On a few occasions there are direct French–English translations, e.g. 'neuf' to 'new'.

The Duchess of Cleveland defends this list as she says that many of the additional names can be found in the *Black Book of the Exchequer* (Liber Niger Scaccarii) of Henry II and from other monastic cartularies and the *Domesday Book*. The author has made no attempt to corroborate this claim as it would entail a huge amount of work.

For comparison with names in the *Domesday Book* we have some indirect connection via the later lists of Dives and Falaise as they both extensively used *Domesday* to scour for names.

The firste volume of the
*Chronicles of England,
Scotlande, and Irelande.*
Public Domain

Duchesne (1619)

André Duchesne (1584–1640) produced a Roll shorter than Holingshed's in his *Historiae Normannorum* of 1619, and at first glance it appears much like a shortened version, with some names seen in Auchinleck and Holingshed omitted. It does however contain names not seen in Holinshed, but only once duplicates a name found in Auchinleck alone. Although new names and duplicates of these and of Holinshed's names do appear there are runs of numerous names missing giving the appearances of a somewhat rushed or botched job. The Duchess of Cleveland was not impressed, but she does repeat a number of names that appear solely in the Duchesne list and not confirmed by any of its precursor lists or later lists. These must be quoted with added circumspection as they are dubious.

4 A CRITIQUE OF THE ROLLS OF BATTLE ABBEY

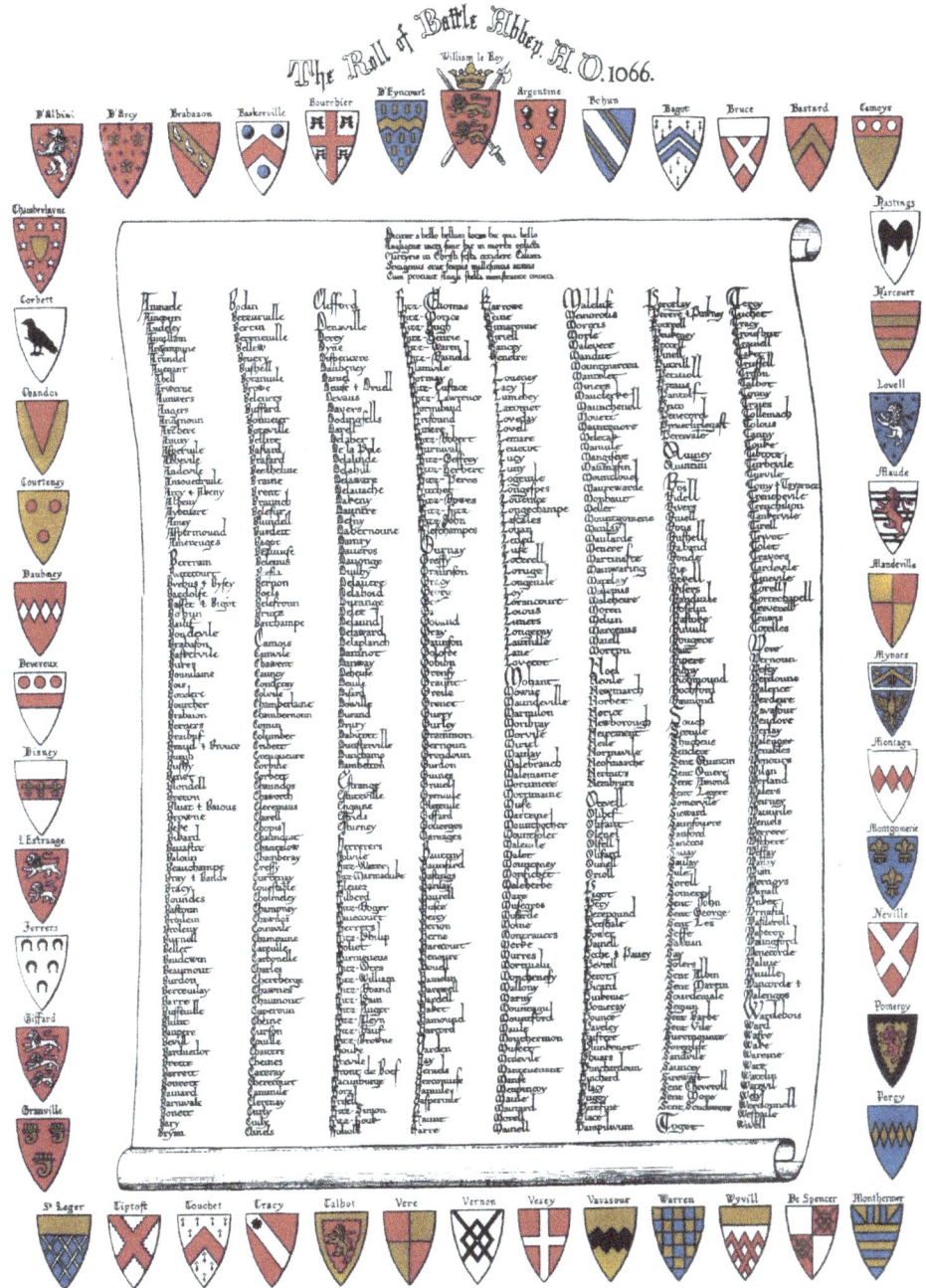

A version of Holingshed's Roll as sold in Battle Museum of Local History.

It is clearly modern. There are about 800 names. In the appendices to this book this number of names in 'Holinshed' is reduced to under 650 by removing duplicates.

Dives and its De Magny additions (1862)

The Roll of Dives is the 1862 Roll made by Léopold Delisle in anticipation of the 800th anniversary of William the Conqueror's original departure of his invasion fleet from Dives-sur-Mer. William's perhaps unintended destination after leaving Dives on or about 13 September 1066 was to be St Valéry-sur-Somme where he was forced to wait for a favourable wind before finally departing for Pevensey and Hastings on the other side of the English Channel on 27 or 28 September.

> … At the foot of the hillside, at the mouth of the River Dives, Duke William gathered together the fleet that was to transport his powerful armed forces towards the English coast … after having camped for a month on these banks before embarking …

The list is interesting and contains 485 full names or 473 family names. In the appendices one list of full names is listed but elsewhere only the family names without duplications are listed alphabetically to enable list comparisons.

A report on the inauguration of the Roll of Dives can be found in Burke's *The Vicissitudes of Families,* third series. This stated that the compilation of a Roll of William's Companions, in the Church of Dives-sur-Mer, was inaugurated on 17 August 1862 with a plaque being fixed inside the Church of Nôtre Dame, above the main entrance.

Before this, an international academic meeting led by Monsieur de Caumont, chairman of the Société Française d'Archéologie, with the approval of the Bishop of Bayeux; Monsieur Renier, vicar of Dives; Count Foucher de Careil, member of the Conseil General; Monsieur Arnet, and the Mayor of Dives had compiled the list of 485 names. The results were from the research of Léopold Delisle, who unfortunately left no records of his sources. Burke clearly notes that the Roll of Dives differs in intent from that of Battle Abbey. It was compiled from the names of those who were enablers and assemblers at Dives as well as those who followed on and helped William conquer all of England.

Edouard, Compte de Magny, added 51 names to the list when writing the *Nobiliaire de Normandie* (published only a few months later in December 1862), so it appears that he may have had access to Delisle's list before it was installed at Dives. He comments that his list is not always in accord with that of the Société Française d'Archéologie installed at Dives. On closer inspection it appears that he only adds twenty or so names once variations of spelling, etc. are taken into account. The two lists – the original of Dives and de Magny's additions – have been listed in alphabetical family name order for comparison in the appendices.

The plaque at Dives
Modified from http://www.rgcrompton.info/d/1066dives_roll1.jpg

Falaise (1927)

The Falaise Roll appeared in order to celebrate the 900th anniversary of the birth of William the Conqueror, which was apparently celebrated at Hastings, Bayeux, Falaise and Caen during June and July of 1927. It is not actually known if 1027 was his birth year. William 'the Bastard' was born at Falaise in 1027, 1028 or 1029 – there is no birth record, and calculation of his birth year varies according to other recorded life events, e.g. his recorded age at the departure of his father to Jerusalem (seven or eight in 1035) and the record in *De Obitu Willelmi* which states that at September 1087 he was 59. Even this stated age could have been incorrect.

To organise the birthday ceremonies an international committee called the Comité Guillaume le Conquérant was set up with présidents d'honneur: Henry Chéron, a senator for Calvados 1913–1936 and a former minister of agriculture; Jackson Crispin, a member of the Historical Society of Pennsylvania; Lord Eustace Percy, British MP for Hastings 1921–1937, who was President of the Board of Education 1924–29, becoming in 1953 Baron Percy of Newcastle, of Etchingham in the County of Sussex; Général Gouraud, military governor of Paris; and A. Bussière, préfect of Calvados; with M. Macary a teacher at Falaise College as secretary; plus 16 other members. The objective was to form a list of those companions of William present at the Battle of Hastings including those who could be strongly assumed to be there even though there was no documented evidence. We are told that all the relevant texts and charters were searched, and use was made of existing rolls with care and discrimination. Eventually a bronze tablet inscribed with 315 individual names was installed in the chapel of Falaise Castle in 1931. However 92 formally accepted names were not ready in time to be included. All 407 names are included in the appendixes.

It should be noted that the Falaise list did not meet with wide acclaim in the United Kingdom and was discussed with critical circumspection by the Society of Genealogists in 1932. The paper about this meeting is reprinted in Camp's book, which also contains reprints of further useful articles and in addition a close and comprehensive analysis of eight rolls including all those above except Auchinleck.

Analysis and Comparison

Camp used a numbering system to identify in which lists the 3,000 or so names that he found occurred. Almost the same overall number of names that the author has found. On inspection of Camp's names, similar scatterings and non-consistency between all eight lists are as apparent as they are in this study. Camp's name list adds those from Brompton's *Chronicle* where there are name couplets similar in appearance to but differing from those of Leland I. The *Chronicle* is prefaced in old French for which the author has made a liberal translation:

> You who want to know the names of the lords of the sea who came with the conqueror, the great, strong William the Bastard, here I give you their surnames as I found them written. Of necessity some proper names are not there, because they made changes hither and thither: Like Edmunde to Edwarde; Baldwyn to Barnard; Godwyne to Goddard; Elys to Edwyn, and consequently all other names, as if they must elevate the sound of the surnames which have not been continuously altered. You, when copying them at this time take heed, yes, your eyes will see the changes.

So even the author of Brompton's *Chronicle* was uncertain of the former names of those on his list and the tone of his note appears critical of what he found. It may even be that the couplets are alternative names for the same person – and some obscure names at that. It was printed in 1652 but ascribed to 1436 with 244 names – or rather possibly alternative names for 122 individuals. Leland may have seen this list on his pre-Dissolution travels at Jervaulx Abbey, where Joannes Brompton was Abbot from

1436–64. If so it may have confused him, just as it confuses today. For completeness this list may be seen as a copy in the appendices, but it is not used in the analysis here.

Camp also copied Guillaume de Talleur's list and another list of 315 names from a study by Loyd. The last is very clearly a list of families who benefitted hugely from the Conquest and may still do so today. Research by Clark has shown that the descendants of people who in 1858 still had Norman surnames were still substantially wealthier than those who did not in 2011. Loyd's list is a fine piece of work and it very usefully locates the geographical origins of some early Anglo-Norman families in Normandy and this data has been useful in the analysis. It is very clearly not a list of Companions; therefore the names from this have not been included in the numbers here.

The biggest problem with the names is their significant variation in spelling. Clearly the names will have been initially transcribed from old parchment rolls, charters, etc. and the initial transcriptions must sometimes have been faulty and even vary in spelling between sources. Subsequent iterations will also have generated faults and indeed some more, hopefully very few, may have been generated accidentally in this study.

An example will help to illustrate this. In the table below are the variations of spelling found for the names, Montague (*Mont agu*), Mowbray (*Montbrai*), Thouars (*Thouars*, unchanged) and Waterville (*Vatierville*) (*The original geographic names are in italics, after Loyd*)

Mont agu	Montagu	Mountagu	Montagu	Mortagne	Maintaigu	Montaigu		Montaigu	
Monbray	Moubray	Moribray	Moribray	Moubray	Mowbray	Montbray	Montbrai	Montbray	
Tours	Tows	Tauers	Thouars	Thouars	Thaon	Thouars	Thouars	Tours	
Vatteville	Vayyruile	Wanneruyle	Wareuyle	Wamervile	Waterville	Wateuile		Wateruile	Wateuyle

In these examples can be seen the variety of possible confusions between the scribed lower-case appearances of some letters. Words have also been spelt phonetically as heard by various clerks down the centuries, just as we find names varying in old parish registers. For example 'Ville' can be spelt 'Uyl'. So it is easy to see how a name like Coursy can quickly become Cussy or Cressy, and Deverelle to become Deuerel or Deuile.

The appendices to this chapter contain over 3000 names in total. This total is from ten lists of varying length with many duplicates both between lists and from within lists with some names also duplicated to quintuplicated or more because of significant spelling variations. There are also large numbers of singletons – single entries with no match between lists. When fully compared the 3000 or so names compress to 1407 different names shared over the lists, with significant numbers (722, 51%) only being represented once. The maximum number of times a single name (or a variant of it) appears is 10.

Frequency	Number	Frequency	Number
1	722	2	250
3	175	4	113
5	48	6	39
7	28	8	13
9	8	10	4

When looking at names in the appendix some words will appear subtly different, but it becomes slightly clearer after a while when the 'eye' gets tuned in and/or the words are mentally rehearsed with French pronunciation. Loyd's book is also helpful in this context. Many words which look different must be linked: For example Sanzaver becomes Sein Saviour or Saint Saviour; Peukey, Pinkenie, Picquini, Picvini, Piquiri, Pinkeney and Paiteny must all be the same place; as must Creuequer, Criketor, Crevecoeur, and Criquetot. Qu and K become confused in the last example as both are pronounced as a K in French.

The *Roman de Rou* list, as would be expected matches well across the listings. As it, and the works from which it drew, have almost certainly been used as sources for both the older and the newer works this is not surprising. But caution is still required – it may have been overdepended upon as it cannot be fully verified.

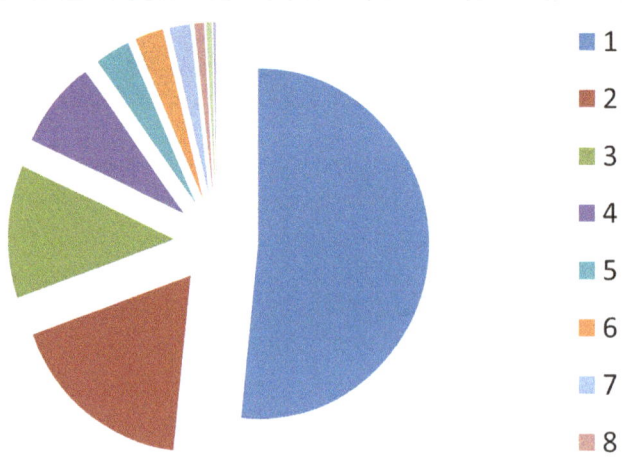

An exploded pie chart of the frequency of a name or its variant being mentioned
©BDHS

Conclusions

It is worth commenting about how the names from the various Rolls match to those of some Anglo-Norman family names between 1066 and 1205. These are the names of some of those who settled in England. Of the 315 family names Loyd and his editors list and match to place names in Normandy only 156 match to names derived from Norman place names on any of the Rolls. Conclusions should not be jumped to about this, but it may reinforce the suggestion that a very good number of Normans followed on after the initial Conquest to settle in England and their names should have no place on a Companions Roll. The lists need to be used with extreme caution for genealogical studies. The admitted use of Domesday names to expand the Dives and Falaise rolls begs the question of just how involved in the events of 14 October 1066 were those given land after the Conquest?

Not every Norman family sent warriors to Hastings. We know that Normandy could be a turbulent, indeed somewhat anarchic, place and that William carefully left Normandy in the good hands of his wife Mathilde and oldest son Robert Curthose with assistance from other trusted nobles, including Roger de Beaumont and Roger de Montgomery. These caretakers would certainly have received some share of the spoils of England in due course for their diligence. There would also be those who built the boats and piloted them across the Channel, and those left to guard the camp at Hastings and the garrison left to defend the western flank at Pevensey, who could be defined as Companions but did not fight in the battle. There were even some, such as the known companions Auffay and Thouars, who refused English lands offered by William, but were undoubtedly otherwise well rewarded.

It could be thought that only those names with strong cross-listings should be considered as having had any significant involvement in the Norman Conquest – either as a true Companions of William in the invasion and battle, or significantly involved in its preparation back in Normandy – or in the first stages of subduing, colonising and organising the new Norman-English kingdom after the Battle of Hastings. But even that idea does not run, as some significant names have very few listings. Camp, Round and others have pointed out, sometimes in no uncertain terms, that there is unfortunately an inextricable mix of fact with fiction in these rolls and further proof of involvement, certainly more than the mere presence of a family name on a dubious list should be sought to claim a family Companion at the Battle of Hastings in 1066, at a place now called Battle.

5
Not just Battle Abbey: other religious houses in eastern Sussex to 1538

Religious communities are a requirement of the social nature, both of men and of religion itself

Pope Paul VI (1897–1978)

The term 'other religious houses' encompasses amongst other institutions more than seven hundred hospitals, some run by religious orders, others by secular monks and nuns, founded in England between the Norman Conquest and 1538. Their name was derived from the Latin hospitalis, meaning being concerned with guests who needed shelter, for one reason or another. Some were only for pilgrims; some almshouses for the aged poor; some provided care and primitive treatments for sickness; and some were for lepers.

All would have served to support their communities, in sickness, health and old age. Illness was seen in those times as linked to the sins of those who were sick, and those in hospitals run by monks and nuns were given regular access to mass and prayer, both by listening and taking part. Religious beliefs also covered miraculous healing, holy wells and springs, relics of saints and other cures. Illness then, as for many still today, might have involved travel on pilgrimage in the hope of healing. This in turn could be a source of income for abbeys in possession of saintly relics, holy wells or other supposed cures –hence the need to provide hospitals to accommodate pilgrims. And one should not ignore the fact that monks and nuns had herb gardens and could be experts in healing with a deep knowledge of effective medicinal herbs.

Without the charity of religious houses, the poverty of the people would have been even worse than it was, and the hospitals that provided shelter and care for the elderly and alms for the poorest section of society would have provided a rudimentary social support system that all but disappeared after the Dissolution.

Battle Abbey was associated with two external hospitals. One, run by the almoner, just outside and in front of the Abbey gate, was undoubtedly for pilgrims or perhaps at first for those visiting the new Abbey, which was a building site and was first mentioned

5. NOT JUST BATTLE ABBEY: OTHER RELIGIOUS HOUSES IN EASTERN SUSSEC TO 1538

in 1076. It was replaced by a new hospital or house for pilgrims under Abbot Odo (1175–1200) and then was completely re-built again in 1443–5 with its design based on a Wealden hall house. In about 1538 an upper floor, hearth and chimney were added. This building with even later modifications is what can still be seen today across the road from the Abbey gatehouse. Its recent owners have sometimes called it the Pilgrims Rest.

The second Battle hospital, run by the Abbey infirmarer, was beyond the watch croft which marked the south-eastern town boundary at the top of what is now Battle Hill at Spitalfields. This is the Starrs Green area and two cottages there are still called Spittle Cottages. This hospital was dedicated to the blessed Thomas the Martyr, the name of which we know, as in 1345 one Alan Payn was accused of breaking into the buildings of the hospital of the blessed Thomas the Martyr in the vill of Battle. He stole a silver chalice and other goods. This hospital was undoubtedly for infectious diseases and leprosy. The two hospitals are confusingly dealt with as one in the *Victoria County History* (*VCH*) of Sussex Volume 2. The infirmarer also ran the Abbey's own infirmary to the east of the cloisters for sick monks within the Abbey precinct, but this was part of the Abbey itself.

But clearly Battle Abbey, a Benedictine monastery, was not the only local religious house associated with external influences and which influenced the affairs of eastern Sussex. These other houses, which include minsters, more hospitals, friaries, priories, a collegiate church and two other local abbeys cannot be ignored in a book which covers this period in eastern Sussex. Nor can the influence of the Abbey of Fécamp in Normandy. Two of these religious houses go back to Anglo-Saxon times when in 772 a minster was set up at Bexhill, and there may have been a contemporaneous minster at Peasmarsh. In pre-Conquest times the Benedictine Fécamp Abbey had influence within the manor of Rameslie from 1017, and in the post-Conquest era, Fécamp must have been involved in founding a hospital at Playden, just outside Rye. Before that they almost certainly would have established the very first church at Rye and churches and a hospital at Old Winchelsea, and probably the original churches of All Saints and St Clement in what is now Hastings Old Town, which area was at the time within their manor of Rameslie. These may have been wooden churches, replaced after the Norman Conquest with stone buildings.

Following the Conquest and the establishment of Battle Abbey, later houses developed in Hastings including the Augustinian Hastings Priory and what was probably a secular order of the Hospital of St Mary Magdalene. The Augustinian order was founded in 1254 by the merger of several smaller orders in Tuscany who were following the Rule of St Augustine, written by St Augustine of Hippo in the 5th Century. The Hastings Collegiate Church of St Mary in the Castle, a secular body which provided monks to take services in local churches as well as observing their own devotions and which also probably took over the minster roles of Bexhill and

Peasmarsh, was founded by Robert, Count of Eu and Lord of the Rape of Hastings in about 1090.

The Cistercians founded another abbey at Robertsbridge. At first it was near Salehurst but then they moved to another site about a mile (1.4 km) from the centre of Robertsbridge. The Cistercian order, also known as white monks, were founded in 1098 and named after the original establishment at Saint-Nicolas-lès-Cîteaux, south of Dijon, France. They were a stricter breakaway group from the Benedictine order. Nearby Lewes Priory was also Cistercian.

Franciscans friars (also known as grey friars), from a relatively new order, came over the English Channel sometime in or after 1224 and established a friary at Old Winchelsea. This was possibly as part of the first group sent directly by St Francis in 1224; Pratt says that they came from Fécamp Abbey – a Benedictine abbey – although it is possible that this was a splinter group. The Franciscan order was founded in 1209 by St Francis of Assisi. Greyfriars priory was well established in Old Winchelsea by 1245 when it was recorded as benefitting from a will. When Old Winchelsea was inundated by the sea after the great storms in the late 13th century, with its final destruction in 1287, they moved up the hill to a new priory in New Winchelsea. The new town was founded under the sponsorship of Edward I to replace the lost township and to serve its harbour, which at that time remained an important strategic naval base. It is believed that after Old Winchelsea's loss of its churches to the sea, that it was Edward I, rather than Fécamp Abbey, who soon sponsored the building of the new churches of St Thomas and St Giles at Winchelsea. Much later to the Franciscan's dismay, the Dominican black friars were also allowed establish a friary at New Winchelsea by Edward I's son, Edward II.

At Rye in about 1263 a 'Friary of the Sack' was established, but it was short lived. An Augustinian friary followed sometime before 1350, but its original building stood below the eastern cliff and became unsafe due to flooding, so in 1378 it moved within the walls of Rye town.

Pevensey is not to be left out. A hospital was developed at Westham. and a small Premonstratensian abbey was started up in 1180 at Otham about three miles (5km) west of Pevensey, situated just north of the A27 Pevensey to Polegate road, but shortly after 1200 it moved to Bayham, just within Sussex near Lamberhurst. There it merged with another small group of white monks from Brockley (now in Lewisham, south London). The Premonstratensian Order combines the contemplative with the active religious life and was been founded in the valley of Prémontré, near Laon, France, in 1120 by St Norbert, later Archbishop of Magdeburg in Germany.

5. NOT JUST BATTLE ABBEY: OTHER RELIGIOUS HOUSES IN EASTERN SUSSEX TO 1538

An alphabetical overview of houses not under the control of Battle Abbey: information is mainly from Knowles and Hadcock's *Medieval Religious Houses* and *VCH Sussex* Vol.2				
House name	Order or Dedication	Founded	Closed or Dissolved	
Bayham Abbey	Premonstratensian (Whitefriars	1199–1208	1525	A small Premonstratensian house from Brockley was moved here in about 1207, with the canons moving before that in abt.1199 to build the new abbey. They were joined by the canons from Otham near Pevensey in 1208–11. There were 20 canons by 1315, but in 1500 there were only ten plus the Abbot.
Bexhill Minster	St Peter	772	After 1066 a new church was developed. This may not have been on the same site	Founded by King Offa. The minster was possibly not on the site of the present St Peters. But the Saxon Church of St Peter was about 40 feet (12m) long by 20 feet (9m) wide and the first Norman additions were made in 1086. One prebend was later attached to Hastings College of St Mary in the Castle which received support from the churches associated with Bexhill and the chapel of Bulverhythe.
Hastings Hospital	St Mary Magdalene	Before 1293	After 1600 became a charity	For a master and poor or infirm brothers and sisters.
Hastings College of St Mary in the Castle	Secular	1090	1546	Founded by Robert d'Eu, earl of the Rape of Hastings. Became a Royal college. It has a complicated history tied into Royal and Rape events. There were between 8 and 10 priests, with the same number of prebends.
Hastings Priory	Augustinian	1189–99	1536. Sea damaged. Moved after 1413	A small priory for about five canons. Eventually damaged by the sea and moved to Warbleton. Dissolved 1536.
Michelham Priory	Augustinian	1229	1536	For 13 canons. Five survived the Black Death. There were nine in 1536
Otham, Hotteham, or Oldham Abbey	Premonstratensian ?St. Lawrence	1180–7	1208–11	This tiny abbey was moved to Bayham. After that it became a grange with a small chapel, probably served by a canon from Bayham.
Peasmarsh Minster	?	8th century	New church on same site after1070	A prebend attached to Hastings College of St Mary in the Castle seems to have been partly endowed from the churches and endowments of the old Peasmarsh minster. The present church of St Peter and St Paul stands on the same site and dates back to 1070.
Playden Hospital	Benedictine	Before 1249	1521	For a priest master and poor or infirm brothers and sisters. By 1442 the building was in ruins. The 'building' passed from Fécamp Abbey to Syon Abbey in 1461 and to Westminster Abbey in 1502. It was so derelict by 1521 that it was appropriated.
Robertsbridge Abbey (1)	Cistercian	1176	13th century	The first abbey was moved from Salehurst to a new site in Robertsbridge.
Robertsbridge Abbey (2)	Cistercian	13c.	1538	There were nine monks in 1418, and the Abbot and nine monks in 1538
Rye Friary (1)	Augustinian	Before 1350	1378	This early friary was threatened by flooding on the east side of Rye and was moved.
Rye Friary (2)	Augustinian	1378	1538	What persists of this building is off Conduit Street within the old town walls of Rye.

An alphabetical overview of houses not under the control of Battle Abbey: information is mainly from Knowles and Hadcock's *Medieval Religious Houses* and *VCH* Sussex Vol.2				
Rye Friary of the Sack	of the Sack or De Penitentia	About 1263	1307	This order was disbanded at the 2nd General Council of Lyons in 1275. Surviving brothers were obliged to join one of the four major orders by 1317. The building stood near the south-west corner of the town churchyard and only small parts of it persist in the structure of the much rebuilt house that stands there today.
Westham Hospital	Hospital House of St. John the Baptist	Probably considerably before 1302	Not suppressed evolved into a charity	Possibly founded by Lords of Pevensey Castle. For the poor, aged and sick. Endowed with 30 acres of land. The surviving charity 'Hospital of St John The Baptist' objectives remain: 'for the benefit of almspeople of the ancient parishes of Westham, Pevensey and ancient liberty of Pevensey...'
Winchelsea Friary (Old)	Franciscan	Before 1245 but after 1224	Destroyed by the sea	Founded by the new order of Franciscan monks
Winchelsea Friary (New)	Franciscan	Relocated abt. 1285	1538	The Franciscans built a new priory
Winchelsea Friary	Dominican	1318, moved 1339 and again 1342	Bef. 1538 when it was found in ruins	Allowed by Edward II. Original site distant from town centre, near New Gate. Moved to a site possibly near the harbour and then again, nearer the town centre. Always small.
Winchelsea	Hospital of St Bartholomew	Before 1292	Combined with St John about 1500	Sited in quarter 39, near New Gate. An alms-house. Patrons became the town of Winchelsea.
Winchelsea (Old)	Hospital of the Holy Cross	Before 1209	Destroyed by the sea	Possibly founded by Fécamp, probably for lepers.
Winchelsea (New)	Hospital of the Holy Cross	Relocated after 1287	? after 1501, about 1520	Near the New Gate in quarter 39.
Winchelsea (Old)	Hospital of St. John	?	Destroyed by the sea	An alms-house. Thought to be the oldest hospital at Winchelsea
Winchelsea (New)	Hospital of St. John	Relocated after 1287	Before 1586	In quarter 34. Patrons became the town of Winchelsea.

Anglo-Saxon Minster Churches

There can be little doubt that the 'planting' of one, probably two, minster churches in the 8th century to act as nuclei for other Anglo-Saxon churches around them, was a large step in the re-Christianisation of eastern Sussex, which had significantly lagged behind Kent. These small monasteries, to be known as minsters, were worldly institutions whose priests were known as 'clerks' or 'canons', who were in modern parlance developing 'outreach' into their local hamlets and villages. The clerks remaining in place just after the Conquest are sometimes mentioned by name in Domesday, holding small parcels of land off which they will have lived. At other times a church is mentioned in the areas covered by the minsters or within the lands of Fécamp Abbey, for example at Guestling. These minsters were subsumed into other institutions post Conquest, but they remained important as the pattern of churches post-Conquest very much followed the arrangement laid down by these precursors. But the recording of churches and priests in Domesday is very erratic.

Peasmarsh

It is known that the prebend of Canon Theobald of Hastings College of St Mary in the Castle was later known as the prebend of Peasmarsh because the lands of Peasmarsh minster made up the bulk of the endowments – these included the lands belonging to four other churches at Iden, Beckley, Northiam, and Playden. A prebend was a stipend which was usually obtained from specific sources, in this case a share of each nominated parish's income.

Bexhill

Much more is known about Bexhill. In a charter dated 772 King Offa provided the assets to support a new minster church to Bishop Oswald (Osa) of Selsey. We have only a later copy of this which may have been somewhat altered when transcribed in the 13th century and an inversion corrected version of this is provided by Porter. This provides some interesting details of the location of the eight hides (or cassati) of land provided in Bexhill (in modern terms eight hides would have been, depending on its quality, up to about 1000 acres or four square kilometres, so not insignificant). There were also assets in other nearby locations to provide additional financial support. The location is interesting as the charter reads:

> These are eight hides relating to the inland of the land of the Bexware (Bæxwarena land, i.e. the land of the people of Bexhill) first to the servants tree, from the servants tree eastwards and up to the old marsh dyke, then south to the treacherous place, along the beach (strand) over against Cooden (Coden) cliff, north to Kayworth or Kewhurst (Kæia weorð) and to the bending stream, north through Shortwood to the landmark beacon, from the beacon to the haunted ford, from the ford along the water to the street bridge, from the bridge up along the drainage ditch to the bedan pool, from the pool along the boundary thus to the servants tree….

This locates this land as being a large parcel north of the Cooden cliffs, not at all the location of St Peter's church in Bexhill old town, which was the nucleus of old Bexhill and sited further east. This conclusion was also made by Ray. The description is also wrong for the old church of Northeye, where there was once a flint chapel dedicated to St James, which faded away in about 1300. The other supporting lands were

> gavel-land appurtenant to Bexhill, namely, Barnhorne, Worsham, on Ibbanhyrste, Crowhurst, on Hricge (Ridge), on Gyllingan, Foxham (somewhere in

Crowhurst), on Blacanbrocan (? Black Brooks in Westfield) and Icklesham, all in Sussex.

In Domesday, two churches are noted at Bexhill, so the known Saxon features at St Peter's, i.e. the stonework uncovered in 1878 works, in the form of flint-rubble laid in herringbone courses, and an intricately carved slab of local fine grained sandstone, can be explained in that it may have been the second church, not the minster, and the slab may even have been moved from the minster when it demised. Tweddle dates the slab to the tenth or early 11th century although it was previously thought to be of eight century origin. He says that it is unique in south-east England in that its decoration comes from mixed periods, and he suggests that it has been derived from an illustration in a Franco-Saxon manuscript such as the Leofric Missal, a service book written in the ninth/tenth century.

But clearly we have no definite archaeological location of the minster. It may indeed have been on the site of St Peter's and the large piece of land reported above may have solely been used for its financial support.

Arrangements similar to those of Peasmarsh may have also once applied to a second canon's prebend at Hastings Collegiate Church – the Bexhill minster had 'parishes' which may have involved pre-Conquest churches in Hooe, Ninfield, Bulverhythe, Bullington (near Worsham/Pebsham) and Bexhill. Because of these linkages it has been assumed that small probably wooden Anglo-Saxon churches had been created in these locations pre-Conquest and that these and the minsters were further developed or replaced by early Norman stone churches in the early post-Conquest period.

Sometime after the manor of Bexhill was returned to the See of Chichester in 1147, it was likely that under Bishop Richard de Wych (1197–1253) the clergy house was enlarged into a substantial bishop's lodging at the eastern end of the diocese. In 1447, at a time of national tensions, Bishop Adam de Moleyns was granted leave to fortify the manor. How much of this was done is unclear. De Molyens himself was an ambitious man with a supplementary role as an international envoy to the pope, but was also involved with and upset Richard of York. He was murdered at Portsmouth in confusing circumstance in 1450. Ownership of the property by the diocese continued until 1559 when it was resumed by the crown and passed into secular hands. After that it was developed into a noble's dwelling. The ancient manor house, with the exception of its barn, coach house and stables was demolished to make way for road widening after 1966. Its remaining ruins can be seen in Manor Gardens. The demolition was maybe a bit premature as a dual carriageway, a small part of the abandoned Folkestone to Honiton trunk-road scheme, bypassed Bexhill Old Town only ten years later.

5. NOT JUST BATTLE ABBEY: OTHER RELIGIOUS HOUSES IN EASTERN SUSSEX TO 1538

The Saxon slab from St Peters church
from www.stpetersbexhill.org.uk

…and Pevensey too?

A small two-celled church, with ruins dated 1100–06, found within the inner ward of Pevensey Castle, may have been the start of a collegiate church, as at Hastings. The size of its endowments, which included another probable minster church and lands at Arlington, the church of St Nicolas, Pevensey and salt and money from the burgesses of Pevensey, support this theory. If so this was never completed as the lord of Pevensey, William de Mortain, was deprived of his lands after being captured at the Battle of Tinchebrai, having fought against Henry I. Rushton has suggested that the church was another pre-Conquest minster and Gardiner that the parish of Pevensey fell within the extensive territory of the minster at Bexhill, so there is a degree of confusion.

There had been ecclesiastical holdings at Pevensey created by one or both of Fécamp and Tréport Abbeys pre-Domesday and the Bishop of Chichester (previously Selsey) had five burgesses providing income within the borough at Domesday. Also three priests were mentioned at Pevensey in Domesday, also receiving rentals from burgesses – in total considerably more than anywhere else in eastern Sussex. Edmer received rents from 15 burgesses, Ordmer from five and Doda from three more. The exact nature of the burgesses own income is not known but it may have been from salt making. At another place called Horsey (not the Pevensey Bay islet called Horse Eye) in nearby Eastbourne Hundred, one hide was held of 'St Martin's church' by a clerk of Fécamp called Roger, but this church name does not correspond to the names of the later churches of either Pevensey or Eastbourne. It might have been land of Battle Abbey.

As we can see from the map overleaf, eastern Sussex appeared to have been well churched in late Anglo-Saxon times. Many of the churches seen today were rebuilt, usually on the same site post-Conquest, but it is rare to find any Anglo-Saxon component. For details of individual churches the reader is directed to the excellent web site: https://sussexparishchurches.org/

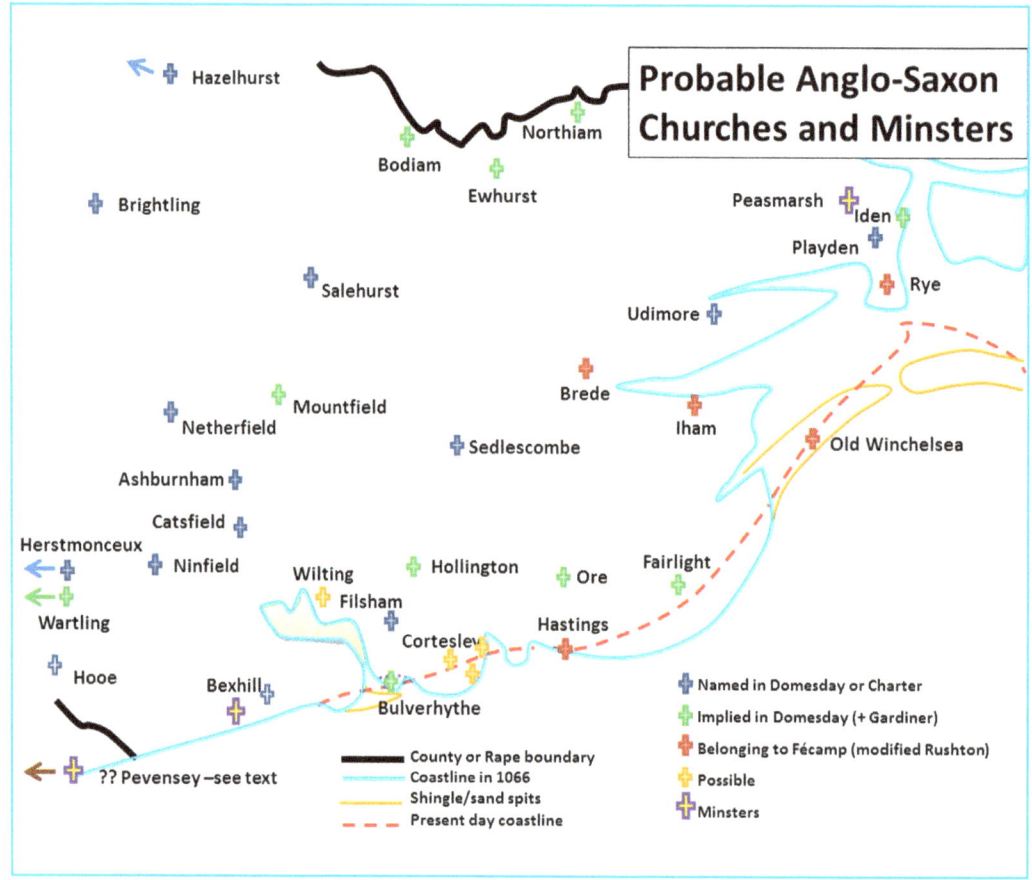

Hospitals

The hospitals at Battle have been described above but there were six more named hospitals, run by friars and nuns, at Playden (only just outside and to the north of Rye), Hastings, Westham near Pevensey, and no fewer than three at Winchelsea.

Playden

There had been a hospital of St Bartholomew in the parish of Playden from the 12th century with a first mention before 1219, seemingly founded with at least the involvement of Fécamp abbey. This mention was in the form of a notification from Abbot Ralf (1189–1219) of Fécamp that the chapel, buildings and lands were to be transferred to the care of the brothers and sisters of the hospital. They were to appoint any future warden as nominated by the mayor and jurats of Rye, who were to submit his name to the Abbot of Fécamp in time of peace, or to the lord chancellor of England if there was war with France, and they in turn should present him to the Bishop of Chichester. Part of the funding was to come from a fair, authorised by the King, from which the Abbey expected a share of the profits. The mayor and jurats of Rye held the hospital seal to prevent fraud and issued a charter to that effect in 1249. From this charter we find that there were then twelve inmates, of whom some were lepers. In 1290 King Edward I granted a charter for a fair which was held on St. Bartholomew's Day in the immediate neighbourhood of the hospital. Unfortunately the hospital had a rather chequered history and by 1442 no master or inmates were there and the building was in ruins. The building passed from Fécamp Abbey to Syon Abbey in 1461 and to Westminster Abbey in 1502, but it was so derelict by 1521 that it was sold for a few shillings, the little money being used towards a new chapel at Westminster. The present modern community hospital at Rye is on the same site and when it was re-developed in 1994 excavations found many items of coins and pottery dating from the 13th and 14th centuries.

Hastings

In Hastings the date and founder of the hospital remain unknown, although the old ruins are said to have 12th century features. It may have been established via the collegiate church. In 1294 the hospital of St Mary Magdalene was gifted land by Petronilla de Cham, widow, of over five acres (2 ha) between what is now Warrior Square and Bohemia Road.

> 22 Edward I., Sunday the Feast of St. Benedict the Abbot.—Grant by Petronilla de Cham of Hastyng, widow, to the Brothers and Sisters of the Hospital of St. Mary Magdalene of Hastyng, of five acres of land in the parish of St. Margaret in Hasting for the healthful estate of her soul and of the souls of Godard, Matilda, Robert, Robert, Robert, William, Richard, and Henry, and of her heirs, parents and friends.'

At least part of this hospital still existed as a wall of an old barn when drawn in 1815, and these sketches show 12th century Norman window features. It was partially excavated in 1862, when the mayor reported that the centre of the building was found full of bones. Protection was granted by Edward III to its master and brethren in 1320, and in 1381 the proctors of the hospital obtained letters of commendation to the clergy of the diocese of Canterbury. The Hastings custumal says:

> The bailiff shall have the visitation of the hospital of St. Mary Magdalen of Hastings once a year; and there shall be in the said hospital brethren and sisters, sometimes more and sometimes less; but no brother or sister shall be received into the aforesaid hospital except by the assent of the bailiff and the commonalty. And the rules of the aforesaid hospital shall be read before the

bailiff at the time of the visitation, at which he shall demand and enquire whether they be well kept or not; and ... the bailiff shall enquire into the life of all the brethren and sisters examined, and if any of them be attainted the bailiff may remove him if he will. And the bailiff by the assent of his fellows if he shall find a man in the said commonalty infirm, and who has conducted himself in accordance with the usages of the ports for all time, and who shall be impoverished ... may put such into the said hospital to partake of the sustenance of the brethren and sisters without paying anything to the said hospital.

Inventories of the stores in the hospital and chapel there were made in both 1525 and 1536. The hospital survived the dissolution and was still in existence at the beginning of Elizabeth I's reign but by 1600 had closed. Its assets, a small estate of a house, a barn and farm lands were occupied by several tenants and the Hastings Corporation decided that the rents would be donated to the churchwardens of St Clements and All Saints parishes to help with the poor rates. In time this benefit passed to the Magdalen and Lasher Charity, which still exists providing relief from poverty and assistance to those in need who are residents of the Borough of Hastings. Its later history is told in Baine's Historic Hastings.

Pevensey/Westham

A hospital at Westham probably existed before the 13th century, possibly founded by one of the lords of Pevensey Castle and endowed with 30 acres (12 ha) of land, but little is known of it. A Pevensey rental of 1292 mentions the master of the hospital of the Holy Cross, but the hospital was named after St John the Baptist, of which the brethren are mentioned in a later rental of 1354. King John authorised a fair at Pevensey, probably to help fund the hospital as it was held around the date of birth of John the Baptist:

> ... and furthermore, we have granted to our aforesaid Barons of Pevensey, that they may there have every year, a fair of seven days duration: to wit, three days before the nativity of St. John the Baptist, that day, and the three days following.

About the middle of the fifteenth century William Slyhand left 40s. and in 1489 Henry Dawson left 6s. 8d to the hospital of St John in Westham. There is little doubt that it was an alms-house as the town custumal says;

> The Men of the Burgage of the Towne of Pevensey have an Hospital of Saynte John Baptiste, in the whiche been brothers or sisters, havynge londes and possessions within the Leege aforesaide, and the same Receyvour and the Men of the saide Burgage have the disposicion of the saide Hospitall, to graunte Corodye, as well to men as to women, as they may consente. And they have to

visit and chaste after the quantitie. And one of the Men of the Burgage alway shalbe Overseer and Superior of that Hospitall, to oversee the expense, and the accompte of the Master of the saide Hospitall. Also the saide Receyvour and the Men may, yf there be to be hadde a Man or Woman of the saide Burgage, the whiche is come into povertie and have not whereof to lyve, and have borne him or her well by all his or her lyffe, that same Man or Woman in the forsaide Hospitall ther sustenances in the same shall take, nothing paying for the same.'

The almshouses that succeeded the medieval hospital of St John the Baptist continued to make provision for the needy of the Liberty of Pevensey and the charity of the Hospital of St John The Baptist remains in existence today, with almshouse bungalows for people in need who are 60 years of age or over and are (or have been) resident in the ancient parishes of Westham and Pevensey including Westham, Pevensey, Pevensey Bay, Stone Cross and Hankham.

Winchelsea

The three hospitals at Winchelsea were those of Holy Cross, of St Bartholomew and of St John. The Holy Cross was clearly founded at Old Winchelsea before 1209, almost certainly under the auspices of Fécamp Abbey within whose manor it lay. Following the inundation of Old Winchelsea the hospital moved to the 39th quarter of New Winchelsea, near the New Gate. This position was well away from the town centre and it was probably a leper hospital. Its original endowment was of one acre of land, but this was subsequently increased to six and a half acres. The last master of Holy Cross, Robert Wrothe, was appointed in 1501 and it disappeared soon afterwards, the mayor and jurats saying in 1570 that it had not existed for 50 years.

St John's was probably even older than Holy Cross: rents were assigned to it from time immemorial. Rentals were received from houses at Great Yarmouth via the Cinque Ports, and in the time of Edward I, John de Romeney, as attorney of the brethren and sisters of the hospital of St John of Winchelsea, received 31s. 6d. (£1.58) from this source. This hospital was nearer the town in the 34th quarter, and its lands which passed to the corporation in 1586 amounted to ten acres. It was under the control of the mayor, who had to visit it once a year and had power to remove any objectionable inmate, and with the consent of the jurats might admit any poor man or woman who had been 'in good love and fame all their time.' So in functional terms it was the almshouse rather than an infirmary.

St Bartholomew's was founded when New Winchelsea was built and stood near Holy Cross in the 39th quarter. It was for brethren and sisters and was endowed with two acres of land worth 6s. (30p). It was under the control of the mayor and commonalty and was another almory as the corporation were able to admit suitable inmates. It and St Johns were probably combined in about 1500 at the St John buildings – a gable end of St John's hospital stands to this day by the roadside out of Winchelsea.

Decline of the hospitals

By 1414 the House of Commons had become as concerned as anyone could be in those days that the hospitals were in decline. We can see this from some of the descriptions above. In a way this had been an increasing problem since the Black Death of 1347–50 when the population had been significantly reduced with the resultant economic problems causing a lack of funds, but also the institutions had been proportionately reduced with respect to numbers of carers: monks and nuns dying in the same proportions as the general population. At the same time, some hospitals had become sinecures for those who ran them and they were caring for fewer people. MPs petitioned King Henry V, who agreed that they should be inspected and properly governed, but left the church to do it. Nothing was done.

By 1540 many of the hospitals had disappeared after their abbeys were dissolved. Some few survived as charities such as at Hastings and Pevensey, or their running was passed to local corporations who had little experience and not much money. The dissolution had profoundly changed English society and the poor suffered, with the sick, beggars and vagrants becoming more numerous and obvious. It would take some time under Elizabeth I before new poor laws were evolved to develop parish based strategies, but the new Protestant élite lacked the sympathetic approach of the previous religious institutions and workhouses started to develop. Medicine was taken over by laymen, who had little idea of the causes of illness. In those early years medical care was still based on old beliefs and doctrines which had actually somewhat regressed from Greco-Roman days and involved supernatural ideas including astrology. Life expectancy remained low with deaths at average ages of 32–35 years.

Priories and Friaries

Hastings

Hastings Priory of the Holy Trinity, which was only ever small, was established in the reign of Richard I (1189–1199) by either Sir Walter Bricet or Walter de Scotney who gave the priory the churches of Crowhurst and Ticehurst. The priory later also obtained more churches at Dallington, Ashburnham and St Michaels in Hastings, the last from Ralph Neville in 1237, and as noted below lands at Michelham in 1229 from Gilbert de Laigle. It was just above where the old Hastings Post Office was on Cambridge Road. Sometime later 192 acres (78 ha) of land were transferred to it from St Michael's parish.

This land was all on the west side of the Priory valley, a very small tidal port at the time, and some of it would have been a typical water meadow so beloved of monastic

5. NOT JUST BATTLE ABBEY: OTHER RELIGIOUS HOUSES IN EASTERN SUSSEC TO 1538

institutions. As the protecting cliffs eroded, the sea encroached until the priory was in danger of being inundated, and in 1413 Sir John Pelham gave a site at Warbleton, and Henry IV licensed the priory to remove there. A small farm persisted on the residual Priory land for many years and was still shown on the Boundary Commission map of 1832 and the OS map from the 1873 survey. The priory had a rocky history and at times it must be wondered what its function was.

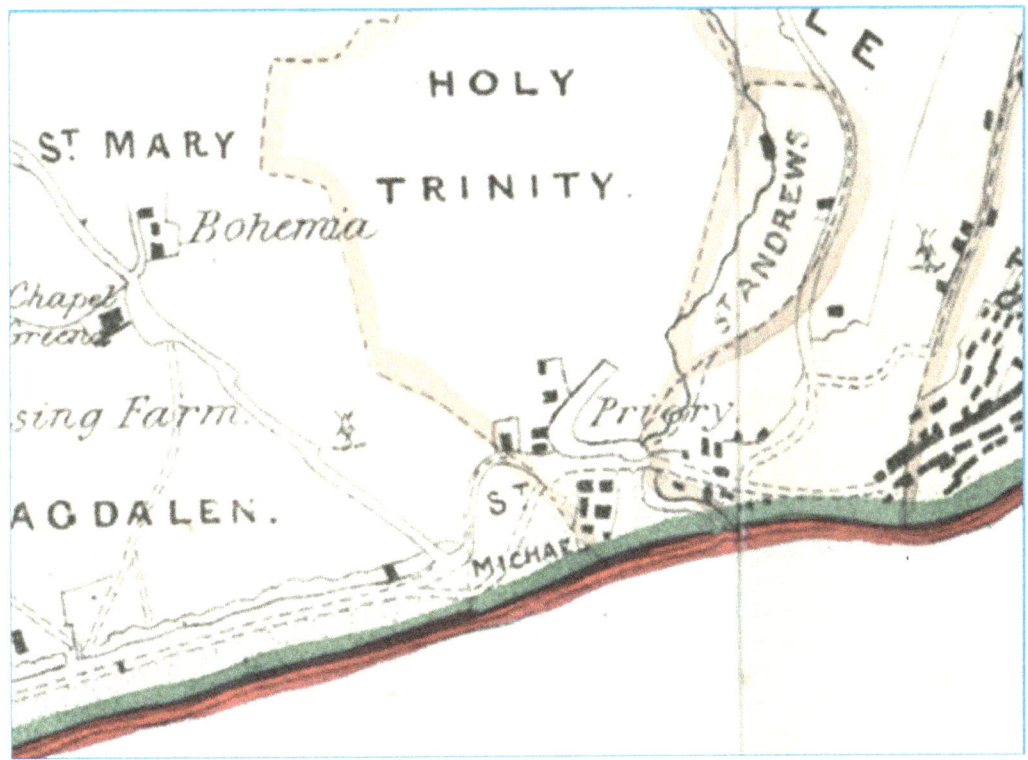

Extract from The Boundary Commission map of 1832
This still shows St Michael's and St Andrew's parishes, the Priory farm on the site of the old Holy Trinity Priory and the site of St Mary Magdalene Hospital.

A small article which seems to be about excavations at the Hastings Priory site has been found in the Sussex Archaeological Society newsletter of May 1973. The Hastings Area Archaeological Research Group carried out excavations at a small Augustinian Priory site, in advance of building works. They found that a late 12th-century chapter house had a blank arcade along its north, south and east walls, consisting of a series of interlaced semi-circular arches supported on foliated capitals. The vault had moulded ribs with dog-tooth ornamentation. The tiled floor of the chapter house had been robbed out but the remains of a crude dais or seat were retained in the centre of the east wall. The walls of the 13th century dormitory, to the north, stood to a height of 4–5 feet (1.5m) above floor level and retained the remains of two doorways and a lancet window. The north range was taken up by the 13th century refectory, which had been extensively rebuilt during the 14th century. Work of the latter period, which included the wall staircase giving access to the pulpit, was of high quality, having double plinths and being faced with small, square, ashlar blocks and courses of squared and knapped flints. The roofs were of West-country slate throughout. The buildings were abandoned in about 1417.

Michelham

Michelham Priory is included here because of its founding family association with the Battle of Hastings and that family's sponsorship of Hastings Priory of which Michelham appears to be a daughter priory. Engenulf de Laigle, accepted as a definite companion of William at the Battle of Hastings, was killed at the battle where he

> with shield slung at his neck, and gallantly handling his spear, struck down many of the English.

His Norman descendants became in time lords of Pevensey Castle and its Rape until 1235 when the links with England came to an end. Gilbert de Laigle, the fourth Laigle lord of Pevensey Rape, founded the Augustinian Michelham Priory at a bend of the river Cuckmere in Arlington parish. The first prior was called Roger. After receiving approval from Henry III in letters patent of May 1229, de Laigle arranged in the following March that Hastings Priory, in order to found the new priory, would receive 80 acres (32ha) of land at Michelham, a wood at Pevensey, 80 acres of marshland in Hailsham, 20 acres (8ha) of meadow at Willingdon and numbers of other grants. After this links seemed to persist between Michelham and Hastings Priories which were both of the Augustinian order. Later in 1300 John, prior at Hastings, was ordered to return to Michelham as a simple canon because of various misdemeanours and in 1402 Richard Weston, a canon of Michelham, became prior of Hastings.

The situation of Michelham on a route across Sussex meant that it received many visitors on progresses through Sussex over the years before its dissolution, including Edward I in 1302 on one of his itineraries. A good history of Michelham Priory can be found on the Sussex Archaeological Society's website.

Rye Friary of the Sack

There was a short lived Friary of the Sack at Rye established in about 1257. The order was forbidden to receive novices and new sites after the Second Council of Lyons in 1274 and died out in the early 14th century. Old Stone House in Rye, on the south side of the parish churchyard, which has traditionally been identified as the site of the Friary of the Sack, survives as a private dwelling. But very little of any original stone building survives. The surviving stone window has a 19th-century replacement with a decorated style head which might be of 13th or early 14th century date. Martin and Martin say that the original stonework of this window is more reminiscent of 14th century than 13th century work.

Rye Augustinian Friary

Rye Augustinian friary was the first successful house permitted following new papal licences of spring 1364, which allowed foundations in towns where 'many faithful' desired them. A community of friars was certainly established quite quickly in 1364 on two acres of land held from the king for a payment of 2s. 10d. (14p) yearly. It possessed both common and prior's seals by 1368. What was very important for the success of such a friary was local support, which was it seems readily given from the town.

The first build was to the east of the town centre but this soon became non-viable. There had been five messuages on the land on which the friary was first built but they and the friary had been 'submerged', possibly after erosion and slippage of a cliff, and were unusable. The friary was therefore relocated within the town walls to le Haltone, on the corner of Conduit Hill and High Street, where their former chapel, but not the whole friary, survives. It largely lacks mediaeval detail, and although east, south and west windows of the late 14th century chapel remain they are blocked. The *Victoria County History of Sussex* says the house at Rye has mid-fourteenth-century details, chiefly windows with tracery of French or Flemish character. A plan of the chapel, which is about 65 feet (20 m) long, is also given in the *VCH*. There was a fairly small quadrangular cloister-type building on the north side of the chapel which does not survive. It is shown in a view of Rye painted by Van Dyck dated 1633. There is quite a bit of detail about both of the Rye friaries in Draper's book.

Winchelsea Greyfriars

Greyfriars at Winchelsea has some rather beautiful surviving ruins of its choir, which are taken to indicate the early size and wealth of this friary. Heritage England in its listing says that it is one of the most impressive examples of Franciscan architecture in England.

This was perhaps aided by the fact that its forced relocation from Old Winchelsea to the new town coincided with a phase of Franciscan re-building in Britain, which often entailed an 'aggrandisement' of their sites, particularly the churches. Although the friars were poor, the local friary was well supported by donations and legacies. In 1413, for example, the Finch family of Winchelsea made a grant so that

> a mass [be] said for Vincent Finch and his wife Isabella on their death and their names [to] be written in the gift book of the covenant among the chief benefactors.

The Chancel of Greyfriars (Franciscan) Priory, Winchelsea
Photo © Keith Foord

Following devastating French raids, the Black Death and the economic decline resulting from the silting of its harbour, Winchelsea became significantly poorer as time went by and support from the Winchelsea community reduced.

The Bishop of Dover was sent to accept the surrender of the friary, and sold the stuff – that is the ornaments and furniture. 'The house is at the king's command and yours,' he reported to Thomas Cromwell.

Following the dissolution, the site was leased to the Captain of Camber Castle, Philip Chowte, who was only interested in making what he could out of the buildings. As he was also tenant of the also dissolved blackfriars' site near the Pipewell Gate it was more convenient to take stone from there to Camber Castle than to rob stone from Greyfriars. This probably accounts for there being no significant residue of Blackfriars and the survival of so much of Greyfriars.

VCH, Pratt's books and the studies by Martin and others contain much information about this friary, its history and relationship with the town.

Winchelsea Blackfriars

When New Winchelsea was founded it had been agreed that there should only be a single friary – the Franciscan one. However, just like between parliaments today, one king would often take no notice of his predecessors' promises and, in 1318, Edward II granted 12 acres (5ha) in quarter 39 of Winchelsea, not far from the New Gate and next to the hospitals of the Holy Cross and St Bartholomew, to build a house of Black Friars. Apparently few worshipped there and in 1339 licence was given for William Batan of South Iham to grant the friars six acres of land nearer the town. This site appears to have been by the harbour, and even less satisfactory than the first and they were in danger of being swept away by the sea. In 1342 they obtained permission to move to yet another part of the town, possibly quarter 6, as but what exactly happened is obscure, as in 1358 the king granted them an acre of land near the church of St Giles and allowed them to take over five messuages adjoining this land. In 1372 the King released them from payment of the rent of 5s. 8¾d. (29p) due for the messuages.

In 1398 Henry Sucton was appointed for a term of three years as a teacher of philosophy and theology, and had permission to make a pilgrimage to Rome. The prior a few years later may have supported Richard II, as in 1402 Henry IV issued orders to arrest him for high treason. His end was probably very unpleasant, although we have no details. Little more information has been found after this until its final dissolution in July 1538, when the Bishop of Dover reported that the house was in ruins and although its furniture had fetched £10, and there was 20s. (£1) rental income, the property would not bring in 10s. (50p) a year. Overall it seems as if the Dominicans had little effect on the life of the town.

Hastings Collegiate College of St Mary in the Castle

Collegiate churches were secular and not associated with any particular order. As well as their own devotions they served churches in their neighbourhoods. This collegiate church had a chequered history and had many more downs than ups in this history. It was founded in 1090 by Robert, Count of Eu and lord of the Rape of Hastings, and was built within the walls of Hastings Castle on a windy sandstone promontory now called the West Hill, between what is now Hastings old town and the centre of modern Hastings. The somewhat restored ruins of the church can be seen today, but it is difficult to envisage the total setting at its active phase as about 2/3rds of the Castle has fallen into the sea after cliff erosion. Its absolute peak was very early when William II (Rufus) held court there in 1094 as he waited with an army to cross to Normandy. Archbishop Anselm of Canterbury consecrated Robert to be Bishop of Lincoln whilst there, and the assembled throng took a day outing to Battle to consecrate the first part of the Abbey church at Battle.

Some have claimed that there may have been an earlier collegiate establishment at Hastings, as in trying to prevent a visitation by Bishop of Chichester in 1299 the canons claimed a foundation of Edward the Confessor, and said that William the Conqueror gave the Castle and chapel with the prebends directly to the count of Eu.

This claim of foundation from the Confessor was not supported. But the King still stopped the Bishop from visiting, as after Countess Alix of Eu had opted to retain her lands in France over those in England in 1243 and after her death in 1267, the church had passed to the crown and became a royal free chapel, independent and outside of the See of Chichester. This status remained until 1446 when it was granted by Henry VI, along with the Rape of Hastings, to Sir Thomas Hoo. After this it was decreed that the church should be exempt from visitation by the king or any other person except the Bishop of Chichester and his official. This arrangement was confirmed in 1460.

Following its foundation, ten prebends were established to fund overall functioning and the canons of the college, and it probably took over the roles of the local minster churches. From about the beginning of the thirteenth century the prebends seem to have been as follows: Bulverhythe, Brightling, Crowhurst (sometimes with Ticehurst); Hollington (with Ewhurst and Bodiam), Marlepast, Peasmarsh, Stone, Thurrock; and the combined prebend of Wartling, Hooe, and Ninfield which was divided into three separate prebends; finally, there was the prebend of Salehurst, which from 1333 onward was held by the Abbot of Robertsbridge. Later these prebends gradually diminished in number.

The overall history of the College is one of inexorable decline as its fabric and the canons' houses deteriorated within a derelict castle. The Castle was slighted by King John to prevent it falling into his enemies hands, was raided by the French and robbed by the people of Hastings. It had little function as a redoubt and was under constant attack by nature as the southern face of its cliff inexorably fell away. Eventually the canons were the only inhabitants. It survived the dissolution, but was suppressed in the last year of Henry VIII and was given to Sir Anthony Browne, who already held the Battle Abbey and Syon Abbey lands. Some collegiate churches evolved into renowned schools or universities, but that was not the case at Hastings. The whole rather sad story is well covered in the *VCH*.

Abbeys

Otham/Bayham and Robertsbridge Abbeys

Although eastern Sussex contains the famous Benedictine Battle Abbey which had great local influence it cannot be ignored that there were other abbeys in the area. These were Otham Abbey, which later moved and merged with another small abbey to become the Premonstratensian Bayham Abbey and the Cistercian Robertsbridge Abbey.

Otham and Bayham

Otham Abbey was tiny and was situated at Otham, also previously known as Hotteham or Oldham, about three miles (5 km) west of Pevensey. It was founded by

5. NOT JUST BATTLE ABBEY: OTHER RELIGIOUS HOUSES IN EASTERN SUSSEC TO 1538

Ralph de Dene of West Dean near Seaford on his own land in about 1180, which he gave to the canons of the Premonstratensian order at St Mary and St Lawrence, the grant suggesting that there was already a small chapel there. The geographic position of Otham is not very good and low lying on the fringes of marshland. After about twenty years, proposals were made to the Abbey to move. The first site offered was at Hellingly, but in about 1205 Sir Robert de Turnham, said to be a favourite of Richard I, decided to cofound an abbey at Bayham, then called variously Begham, Beigham or Begenham, on the borders of Sussex and Kent, and arranged for a small group of Premonstratensian monks who had settled at Brockley in Kent to move there. Brockley had been founded by Michael, brother of Robert and Juliana, widow of Hugh Bigod, earl of Norfolk. To swell the numbers of monks he also obtained the consent of Ela de Sackville, daughter of Ralph de Dene, the patron of Otham, to move the Otham monks as well. After that Otham remained as only a small grange of Bayham Abbey, served by perhaps a couple of monks. In the *Taxatio Eccesiastica* of 1291 the Abbot of Bayham is shown as having income of £2 10s 2d (£2.51) from 'Oteham'.

Heritage England list a Grade II* small chapel, dedicated to St Lawrence, which originally formed part of Otham Abbey. This is at the time of writing used as a wedding venue. Iit is described as a small building, aisle-less in plan and 10m long by 7m wide built of flint and greensand with greensand dressings with repairs patched in red brick. The roof is of slate on old oak timbers. It is dated of about 1350, so must have been at least partially re-built.

So Jordan, the Abbot of Otham, became the first Abbot of Bayham, and building started after 1199 or more likely sometime in 1208–1211 when King John was finally bribed with two horses of price to confirm all the various grants involved. Apparently building progress was slow and was still ongoing in 1234, but was probably nearly finished. It was built of local sandstone. As the two contributing Abbeys had had different mother houses the Abbey became a prestigious direct daughter of Prémontré Abbey, thanks to the efforts of its second Abbot, Reginald. Over the next years considerable numbers of further grants were made to Bayham, so it was financially well provided for, but monastically it did not receive many enthusiastic visitations (inspections from the local diocese) and seemed to have more than its share of naughty monks. There also seemed to be a rapid turnover of monks in residence, but there is some suggestion that it may have been normal in the Premonstratensian order to move monks around between establishments. The Abbey church was extended in the late 13th century, and a gatehouse was added in the 14th. Bayham Abbey had royal visits on at least two occasions: in 1299 by Edward I and in 1322 when Edward II stayed overnight on his way to Battle Abbey.

Bayham did not last to the dissolution of the monasteries. It was dissolved in 1524 by Cardinal Wolsey along with 39 other minor houses, to provide funds for Wolsey to found new colleges at Oxford (Cardinal, which became first King's and is now Christ Church) and in his home town of Ipswich.

At that time Bayham's annual income was reckoned to be £152 9s. 4½d. (£152.47). The monks and local people resisted and there were protests before Wolsey prevailed. This suggests that the Abbey was well regarded locally and would of course have been a source of employment. When Wolsey fell from power in 1529, the Abbey reverted to the crown, but the little chapel at Otham may have continued for another 20 years or so as a parish church. The Ipswich college was demolished in 1530 and only Wolsey's Gate, the waterside entrance remains.

The Bayham buildings were largely destroyed after 1547. Today the Abbey ruins are enclosed by a moat on three sides, with on the west side a bank and ditch. Only parts of the monastic buildings survive. The best-preserved feature is the south wall of the church nave, with three large arched windows, braced by thick buttresses. Also parts of numerous outbuildings survive, including the bakehouse, mill, brewhouse, stables, stores, and barns. There is a detailed history of the Abbey by Cooper published in 1857 and Rigold wrote a description and brief history of it in 1974, updated by Coad in 2016.

Robertsbridge

John, Count of Eu and lord of the Rape of Hastings, retired to the Abbey of Foucarmont in Normandy and died there in 1170. He had married Alix d'Aubigny who was daughter of William d'Aubigny, Earl of Arundel and Alix de Louvain, Dowager Queen of England, the widow of Henry I. After John's death she married Alured de St Martin, and he and Alix are jointly credited with founding Robertsbridge Abbey in 1176. To support the Abbey, Alured also gave some estates in Ewhurst, Sedlescombe and Pett Level and others all previously held of Geoffrey de St Martin and his heirs. There is some indication that the St Martin family may have been planning this move and accumulating the assets to do so since 1161. A relative, possibly also involved with the foundation of the Abbey, Robert de St Martin, may have built the first bridge over the Rother, which Mawer and Stenton accept probably led to the future name of the settlement of Robertsbridge.

Alured de St Martin had been one of John of Eu's knights, but by 1176 he was also sheriff of Sussex and a steward (dapifer) to Richard I. Alured had witnessed the Treaty of Falaise made at Falaise Castle between the captive King William I of Scotland and Henry II in December 1174. William had been captured at the Battle of Alnwick during an invasion of Northumbria and was being held at Falaise whilst Henry sent an army north and took several Scottish castles, including those at Berwick and Edinburgh.

The original location of the Abbey was in the vill of Salehurst, and the first Abbot recorded was called Denis. A later charter of 1314 describes a chapel, dedicated to the Trinity, Holy Cross, St Mary and St John the Evangelist, in Salehurst as being on the spot where the Abbey was originally founded. The community was able to increase its land-holdings, but just as now there was periodic flooding in the Rother valley which has been put forward as the reason for moving to a new site. So some time during the 13th century, about 1250, the Abbey did move to a new site on the south side of the River Rother, one mile (1.4 km) from the centre of Robertsbridge. Harris has pointed out that the new site was only 10m above mean sea level, whereas the old was 20m above mean sea level and which implies that flooding was not the issue and he proposed that the re-siting was more likely to be to obtain a better water supply and/or that it was a better site for enlargement of the Abbey estate after the receipt of generous bequests. Indeed the Abbey expanded and later purchased more land at Playden and Bexhill from the Abbey of Tréport and also obtained the advowsons of Salehurst, Udimore and Mountfield. They were often at odds with their neighbours, including Battle Abbey, over many years about land ownership as evidenced by a large trail of charters.

As noted above, in 1192 Abbot Denis of Robertsbridge was sent together with the Abbot of Boxley to search for King Richard who had been captured and was being held for ransom on his way back from the Holy Land. It may have been the connection with the royal family by the Abbey's founder that led to the choice of the Abbot for this task. Whatever the connection the Abbot of Robertsbridge was clearly well regarded as he was chosen for the task of king's messenger three more times as discussed in Chapter 3. The story of Henry III's unhappy visit to Robertsbridge before the Battle of Lewes is also covered in this chapter as is a brief visit by Edward I.

Robertsbridge did not exist when the Abbey was founded but was developed after 1220 possibly as a new settlement encouraged by the Abbot, who in around 1250–60 developed his own Hundred of Robertsbridge and created the posts of constable, ale-conner and street-driver. A rental probably of the late 13th or early 14th century includes several tenants, and Robertsbridge market became a significant centre for trading and manufacturing by about 1300, possibly at the expense of Salehurst market.

Of interest is the Robertsbridge Codex (of about 1360) which is a 14th century musical manuscript. It contains the earliest surviving music written specifically for keyboard. It was discovered in a bundle with an old register from Robertsbridge Abbey at Penshurst Place in Tonbridge in the mid-19th century. Originally it was thought to date from about 1325, but later, about 1360, was thought more likely. It contains six pieces, three of them in the form of the 'estampie', an Italian dance form from the 14th century, as well as three arrangements of motets. Two of the motets are from the *Roman de Fauvel*. This is a musical form of a French poem by Gervais du Bus that is regarded as important by music historians. This poem satirizes social corruption in political and religious life. Its hero is a fawn (French: fauve) coloured ass called Fauvel, the letters of whose name were taken from the first letters of the French words Flatérie, Avarice, V[U]ilanie (depravity), Variété (fickleness), Envie, and Lascheté (cowardice).

Folio from the Robertsbridge Codex
Detail from BL Add. Ms.28550 via https://assets.classicfm.com/2017/10/robertsbridge-codex-1488817419.jpg

In Parrish we are told that all of the music is anonymous, and is written in tablature. Most of the music for the 'estampies' is for two voices, often in parallel fifths, and also using hocket technique The source is probably English.

Robertsbridge Abbey seems to have faded somewhat towards the end of the fourteenth century. In the 15th century a general Royal Charter dated 14 July 1437 was received:

> granted at the request of the communities of the kingdom made in the last Parliament, and with the assent of the lords spiritual and temporal in the same Parliament assembled, pardoning the Abbat and convent for all kinds of transgressions and offences committed before 2 Sep: 10 H. 6; and for all alienations, donations, and purchases made - by them of lands and tenements held of him or any of his progenitors. Kings of England, in capite, and all

5. NOT JUST BATTLE ABBEY: OTHER RELIGIOUS HOUSES IN EASTERN SUSSEX TO 1538

alienations and purchases in mortmain made without license; remitting all fines and amerciaments, reliefs and scutages, and all demands he had against them before the day of his coronation, and all securities for peace ; pardoning offences against the statute in receiving papal bulls, and releasing to them all jewels which had been deposited with them as security for war-loans, and for the expenses of the passage of the late King to the vill of Harfleure and parts of France and Normandy, unless the same be redeemed within a year of the 7th of March last ; but upon this condition that the Abbat shall not put forward any further demands in respect of the late King's wars and journeys over and above what may be due to him for custody of the castle and vill of Calais, and the marches there in the late King's time. Tested at Westminster 17 July, 15 H,6'.

In 1437 Henry VI became 16 and assumed the reins of government from a king's council. The charter above may be related this this fact and the costs of the ongoing war with France.

It is notable that Robertsbridge Abbey did not support the Cade Rebellion and that the Abbey fair had been the subject of an early attack by Cade's supporters in 1449. This suggests that the Abbey was not very supportive of its community at that time. Battle's Abbot and his Abbey did support Cade as did Lewes Priory, and afterwards both received Royal pardons.

At its Dissolution in April 1538, the net annual income of the Abbey was £248 and there were twelve monks. The site was acquired by Sir William Sidney of Penshurst, Kent and the remains of the Abbey were later incorporated into Abbey Farm. The remains include a rectangular stone south range, incorporating the Refectory or Frater. This features a pointed recess and three round-headed windows. At the east end of the range is what is thought to be the calefactory or warm room and a 14th century vaulted passage. To the west is the Abbot's house with a medieval undercroft dating from about 1250, incorporated into a Grade I listed residence.

A good general history of Robertsbridge Abbey is given in *VCH*. There is no modern definitive history of Robertsbridge although there are several websites which give very useful information, mostly focussed on the Abbey. The most comprehensive article about Robertsbridge Abbey is probably Cooper's. A small more general history of Robertsbridge and Salehurst parish was written by Piper and published in 1906.

He is a lion by his pride and ferocity, but by his inconsistency and changeableness he is a leopard

The Song of Lewes, about 1264

Edward I, 1272–1307
Unknown artist oil on panel, 1597–1618
22 7/8 in. x 17 3/4 in. (580 mm x 450 mm) uneven
Purchased, 1974 NPG 4980(6)
© National Portrait Gallery, London

6

The Great and Terrible King Edward I and his son: Battle and the Cinque Ports of eastern Sussex 1272–1327

Edward I cannot have had particularly fond memories of eastern Sussex after his visits as the Prince Edward during the Second Barons War before the Battle of Lewes on 14 May 1264 and its aftermath. These visits have been described in the section about Henry III in a previous chapter. The First Barons War (1215–17) was against King John (d.1216) and rolled over into Henry III's reign and the local events of this have also been described above. Prince Edward had been captured at Lewes and was initially sent to Dover Castle to be guarded by Henry de Montfort, thence to London.

Just over a year later, after the Battle of Evesham (4 August 1265), with the rout of the barons, in late 1265/early 1266 Prince Edward had attacked Winchelsea from the sea and land. The sea attack was with a navy recruited mainly from Yarmouth and the east coast, Winchelsea's traditional rivals. This was because Winchelsea had not apologised for its role in the 2nd Barons War. Armed retribution was exacted and some citizens of Winchelsea executed. Winchelsea revolted again in 1267 to no avail; the leaders were taken to Rochester and never seen again.

After these events, the town was pardoned and it was guaranteed its land and liberties. Edward had recognised that he and his father would need the town's support for a harbour and ships for the royal fleet and took an unusually forgiving stance. This act did not go unrewarded as from that time forward the town, in spite of its anarchic tendencies from time to time, generally cooperated with the crown to mutual benefit.

Henry III died at his Palace of Westminster on 16 November, 1272. Edward had left England in 1270 to join what is sometimes called the Eighth Crusade and eventually returned in 1274 as King Edward I to London, being crowned at Westminster on 19 August. He was in fact the fourth King Edward of England, but the first since the Conquest over 200 years ago.

Winchelsea must have been little more than a tiny fishing village at first, possibly with origins in the 9th century. Eddison considers that Old Winchelsea could not have been of much significance as a harbour much before the end of the 12th century, when it rapidly enlarged in both size and importance. For a while it became the preferred English port on the route from London to France, but sadly Old Winchelsea's demise was as quick as its rise. During several great storms of the late 13th century, there was a shingle bar breach in 1250.

Winchelsea first appealed for help in 1272 as Old Winchelsea was becoming unviable because of the changes to the shoreline. The historical geography of the time has been summarised by Foord and Clephane-Cameron and is described pictorially below. Old Winchelsea was to be completely lost to the sea along with its shingle bank after 1287. Edward must have been briefed about this in 1272 and, although he may have had some residual antipathy towards Winchelsea, it did not last long as he clearly appreciated the strategic nature of the ports of Rye and Winchelsea, and would have realised that the latter still had potential, albeit severely damaged. Both still retained the sheltered large lagoon of the Rye Camber and both still had ship-making skills. He would also have been aware that Hastings was decreasing in its attractiveness as a port due to its own damage from the sea and its now more open position with lack of a large port.

Even so, Edward I did not visit Winchelsea to assess the situation for nearly two years after his return to England. Arriving from Lewes via Laughton, Edward was at Battle Abbey on 1 July 1276, for which visit the Abbey bought a prodigious quantity of beef and emptied its fishpond of fish. The next day he went on to Winchelsea to inspect the sea damage, after which he moved on rapidly to Romney in Kent.

He did not act immediately, but in 1280 he issued instructions that Winchelsea should be rebuilt and this is discussed below after discussion of other further events in eastern Sussex in this period.

Baines reports that Edward visited Hastings 1274 and made 'certain sea laws'. In Twiss' *Black Book of the Admiralty* Vol. 1 is a transcription of the Old French record. It and the English translation both mention King Edward I but in neither is there a precise date or place. There is a side note by Twiss that:

> an Act was made at Hastings by Edward I that no contract concerning port pleas should be tried elsewhere than in the Admiral Court.

The dating appears to rely indirectly on an old record made just before the time of Henry VI, i.e. in the early 1400s, by one Thomas Rowghton of Rowghton who may have been a registrar of the Admiralty Court. This claims that the Act was made during the second year of Edward I's reign. This gives some difficulty as the second year of his reign ended on 16 November 1274 and he did not return to England until 2 August 1274 when he landed at Dover. After this, there were only two small gaps

12th Century

The shingle banks were well established but already there was silting and 'inning' of the lagoons. Shingle blocked Bulverhythe which slowly became a fresh water marsh. A breach in the shingle bar allowed the Brede and Tillingham rivers to exit to the sea via this. The Rother channel was silting and the Rhee wall was constructed to try to keep Old Romney harbour clear.

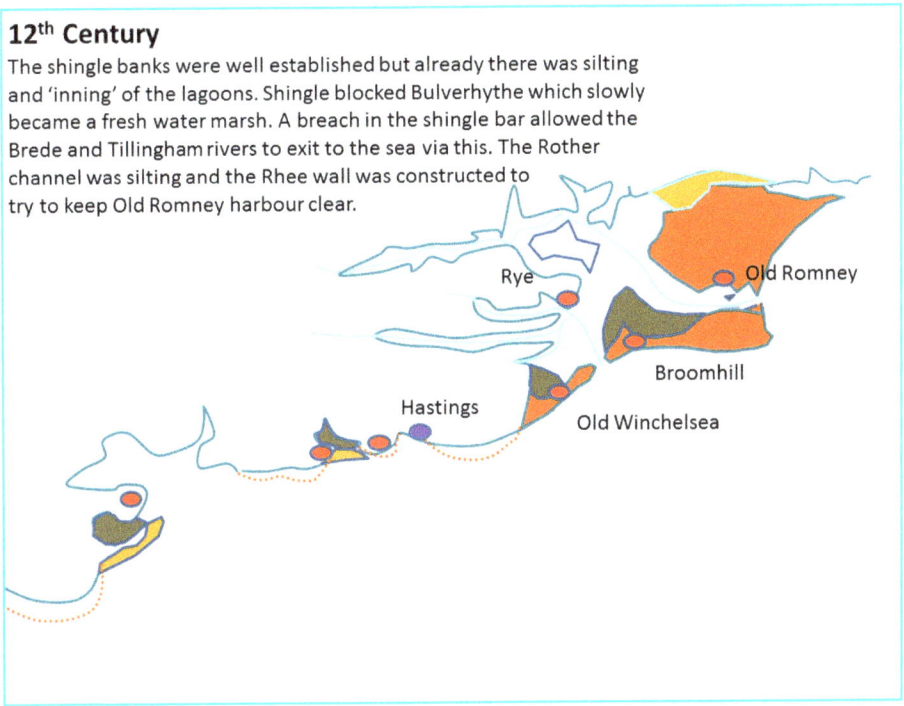

13th to 14th Centuries

In mid and late 13th c. There was a series of great storms, Old Winchelsea flooded, then it was lost together with the shingle bank, which allowed severe flooding of the whole Rye Camber and the estuaries. The lost shingle was moved eastwards and re-deposited at Dungeness, where it also blocked the exit of the Rother at Old Romney. The Rother diverted south. This may have been the time when Hastingceastre was also lost. Bulverhythe converted to freshwater marshland and farming. The Rhee Wall had been constructed to try To keep Old Romney harbour from silting up...to no avail.

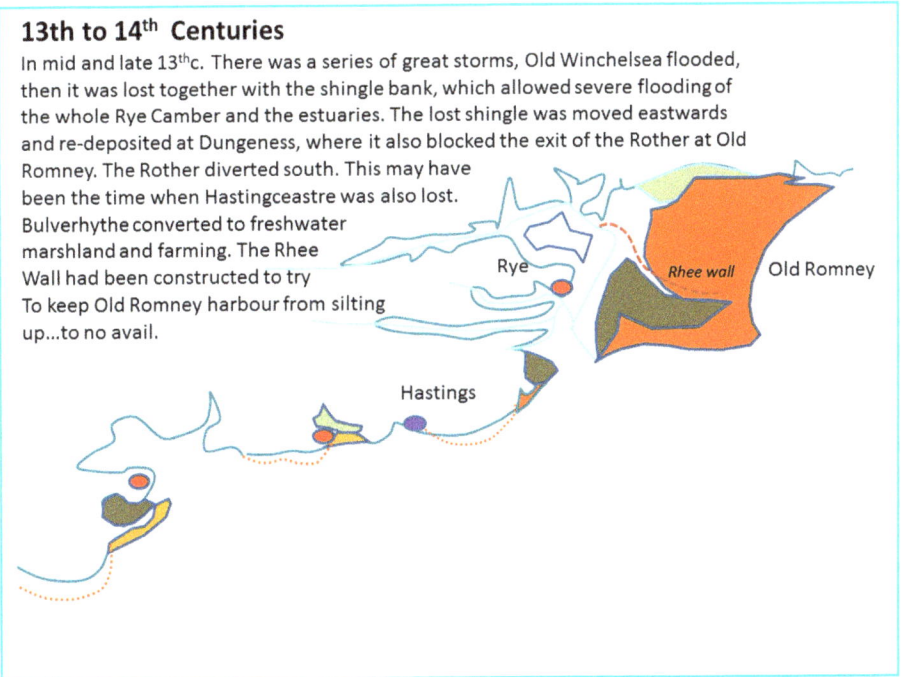

Both maps © BDHS

in his itinerary: firstly between 2 and 5 August when he was at Canterbury; secondly between 7 and 10 August when he visited Tonbridge and Reigate, then moved north through Croydon to London. He stayed in Windsor for a while then visited Hampshire, returned to London and then went northwards towards Northampton and Fotheringay. There is no record at the time that he came to Hastings, but it is not an absolute impossibility that he may have visited when he was nearby in Kent. There is an almost direct parallel to this dilemma also relating to sea laws which King John made, also believed to have been declared at Hastings.

Another later referral to sea laws affecting the local Cinque Ports may be to the so-called Apocryphal Statute or the *De Officio Coronatis* of 1275, which contained instructions to coroners about wrecks and treasure trove, particularly the rules about getting the permission of the King to hold items from shipwrecks and their specific rule modifications for the Cinque Ports.

Much of the first part of Edward's reign was dominated by campaigns in Wales. He invaded in 1277, defeated the Welsh, and the Welsh lords swore fealty to Edward who built a ring of castles to enforce his authority. The ships of the Cinque Ports took an effective part in this Welsh campaign including blockading Anglesey and ferrying troops over the Menai Strait. Edward soon recognised this, as in 1278 he issued a great charter to the Cinque Ports which included:

> The King confirms to the Barons of the Cinque Ports in recognition of their past faithful service, and their recent service in the Welsh army all their freedoms including immunity from toll and custom and from the jurisdiction of shire and hundred, and the right to trove by land and sea. In return they are to provide 57 ships for 15 days each year, upon the summons of the King.

Clearly the Cinque Ports had at least partially redeemed themselves in the eyes of Edward. The share of the eastern Sussex ports to the 57 ship total to be provided by the ports in 1278 was: Hastings six ships; Rye five; and Winchelsea ten. A further charter was issued and recorded in the Calendar of Charter Rolls, 18 Edward I, 12 February 1290.

Arms of the Cinque Ports

After a Welsh rebellion Edward invaded Wales again. The Cinque Ports fleet was involved this time in the creation of a temporary bridge across the Menai Strait to enable the English garrison to attack the Welsh rear. After Edward won Wales it was brought into the English legal and administrative fold and the Welsh leaders were executed.

These wars certainly distracted Edward as many other items before his court were left aside. Battle Abbey was caught up in this. By 1279 Edward had still not confirmed the full Battle Abbey charters, prevaricating with adjournment after adjournment, and in fact he never would. Battle was not alone in this, but it threw the associated administration of local Battle justice into a degree of confusion. A special eyre court (assizes) session had been last held in Battle in 1271 with the Abbey's monk-lawyers sitting with the itinerant royal justices. But the justices did not know what to do after Henry III died in 1272, and it was not to be until 1286–7 that Edward I agreed to special eyre sessions in Battle. In the meanwhile Battle had nearly lost this right, the justices having unilaterally declared in the absence of clarity from the King that the right to hold this special court was time-expired.

Battle's Abbot Reginald of Brecon, who had been elected in 1261 resigned or died in 1280–1 and Henry de Aylesford was approved by Edward I as Abbot, by letters patent, on 28 May 1280. Abbot Henry in turn died in 1297, and was succeeded soon afterwards by John de Taneto, or Thanet who, according to the patent rolls of Edward I, was approved on 30 January 1298 and resigned in 1307, the same year that Edward I died. So during Edward's reign three Abbots held the abbacy of Battle. All three had had John of Whatlington, who was to be the next Abbot, as an able aide.

By charter of the 9th (1281) and 26th (1298) years of his reign, Edward I confirmed the agreement of King John concerning the custody of Battle Abbey during vacancies, and added some other privileges;

> as that the Abbot should have right to all fines and amercements of his tenants in the town of Battel, which had before been received by the king's clerk of the markets ; together with the assize of bread, and of weights and measures; and also the cognizance of all trespasses committed within a certain extent of the Abbey precinct.

Eventually Edward became more attentive to England's strategic naval needs and in 1280 gave instructions to acquire land on the hill of Iham on which to build a new town of Winchelsea. On 11 November 1280 he issued instruction:

> Commission to Ralph of Sandwich, king's steward, to extend and buy or obtain by exchange certain lands of John of Langherst and John le Bon (Bone of Wickham) which are suitable for the new town of Winchelsea, which is to be built upon a hill called Yhamme, the old town being for the most part submerged by the sea.

In 1283 he issued instructions to start building New Winchelsea and the freehold of a new town was granted to the barons of Winchelsea in 1288 (the burgesses of the Cinque Ports towns were often known as barons). Accepting this, the barons stipulated that no other religious establishment should be accepted in Winchelsea other than the Greyfriars who had been established in Old Winchelsea. The site was to be on the hill of Iham some three miles (5 km) or so inland from Old Winchelsea, whose site was by that time almost completely lost to the sea. All the land for the town was acquired in late 1283 by the king's commissioners, Henry le Waleys, Gregory de Rokesle and Stephen de Pencester by purchase or exchange. It totalled about 151 acres (61 ha), of which approximately 87 acres (35 ha) would be built over. The settlement of Iham, still owned by the Abbey of Fécamp, remained outside New Winchelsea and Edward kept a large area of 12 acres (5 ha) near St. Leonard's Church for himself. The town was 'planned' and laid out as a regular grid – modelled perhaps on French bastide towns.

By the 1292 rental there were 690 property holders in New Winchelsea, which might equate to a population of about 3500, or maybe 5000 if there were sub-lettings – a very large town at that time. New Winchelsea had stone gates at each of its four main points of entry. The Land Gate, Strand Gate and New Gate can still be seen and passed through to this day. It also had three churches (St Thomas, St Giles in Winchelsea itself and St Leonards at Iham), other religious institutions including the Franciscan (Greyfriars) monastery and hospitals which re-located from Old Winchelsea where they had been founded in 1252. It may have been encircled by earthwork and palisade defences linking the four gates. The new harbour was on the river Brede.

The port of New Winchelsea which Edward sponsored proved to be a key Cinque Port for another 80 years or so, but gradually it silted up and was further obstructed by ballast jettisoned from ships, so that by 1380 the town was in severe economic decline and Rye became the predominant local port. Winchelsea was also severely affected by frequent French raids and was depopulating. In addition, the Black Death visited as it did many places. The development and decline of New Winchelsea is an extremely interesting story, but far beyond the scope of this book. Two books of particular interest on this topic are one authored by Martin and Martin and another edited by Martin and Rudling. Lilley, Lloyd and Trick have also published detailed work via the Archaeology Data Service. Edward I's next visit to eastern Sussex was 19 July 1285: to Uckfield, then on to Lewes for 20/21 July. During the next three years (1286–9) Edward was in Gascony for much of his time.

In 1295 ship service was commanded from the Cinque Ports for an expedition to Gascony by Edward's brother Edmund. This time Winchelsea supplied thirteen, Rye seven and Hastings only three ships, a further sign of Hastings' continuing decline. About 600 mariners of Winchelsea were required to crew their ships. Later that year, Edward I undertook a visit to his fleet and stayed at Udimore between 1–17 November 1295, visiting Winchelsea 20–21 November, back to Udimore on 21 November, then to Winchelsea again on 22 November and then travelled on to Robertsbridge the same day, after which he returned to London.

Also in late 1295 there was a new Archbishop of Canterbury, Robert of Winchilsey, who it is believed was indeed a son of the town of Winchelsea. With direction from the Pope, the new Archbishop was sternly to resist the financial demands that Edward tried to place upon the church. To say that he and Edward I had a stormy relationship would be an understatement.

Arms of Robert of Winchilsey from a stained glass window in Canterbury Cathedral.
Barrée of six, Gules and Ermine, in chief three cinquefoils, Or

In 1297 Edward was at Lewes on 28–29 May, at Mayfield on 30 May and then into Kent, almost certainly to meet the Archbishop of Canterbury. Later, on 8 August 1297, he returned to eastern Sussex, to Robertsbridge, then on to Brede, where he held a court, then Udimore on 9 August where he stayed again for quite a while assembling the English fleet and army from 9 to 17 August. After a quick visit to Winchelsea over 17–18 August, he popped back to Udimore then stayed in Winchelsea 19–22 August before he left for Flanders on a ship called the Cog *St Edward* with a fleet of 305 ships, including 73 from the Cinque Ports. The barons of England had demanded yet more redress of the principles of Magna Carta, which Edward had often ignored, before they would give him extra money or go with him on this expedition. Edward was not amused, but agreed and the deed was sent after him and sealed at Ghent. His continued benevolence towards Winchelsea was also sorely tried as the men of the Cinque Ports and Yarmouth resumed their long standing feud, with the portsmen burning 20 of the ships from Yarmouth and killing as many as 171 of their crews on landing at Swyn, an estuary on the coast north of Bruges in Flanders. Was this revenge for the attack on Winchelsea in 1266?

At St. Albans in 1298 the king issued two more Charters to the Cinque Ports;

> The King orders that, in consideration of the great expense of maintaining the fleet of the Cinque Ports, all the Cinque Ports and all who claim their liberties should contribute to the cost.' and 'The Barons of the Cinque Ports are granted freedom from taxes upon their ships and rigging, privileges in their trade with Ireland and, if they held land outside the franchise of the Cinque Ports, have freedom from the payment of certain feudal marriage dues to the King and to marry according to the rights of the Cinque Ports.

The Cinque Ports fleet was also involved in Edward's wars in Scotland in 1296, 1299, 1300 and 1303, normally for transport of food, materials and soldiers, but also for blockades, being particularly involved in the blockade of Berwick-upon-Tweed which Edward I took in 1296. The ports fleet was assembled for active duty in the Rye Camber in June 1300 under Gervase Alard of Winchelsea, the first recorded mayor of Winchelsea, who had been appointed Admiral of the Western Fleet. In 1306 26 ships of the fleet were involved, some of which will have been from eastern Sussex ports, but mainly Winchelsea, Hastings only sending one ship on this last occasion. However the

Old manuscript marginal drawing of a medieval sea battle

men of Winchelsea, feisty as always, on one occasion which cannot be precisely dated, refused to prepare their ships as the

> king's clerks had broken the debt tallies and had failed to pay the kings debts or given any allowance or any other thing at which they are much displeased.

During the Scottish campaign of 1302 Battle Abbey was commanded, along with 20 other towns all of which were coastal, but no other abbeys, to send a ship with men and necessaries to Newton-on-Ayr. Presumably the Abbey arranged this via Winchelsea as the Abbey held lands near there.

In 1299, in echoes of Battle Abbey's previous feud with the Bishop of Chichester, Chichester tried to force on the Royal Free Chapel of St Mary's in Hastings Castle his right to select the canons there. This was fought off and in 1301 the Warden of the Cinque Ports intervened, supported by the King and Parliament, with the Constable of the Castle being instructed by Edward I not to allow a visit by the Archbishop of Canterbury. Likewise the Archdeacon of Lewes was kept out in 1302.

Edward's penultimate visit to eastern Sussex was in 1302 – to Lewes on 13 September, then Michelham Priory on 14 September, Herstmonceux on 15 September then overnight at Battle Abbey on 15–16 September from where he sent two letters, one to Sir Roger Brabazon about a legal case involving his aunt and another jointly to the Earls of Lincoln and Savoy about negotiations with the King of France. He also confirmed an appointment of a priest to a church in Worcestershire and made two legal orders. After that he travelled to Newenden in Kent, from whence he sent the order forbidding the Archdeacon of Lewes from visiting St. Mary's, Hastings. This order was dated 15 September so probably was written at Battle but sent from Newenden, a manor that belonged to the Archbishop of Canterbury.

The village and manor of Herstmonceux was situated around the church and present Castle site, south of today's village. In about 1300 the manor was occupied by the Monceaux family. John of Monceaux's daughter Maud married a John de Fiennes whose family eventually built the Castle. The visit by Edward in 1302 must have been a quieter affair than his previous visit with his father and an army in 1264. He completely missed out the eastern Sussex Cinque Ports, but his onward trip was to Canterbury once again undoubtedly to argue with Archbishop Robert Winchilsey.

His final visit to eastern Sussex was a tour of Lewes, a short return side trip to West Dean, then on to Horsted, Buxted and Mayfield between 23 and 28 June 1305 when he also went on to Kent, probably to argue with the archbishop yet again. The reason to visit West Dean is obscure, but it appears to have been a manor in the hands of the Heringod family whose arms we are able to find: '*Azure cruzily with six herrings Or*'. It has been suggested that Alfred the Great once had a manor there, when it was called just 'Dene' and that ships were able to get up the Cuckmere valley at that time. Maybe Edward was 'checking it out' to see if it was still a viable haven.

Arms of Willem Heringod about 1270–80.
Redrawn: based on BL Add 77720

Edward I travelled a lot, but nothing like as restlessly as King John. He would make visits to places for hunting and to visit shrines, and obviously he extensively campaigned in Wales and Scotland. But another reason for royal itineracy was economic, for it was cheaper to be given hospitality, food, drink and fodder by bishops, abbots and others who must have dreaded the costs of such a visit – for the royal household may have numbered up to 500 men and horses and twenty or more wagons as it travelled to visit outlying royal manors. A further reason was political, for the itineracy made royal authority a reality to the people. Speed of travel varied. It was possible to travel over 20 miles a day between venues, but up to 15 miles a day was normal. The visits were seemingly marked by very few ceremonies, such as formal entries to towns.

The King's itinerary would often have no regular pattern of travel, and plans were not made long in advance, although the longer visits by Edward I to Udimore must have been planned. Looking at his visits to eastern Sussex plotted on the map below, based on Gough's *Itineraries*, the visit with his father Henry III of May 1264 during the Second Barons War and the visits to Udimore in both 1295 and August 1297 clearly had structured purposes (the length of the longer stays is marked in the diamonds in days, other stays ranged from ½ to 2 days maximum).

The other visits often passed through Robertsbridge, normally having come from or going to Chichester and Arundel. The visits of 1276, 1285, May 1297, 1302 and 1305 have the appearances of perambulations, but more likely had political motives to rally support and finances for wars in Scotland and France. This is suggested by his visit to Mayfield as there was a palace of the Archbishop of Canterbury at Mayfield, within his Deanery of South Malling Peculiar within which Uckfield and Buxted also

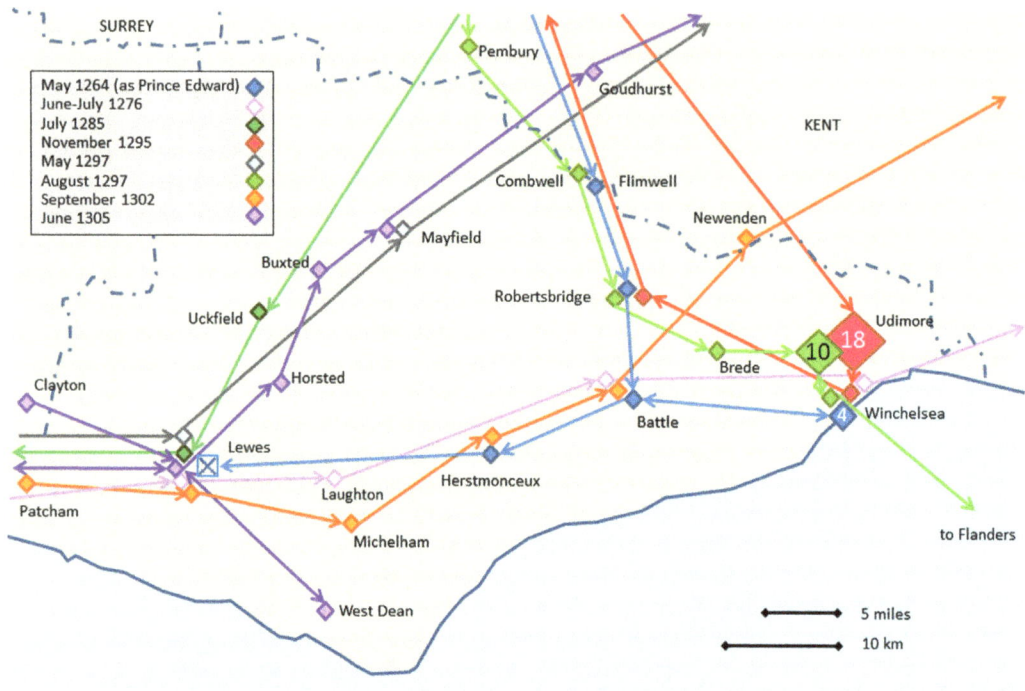

The itineraries of King Edward I in eastern Sussex   © Keith Foord

lay, as well as going to Canterbury before returning to London.

As the Scottish wars were so expensive, he increased taxes in 1305 and included the Cinque Ports in this request. Although this was not the first time they had been asked, it was against the Cinque Ports constitution to pay such taxes. However, the Courts of Brodhull and Guestling met and they agreed to pay 2,000 marks (£1333, over £1 million at 2016 values), of which Hastings paid 700 marks and the other ports 1,300 marks between them. Archbishop Robert Winchilsey also resisted but Pope Boniface VIII, who would have supported him had died and the new Pope Clement V promptly suspended him.

Edward's stays at Udimore were at Court Lodge, which belonged to Sir William of Etchingham, next to the church, both within a moated enclosure. He will have undoubtedly have used St Mary's Church at Udimore for any devotions. A church stood on this site at Domesday, but the existing church has much remaining from Edward's time including the 12th–13th century chancel and tower.

Pevensey had suffered from the same harbour problems as the other ports with gradual blocking of its entrance and silting up and inning for farmland. The salt panning trade had disappeared. A rental of 1292 lists 46 burgesses, holding 62 tenements with another six lying empty, but after this it went into decline. Pevensey Castle remained in crown control from 1268 to 1372 after the Second Barons War.

Udimore St Marys Church
Photo: ©Keith Foord

It would have been of some strategic importance against the French but, although he owned it, Edward I did not visit.

King Edward I died on 7 July 1307 aged 68, at Burgh by Sands, Cumberland, near Hadrian's Wall. Having mustered an English army at Carlisle, he was on his way to confront Robert the Bruce. A monument was erected in 1685 to mark the place where he died; this is signposted and can be reached on foot. His body lay in the village church until taken for burial in Westminster Abbey where it was placed in coffin of black Purbeck marble within an austere plain tomb of the same material. For some reason this was opened in 1774 and the length of his body was measured as 6 feet 2 inches (1.88 m). Clearly he was very tall for the age, would have had a commanding presence and was well suited to his nickname of 'Longshanks'.

Postscript

There is a curious final anecdote about Court Lodge, Udimore. There was an old building on its site dating from the mid-15th century. It was saved from demolition and was moved piece by piece to a new site in Groombridge, between Tunbridge Wells and East Grinstead. This is not the earlier, 12th or 13th century, manor house which was presumably on or close to this building and used by Edward I and his grandson Edward III when reviewing the English fleet off Winchelsea in the lower Brede estuary. For further reading about this see the summary by Martin and Martin in *British Listed Buildings: Court Lodge, Speldhurst*, their full report in the *Rape of Hastings Architectural Survey* (1987), and some *Country Life* articles of 1920 and 1963.

Edward II, 1307–1327

Edward II at his coronation:
Extract from BL Royal MS 20 A ii

Edward II was the fourth son of Edward I, but his three brothers had pre-deceased him. In 1308 he married the 12-year-old Princess Isabella of France. But he tends to be remembered for his dalliances with men, civil war, wars in Scotland and Gascony, later abandonment by his wife Isabella, being forced to abdicate and his reportedly rather unpleasant regicide. As always, conspiracy theories abound around his sexuality and his death including one in which he escaped from imprisonment in Berkeley Castle and fled to Italy via Ireland and another that he was just forgotten.

In 1310 Edward granted a Monday fair and an annual market to Bulverhythe, but as always it took some years for the new King to confirm Battle Abbey's charters – this time five. In October 1312 Edward II confirmed the charters in two dossiers that contained six charters of William I, two of William II, four of Henry I and the 1270 charter of Henry III. The Abbot paid £50 for one of the dossiers, but we are not told the price of the second. These dossiers which were well crafted in legal terms turned out to be particularly useful bases for future confirmations in 1348, 1400, 1412 and 1414. Buoyed by legal success, the Abbey pushed for further writs to reclaim rights that conflicted with other lords' claims or had been interrupted, with mixed success.

The three charters of Edward I of 1278 and 1298 to the Cinque Ports were confirmed with additions by Edward II in 1313. Two years later in 1315 Edward and Isabella visited Hastings and Winchelsea. At Winchelsea they bought a large quantity of wine, six tuns in all – nearly 6000 litres. Three years later the king was to approve the establishment in the town of a church and houses for brothers of the Dominican

(Blackfriars) order, who apparently were not welcomed with open arms. In 1324 Edward II was a guest at Battle Abbey and the Abbot managed to get a warrant to have jurisdiction over weights and measures and the quality of bread and ale within the banlieu, a small, but probably significant victory. Also in 1324 the manor of Brede was temporarily taken into Edward II's hands from the Abbey of Fécamp because of escalating hostilities with France and, at the same time, special wardens were appointed for the defence of Winchelsea and Rye.

Edward II's reign was clearly a difficult one. There was war with Scotland throughout and relationships with France were tense. Raids on coastal towns and piracy continued in the Channel. Ship duty to transport men and arms particularly to Gascony was called for frequently from the Cinque Ports. Isabella was sent to France to negotiate a peace treaty in 1325 and refused to return. She had become 'involved' with Roger Mortimer who had previously led the Marcher lords in a revolt against Edward. In 1326 they invaded England together with a small army. Edward's regime collapsed and he fled to Wales, where he was captured in November. He was made to abdicate in the following January.

There have been as many plagues as wars in history; yet always plagues and wars take people equally by surprise.

Albert Camus (1913–1960)

7
Warrior Abbots, Wars, Revolts and the Black Death: Edward III to Henry VI's usurpation 1327–1461

Edward III

The 14-year-old Edward III was crowned in Westminster Abbey on 1 February 1327. England was now run by Mortimer and Isabella, a situation which rapidly became intolerable. Edward III married Philippa of Hainault in 1328 and they had a son in 1330 who would become the Black Prince. Soon after this, Edward arrested Mortimer and had him executed for regicide. He excluded Isabella, who was kept in a degree of luxury out of the way until her death in 1358.

War with Scotland broke out again in 1332 and ended in 1338, when a truce was made to avoid war with Scotland and France at the same time. Before 1337 French raids were still occurring along the coast and in that year the One Hundred Years' War broke out with France. Events during this interminable war left deep social and economic scars on eastern Sussex. The people of eastern Sussex were truly hard pressed in many ways during these difficult times and took part in major revolts. The only bright spot was the granting of a market to Wartling in 1337. The way Battle Abbey related to the surrounding population and managed its estates also changed, moving from abbatial lordship to arm's length management. The Hundred Years' War stretched from 1337 to 1453 and placed a disproportionately large economic, social and military burden on the Hundreds of eastern Sussex. The dating of the long conflict which brought misery to both England and France hinges on two events. In 1337 Edward III responded to the loss of the Duchy of Aquitaine to France by challenging Philip VI for the French crown. It finally ended in 1453 when England irrevocably lost Aquitaine to France, at the Battle of Castillon, east of Bordeaux. Events during the early years of the war showed harbingers of the future. French raids on the coast between the Isle of Wight and the Thames became more intense. The Sussex coastal ports were particularly targeted. In 1339 the French partially burnt Hastings and further damaged Hastings Castle, which was already in a very poor state of repair.

Arraying of troops for shipment to France additionally placed a heavy burden on the east Sussex littoral. Many peasants fled from land near the shorelines and estuaries, leaving land uncultivated. Society became strained with murderous salvaging of wrecked ships, smuggling, piracy, constant threats and assaults, sheep-and-cattle theft and groups of thieving vagabonds.

Even these events became greatly overshadowed by the outbreak of the Black Death in England, which took a major toll of the population. The Black Death visited between 1348 and 1351, but it did not go away completely and episodically reappeared in perhaps less virulent form six times until about 1400. It had reached Sussex through the Cinque Ports and spread rapidly. At Battle Abbey the numbers of monks decreased from 52 in 1347 to 34 in 1351–2. The Abbot was one of those who died from the Black Death in 1350. In the early 1300s the population of Battle has been estimated to have been around 2500, but after the Black Death it had fallen to an estimated 1500. In Wartling 70 people died. The nearby villagers of Hooe fled, terror-struck at the news that the Black Death might be approaching their village. In England the plague was to kill 1.5 million people out of an estimated total of 4 million between 1348 and 1350, just over a third of the population.

After the first violent phase of the Black Death, the barons and royal court tried to stop the economically inevitable wage and price inflation by imposing The Statute of Labourers in 1351. This was a law to stop the peasants taking advantage of the shortage of workers by demanding more money. It even prohibited their movement to other areas where things could be better. Peasants were forced to work for the same wages as before. In addition, landowners could insist on labour being performed on their lands, instead of accepting rents from their tenants. Landowners could profit, whilst a peasant's life could be very much harder. However the statute was almost impossible to enforce, and farm wages in England on average doubled between 1350 and 1450.

In Battle one result of the shortage of people and an excess of messuages and tithings was that the town shrank towards its High Street core and surviving wealthy people were able to accumulate properties at the expense of poorer single tenancy holders. Rentals were also lower. The rich took over the more valuable empty messuages and as the Abbey later created more tenancies and sold off messuages they too were taken by the wealthy and quite often this enabled individual dwellings to be enlarged or gardens to be created.

This situation continued into the 15th century. This is illustrated in the following table, which also shows the Abbey withdrawing from direct land management.

7 WARRIOR ABBOTS, WARS, REVOLTS AND THE BLACK DEATH 1327–1461

	1305	**1367**	**1433**
Multiple tenancies held by one person	93	159 (+71%)	196 (+110%)
Tenancies held by single holders	112	88 (-21%)	55 (-51%)
Tenancies held by the Abbey	20	22 (+10%)	12 (-40%)

% expressed as increases or decreases from the 1305 figures

The social and economic stresses and strains imposed on the much reduced population of south-east England by the man-made pestilence of feudal war and the natural pestilences of the Yersinia Pestis bacterium (Black Death) and other then untreatable infectious diseases would help to potentiate the Peasants' Revolt, which had a major focus in Kent and eastern Sussex. With respect to the war and the Revolt this book will lean heavily on a paper by Searle and Burghart and on Searle's abbreviation of this in her *Lordship and Community*.

The Peasants' Revolt was focussed on south-eastern England and Kent and eastern Sussex in particular where there was widespread support for the uprising, not just from the peasants but from many across the widening spectrum of society. There was also a failure of the feudal structures and of the crown and the barons to support the southern coasts and their hinterlands during long periods when the French raided with near impunity.

From its outbreak until 1389 war was being fought almost continuously on a large scale. It became the dominant issue politically and economically, bleeding the country dry. There was a brief respite from war and raids after the Treaty of Bretigny in 1360, but from 1369 until towards the end of the 14th century the Abbots of Battle became warrior monks, the major military organisers and defenders of the east Sussex coast against many raids and the fear of invasion.

In 1337 the king had commanded Battle's Abbot Alan de Retlyng, along with other local landowners, that they defend the coast of Sussex. This burden was placed on the Abbey for a long time as there were many French raids during the war, and the Abbots helped to organise local defences and to provide food and clothing for refugees fleeing the coastal towns and littoral. A royal licence to fortify the Abbey was received just after the start of the war, and the building of the great gatehouse and the defensive walls that we still see today was begun during Alan de Retlyng's abbacy.

> June 9, 1338. License to krenellate the manse of the Abbey of Battle – The king to all his bailiffs and liegemen, to whom, &c., greeting – Know that of our special grace we have granted and given licence on behalf of ourselves and heirs, as much us in us lies, to the beloved by us in Christ, the Abbot and Convent of Battle, that they may fortify with a wall of stone and lime, and krenellate the site of that Abbey, which is of the foundation of our progenitors,

formerly Kings of England, and may hold that site so fortified and krenellated for themselves and successors for ever, without penalty or impediment, from ourselves, or our heirs, justiciaries, eschaetors, sheriffs, or others our bailiffs or officers whosoever. In witness whereof, &e. Witness the King at Lopham, on the 9th day of June. Pat. 12 Edw. III, p2, m.28.'

Also in 1338 Abbot Alan was excused from finding men from the Abbey's manor of Wye to guard the coastline of Kent because he had already sent all his available men to patrol the coast near Winchelsea.

We know from histories of Rye and Winchelsea that the Cinque Ports were called on continuously from 1336 to provide and man ships, for sea-battle with French ships, to ferry armies and to generally defend the coast. Even so, in 1339 the French fleet, after trying to attack the English at Sandwich and finding themselves unable to land there, turned on Rye and burnt much of it down, in spite of new walls, before being chased off to Boulogne, which was then duly burnt by the English who also hanged twelve of the French ships' captains. In 1350, in spite of the ravages of the Black Death, the Cinque Ports fleets led by Edward III and the Black Prince fought and managed to defeat a French fleet in Rye Bay at the sea Battle of Winchelsea.

French hit-and-run raids continued, but the French seriously visited Rye again in 1360, just before the brief peace settled by the Treaty of Bretigny, and landed and spoiled the town, as they did Winchelsea. The Abbot of Battle, by then Robert de Bello – as Alan de Retlyng had died of the Black Death in 1350 along with 17 of his 50 monks – did chase off the French from Winchelsea at this time, but not before significant damage and deaths had occurred. Edward I's new town of Winchelsea had already suffered significant loss of population after the Black Death and in 1358 94 properties were recorded as abandoned and 90 in ruins, a total of 184. By 1363 this total figure had risen to 409 (Homan – quoted by Pratt).

A call was made in 1360 for men of distant counties to be sent to help defend the south-eastern coasts, but few responded. Only if the royal government or their own counties would pay for their time would they even consider helping. England might be a realm, but it was not yet a community. After 1369 and the breakdown of the Treaty of Bretigny the coast remained basically undefended, most of the realm's revenues being spent on the land wars in France, with little national support for coastal defence. The raids by the French increased in frequency and in levels of destruction. The only defence was by local men, who were also expected to raise much of the money for local defence and man the ships to defend the coasts, and could also be conscripted for overseas battles. The Hundreds in single localities just could not support this.

The navy had a permanent core of some 15 royal ships berthed at Winchelsea, with in addition some cogs, galleys and barges. In times of need it was supplemented by ship service from other Cinque Ports, Yarmouth, Bristol and Southampton –

essentially fishing and merchant ships which did not come anywhere near being a true fighting fleet to defend the shores. It was mainly a transport fleet for men and supplies to get the king and barons across the Channel for their rapacious uncoordinated plundering expeditions to France, usually ignoring Normandy from which many attacks were made on the English coast, instead plundering through the easier territory of Champagne and Anjou in an inland arc en route to Brittany.

In 1372 the French allied with the Castilians, who then joined in the attacks on the coasts using their galleys with which they could carry out lightning raids into ports and destroy berthed English ships.

A medieval naval combat
from Jean Froissart's *Chronicles,* 14th century

Richard II

Edward III died in 1377 and Richard II, a son of the Black Prince, became King at the age of ten. During his minority the country was ruled by a council led by his uncle, John of Gaunt. Five days after his accession, the French with their Castilian allies captured Rye again and held it for a while, freely ravaging the surrounding countryside. On this occasion, Abbot Hamo de Offyngton of Battle rallied some defence and fortified Winchelsea, keeping the French at bay. However, the French, after killing 66 inhabitants of Rye, kidnapped three burgesses for ransom and, setting fire to the town once more, promptly sailed down the coast, avoiding Winchelsea, to Hastings, pillaged and burned the town and St. Clement's Church. This church had already suffered from the sea and in 1286 had been rebuilt inland. Now it needed rebuilding once more.

Rather perversely at Rye the king's bailiff acting on orders from the new regency had to hang and quarter those inhabitants deemed most responsible for the 1377 loss of Rye, no doubt 'pour encourager les autres' – it was an example of savage feudal injustice. But some funds were made available to rebuild the walls and to build two new 32 oar galleys to help defend the town. In the next year the men of Rye and Winchelsea raided the French coast, recovered some of the loot from Rye, took hostages and burnt the towns of St. Pierre-en-Porte and Veulettes. The French not to be outdone, came back in 1380 and severely damaged Winchelsea once again. By 1384 this town was partially deserted and desolated, with those who could moving inland, the wealthier taking tenancies in Battle for example.

Rye, Winchelsea and Hastings recovered only slowly from these events. Many families had lost their men, livelihoods, dwellings and some their children, many other townsfolk had fled inland but appear to have received precious little help from the Hundreds there or from the central authorities. In addition many people had now totally abandoned the lands towards the coasts as they were too frightened to stay, and local farming and food production dropped.

After Edward III's death in 1377 and into the 1380s, Richard II's government under John of Gaunt was so ineffective that the French raided all along the southern coasts at will. Rumour has it that, as the Keeper of Pevensey Castle, Gaunt arrogantly refused to garrison it for five years after he took possession in 1372, asserting that he was wealthy enough to rebuild it if a French attack destroyed it. As an illustration it shows the attitude of the regency to the defence of the local population and the coast.

In 1377 John of Gaunt imposed a new tax, the Poll (head) Tax, to cover the cost of the war. This was to be paid by the peasants as well as the landowners. Although this was meant to be a one-off event, it was so successful that it was repeated three more times. The first tax was 4d (2p) from every person aged 14 or over, then it was raised to 4d for the peasants and more for the rich, and finally in 1380, it was raised to 12d (5p) per head. The barons liked the idea of the peasants helping to pay taxes, especially if they themselves acted as tax collectors, with some of the money siphoned off into their pockets. It was much harder on the peasants, who could ill afford to pay, especially as the tax was collected in cash and not in farm produce. By 1380, many were hiding from the collectors and avoiding payment. Royal commissioners were sent out as enforcers. It financially crippled the peasants.

The Peasants Revolt of 1381 followed. Sir Richard Waldegrave blamed the outbreak on the extravagance of the court, the burden of taxation, a weak executive and the cynically accepted inadequate defence of the coasts. Certainly this explains the numbers of men from Kent and eastern Sussex who took part. Much has been written about the revolt after which the peasants were crushed and many executed. But it marked the start of the breakdown of the outdated feudal system, the theory of which did not conform to the new reality of needing to have a united country which would respond positively to threats to its individual parts. Parliament gave up trying to control the wages the landowners paid their peasants. The hated poll tax was never raised again until someone was foolish enough to try it once more in 1989–90. The peasants became treated with a bit more respect and many became freemen. This raised land productivity as the free worked harder than serfs. Incidentally, this would have given them the chance to sell at a newly granted market at Bodiam after 1383.

Battle Abbey remained a centre of some support to the dispossessed and desperate peasants of coast and hinterland. In 1360–74, 1386–9 and 1397–1404 the cellarer of Battle purchased extra food to distribute among the large numbers of poor who came to the Abbey and expenses outran that allocated and they nearly had to curtail their hospitality. But in this context, as a major landowner, the Abbey did much more to help the people than did other religious houses and most of the landed gentry of Kent and eastern Sussex. Even so it was forced to change the way it managed its lands towards the end of the period mainly due to loss of manpower from the dual pestilences of war and disease. It created more tenancies and the governance of the town became managed at arm's length from the Abbey.

Abbot Hamo of Offyngton died suddenly whilst administering mass in 1382 and six more Abbots would be elected before the end of the Hundred Years' War in 1453. The last of the six, Richard Dertmouth, the Abbey and all its servants were pardoned in 1450 for supporting the Cade Rebellion.

Sir Edward Dallingridge of Bodiam, a long term career soldier, had played a prominent role in Sussex, representing the county of Sussex in Parliament on a number of occasions since 1379. In 1385 Richard II granted him a licence to crenelate his manor house. The motivation for his construction of Bodiam Castle was probably a desire to create a symbol of his authority, to promote his social standing, and to capitalise on the fears caused by threat of invasion from France. The Castle was never to be tested by war in this period.

In 1386 the French made preparations to invade England. Their fleet was assembled at Sluys in Flanders where Dutch mercenaries were hired for the fighting. In his chronicle, Froissart reports that the French were so confident of their preparations that they considered the English already crushed. The council of Richard II prepared for the invasion by raising an army of ten thousand men-at-arms and thousands of archers. Commissioners of Array, including Sir Edward Dallingridge, were appointed to raise militias in all the coastal counties. The English cunning plan was to allow the French to march inland for 3 or 4 days and then destroy the French supply ships. The French were to be confronted in battle when their provisions ran low. Of course it might have been better to intercept the fleet at sea and not allow the French the chance to occupy the ports, completely remove any English naval threat and thus gain the ability to re-supply their troops.

The French invasion fleet set out, but England's long-time friend 'bad weather in the Channel' dispersed the fleet. A number of French ships were driven onto the English coast where they were captured and plundered. The survivors of the French fleet returned to Sluys. Another invasion could not be attempted as it was too late in the year and bad weather would continue to be a key factor.

Henry IV

There was a degree of peace between 1389 and 1415, including the last ten years of Richard II's rule, which increasingly broke down. He was eventually deposed and succeeded in 1399 by his cousin Henry IV (son of John of Gaunt), but piracy and raiding remained rife on both sides of the Channel coast.

Just before he died in 1413, Henry IV licensed the Priory of Hastings, which had been severely damaged by the sea, to move to Warbleton on to land given by John Pelham.

Henry V

Henry V became king in 1413 and resumed the conflict with France in 1415 with initial success at Harfleur, then Agincourt and afterwards, which led to the Treaty of Troyes in 1420. This was an agreement that Henry V of England would marry Catherine de Valois, the daughter of King Charles VI of France and that his heirs would inherit the throne of France upon the death of Charles VI. Not that the Dauphin Charles agreed.

During 1416 Henry V dissolved all the residual alien priories in England. This included confiscation of the Abbey of Fécamp's manor of Brede, which was eventually passed to the new Syon Monastery in Middlesex, founded by Henry V in the previous year. In 1422 Henry contracted dysentery and died at the siege of Meaux leaving as his heir a son less than a year old. The eventual breakdown of the Treaty of Troyes began the final stage of the Hundred Years' War.

Henry VI

From 1422 a regency council ran England and, theoretically, France until Henry VI was considered old enough to rule in 1437. He was the only English monarch to manage to have been de facto crowned King of France in 1431, but after that things went downhill. Henry was unfortunately too trusting and pious. After 1429 Henry VI's council, and then after 1437 the very ill-advised and easily led Henry VI, had seen a series of severe defeats in France. The royal treasury had been drained, even with the imposition of another huge tax, from which corrupt tax officials as always took advantage to fill their own pockets.

A descendant of the Monceux family of Herstmonceux, Sir Roger Fiennes, was with Henry V in 1415 at the Battle of Agincourt having indented to serve with seven men-at-arms and 24 archers. After the death of Henry V, he continued to serve in military expeditions to France and in 1439 became treasurer of the household of Henry VI. In 1441 he was given permission from the king to construct a crenelated castle on the site of Herstmonceux manor house. It was not a defensive structure, but a palatial residence in a castle style. He served as a member of parliament in 1439–40, 1442 and 1445–6 and died in 1449.

In 1445, Henry married Margaret of Anjou, niece of King Charles VII, at the price of handing over the territory of Maine to the French. In 1447 Hastings College lost its privileged position as a royal free chapel. Henry VI in that year declared it to be entirely subject to the jurisdiction of the Bishop of Chichester.

Pratt records a tale of a possible burning of both Rye and Winchelsea in about 1448, towards the end of the Hundred Years' War, which unprotected and unavenged, put an end to all local respect for the government which had fallen to pieces. But ships were once again somehow mustered at Winchelsea to transport troops to France in the following year, although it appears that only two years further on not enough ships or skilled sailors were available from poor declined Winchelsea.

Cade's Rebellion in 1450 was an uprising against the policies of Henry VI. Although led by property owners, most participants were peasants from Kent and eastern Sussex. It has been seen as another key moment in the growing political consciousness of the country as a whole, as unlike the Peasants' Revolt of 1381, it was not instigated by the peasantry, although the poorest in society were caught up in it. The protesters objected to forced labour, corrupt courts, land seizures by the nobility and heavy taxation, directly linked to the royal management of the war which had dragged on interminably. Afterwards Cade himself was inevitably hunted down, caught near Heathfield and mortally wounded. He mercifully died whilst being taken to London, but his corpse was still drawn and quartered, before his head was placed on a pole by London Bridge. It is notable that Robertsbridge Abbey did not support Cade and that its fair had been the subject of an attack by Cade's early supporters in 1449.

This suggests that this Abbey may not have been very supportive of its community. Battle's Abbot Richard Dertmouth and his Abbey did support the Cade Rebellion as did Lewes Priory, and afterwards received a Royal pardon, as did many others (see appendices for a list of those from the Rape of Hastings and Lowey of Pevenesey who were pardonned). The number of pardons was very high as to have meted out retribution to the large numbers involved across the whole spectrum of society would have damaged the country irrevocably and significantly reduced royal income.

Although the Battle of Castillon of 1453 is considered the final battle of the Hundred Years' War, a formal peace was not declared for another 20 years. England had been defeated and English landowners now complained bitterly about the financial losses resulting from the loss of their French holdings, but this problem was not to worry Battle Abbey, which had no French connections.

The concept of lordship over the surrounding area by the Abbey had also withered during the long period of war. The number of monks was shrinking and the glories of the past fading. More and more lay people ran the Abbot's council and determined rentals and other matters and the inquest jurors became a ruling clique, a small and self-perpetuating group of Battle oligarchic families.

England was not a contented country and to make matters worse, in 1453 the hapless king had a mental breakdown and Richard, Duke of York, was made protector. The king recovered in 1455, but civil war broke out between the Yorkist and Lancastrian factions. It was the start of the Wars of the Roses. Margaret, Henry's queen, together with the Earl of Somerset, took charge of the Lancastrian cause. In 1460 York, Henry's former protector, was killed at the Battle of Wakefield but his son Edward took up the fight, defeating the Lancastrians at Towton in 1461 and crowning himself Edward IV.

In 1460 the Cinque Ports appear to have supported the Yorkists against Henry and helped capture the royal fleet and its leaders at Sandwich. Shortly afterwards, supporting the Lancastrians, they helped bombard London. They were probably prepared to supply their services to the highest bidder.

Apart from these episodes, eastern Sussex seems to have been mainly a bystander to the conflicts between Yorkists and Lancastrians. Certainly Searle records nothing untoward with respect to Battle Abbey. Pevensey played no part and the Castle there was in any case falling into greater disrepair.

So the events above were covered by the reigns of no fewer than five kings: Edward III (1327–1377), Richard II (1377–1399), Henry IV (1399–1413) Henry V (1413–22) and finally Henry VI who had acceded age 9 months, was usurped in 1461, then he briefly ruled again in 1470–1 before he was imprisoned in the Tower of London where he died shortly afterwards.

8
Wars of the Roses, the rise of the Tudors and the Dissolution of the Monasteries 1461–1538

By Henry VII, the sword of government was sheathed, the remains of the feudal system at last completely swept away
William Campbell, 1873

This chapter covers from the time of the middle of the War of the Roses, with Edward IV having just gained the throne from Henry VI in 1461, to the dissolution of the monasteries by Henry VIII in 1538. Henry would live another nine years after that date, dying in 1547.

Information about direct involvement by kings in eastern Sussex during these years is quite limited. The first part of the period is taken up by the final years of the Wars of the Roses and it can be surmised that the national focus of activity was mostly well away from south-eastern England.

Kings in this period were Edward IV (1461–70); Henry VI (restored 1470–71); Edward IV (1471–83); Edward V briefly in 1483; Richard III (1483–85); Henry VII (1485–1509) and Henry VIII (1509–47).

Edward IV

Edward had only just been crowned, aged 18, on 28 June 1461 when on 22 July he learned that the situation in France had swung in his favour when Charles VII had died and been succeeded by his son Louis XI – a real prospect of immediate French intervention in England had subsided.

Edward IV is recorded as having visited Battle and possibly Hastings twice – firstly in August 1461. Edward left London on 13 August 1461 when he travelled to Sittingbourne, then Canterbury and Sandwich until travelling to Ashford on 20 August, then on to Battle Abbey, possibly also visiting Hastings. After leaving Battle on 22 August he travelled to Lewes and Arundel, then back to Westminster, before leaving again for Bristol, then onward to the Welsh Marches on 4 September aiming to organise a Welsh campaign against his opponents.

Edward IV was defeated by the Lancastrians at the Battle of Edgecote Moor in July 1469. He re-engaged the rebels at the Battle of Losecote Field or Empingham on 12 March 1470. Having won he then chased the rebels south-west towards Exeter but they escaped to France, where they allied with Margaret of Anjou, Henry VI's queen. From Exeter he moved to Salisbury. This episode may have led to his second visit to Battle which was on 3 June 1470. Edward was moving from Salisbury to Southampton then to Canterbury, via Battle. This may have been related to the need to organise ships from both Southampton and the Cinque Ports for a blockade of French ports.

Later in 1470, Edward IV was forced to flee to Flanders by the Lancastrians and for six months in 1470–1471, Henry VI was restored to an essentially puppet kingship, but Edward then hit back with a victory at the Battle of Barnet, and Henry VI was then lodged in the Tower of London. Edward IV followed this with a victory at Tewkesbury at the end of which Henry VI's son, also named Edward, was executed. This was closely followed by Henry VI's own death in the Tower of London on the 21 May 1471.

On 15 December 1471 Edward IV issued a charter of a general pardon to John Newton, Abbot of Battle, for all offences before this date and for all moneys owed before the ninth year of his reign. Similar pardons were issued to others and these must relate to the above events of 1470–71 when Henry VI was briefly restored.

By 1475 Winchelsea's inner port had closed to ships of any size although there was still limited access from the outer port further away across the Rye Camber.

Richard III

In 1483 Edward V of course barely reigned at all and was not crowned, and was 'disappeared' with his brother, probably by Richard III, with Richard taking the throne. No records from Richard III's short reign appear to involve eastern Sussex, although in the chapter about the Rape of Hastings we shall see his interactions with the then lord of the Rape of Hastings, William Lord Hastings, at the Tower of London.

Henry VII

The final victor of the War of the Roses after the Battle of Bosworth Field in 1485 was Henry VII.

He visited Battle Abbey on 17 August 1488, and was briefly at Rye en route from Lewes to Charing. Rye spent £2 18s 11d (£2.85) on the King's entertainment. A year afterwards a new ship was built at Rye for the King, so it was probably a good meal.

Rye seems to have then slowly regained some prosperity at and after this time; maybe because Winchelsea was now in severe decline after its inner harbour had become silted and impossible to access for the bigger ships.

Henry VIII

Henry VII died in 1509 and his son Henry VIII became king.

Winchelsea somehow managed to supply four ships and 15 sailors for Henry VIII's expedition to France in 1513 for the fraternal events of the Field of the Cloth of Gold, probably with some assistance from Tenterden, by now an associate member of the Cinque Ports.

This friendship made with France in 1513 did not last long. In 1522 and 1526 French ships entered the Rye Camber, which was by now protected by a small, round artillery tower, built by Henry VIII between 1512–4 which the first core part of Camber Castle which would not be finished until after 1542.

There is, of course, no doubt that on 27 May 1538 the town of Battle changed forever. It moved from a town that supported and was mainly employed by an Abbey to being the manor of a trusted confidant of and Master of the Horse to Henry VIII, Sir Anthony Browne. It would henceforth have to pay its own way. It is interesting to note that the lands of Syon Monastery and its manor of Brede including some lands in old Hastings formerly belonging to Fécamp Abbey and slightly later the assets of the near-defunct Collegiate College of St Mary in the Castle at Hastings would also be allocated to Sir Anthony Browne, to fill a defensive power gap in eastern Sussex.

The growth of Battle had stalled at the start of the 16th century, and it was now to grow very little until the end of that century. Estate information about Battle at the end of the 15th century until 1538 is available from Searle, with amplification from Martin and Whittick's masterly study, *Building Battle Town,* which extends forwards to 1750, beyond this book's scope. It appears that the centre of the town in terms of house numbers remained static, but at the expense of the periphery which shrank. However, the Abbey was selling off plots around the old market at the junction of High Street and Mount Street and this market itself demised, with commerce transferring to shops along the High Street and Upper Lake. A market was revived in 1566, and this took place on the Abbey Green. The lay subsidy returns of 1524 and 1525 can be cross-referenced with the court rolls. From this it is noted that 25 of the 43 families assessed at £5 and over lived along the High Street, as did six of the wealthiest eight. The house of William Boyes, 76–77 High Street, erstwhile Abbey carter and inquest juror may be one of the largest medieval houses to survive. Some of the more prosperous inhabitants, whose services to the Abbey manor may no longer have been required or were reduced may have left the town.

Robertsbridge Abbey was surrendered on 16 April 1538. Its last Abbot was

Thomas Taylor and there were eight monks. The manor of Robertsbridge included parts of Ewhurst, Northiam, Whatlington, northern parts of Sedlescombe and Brede and it was passed to Sir William Sidney, along with lands in Kent in exchange for lands in York and Lincoln. He had been with Henry VIII at the Field of the Cloth of Gold and was tutor and steward to his son, Prince Edward.

The Austin Friary at Rye was suppressed on 18 December 1538, and the Greyfriars and Blackfriars at Winchelsea also finally disappeared although their buildings were apparently empty and forsaken and in a very poor state. Bayham Abbey had been dissolved 14 years before by Cardinal Wolsey.

The Middle Ages were over for eastern Sussex.

9
Rapes of Sussex and Hundreds of the Rape of Hastings

Sussex is divided into six rapes, a division peculiar to this county
Mark Anthony Lower, 1834

History and Formation of the Rapes

The Rapes of the county into which William the Conqueror divided Sussex after 1066 were part of his early defensive strategic moves to protect against possible Danish and Norwegian incursions, with similar areas elsewhere in England – except that they were not called 'Rapes'. The concept was to last for a very long time.

Saxon precursors to the Rapes have been proposed, possibly formed along the same arrangements as the Lathes of Kent, although the latter appear of older origin and were well-defined areas pre-Conquest. But Lathe courts persisted in Pevensey and Hastings Rapes post-Conquest, which indicates a possible persisting Kentish influence on eastern Sussex. As always in Sussex, so it seems to the author, the pre-1066 concept is historically vaguer and therefore historically more controversial than in Kent, although Domesday definitely refers to their existence in some form in the time of King Edward within its references to fragments of Sussex manors allocated to adjacent Rapes. The system may also have some roots in the Burghal forts system of King Alfred which describes large areas of supporting hidage to each fort. This in turn may have had even earlier roots as even the origin of the name is obscure – although an early North Germanic language precursor is possible as the word *hreppr* in Old Norse can mean a share or an estate held in absolute ownership.

Domesday shows that the English possessions given to William I's barons were usually very scattered, something which was quite common in Normandy and may have been a deliberate method of ensuring that local landowners worked together but did not easily plot together. But Domesday also demonstrates that in certain frontier and coastal districts blocks of territory were granted to single individuals. The best known examples of this are the Scots and Welsh border areas and the Sussex Rapes. All can be better termed 'castelries' for general discussion.

The frontier zone or Marches against Wales was split into the three marcher earldoms, Chester, Shrewsbury and Hereford, and the Scots border was covered by Richmond (the land of Count Alan [Alan Rufus] of Brittany, from before 1071), and in Northumberland by the Bishopric of Durham (the first Prince-Bishop appointed in 1071 by William was William Walcher). On the east coast the mouth of the Humber, vulnerable to Danish invasion, was covered to the north by Holderness, and to the south by Barrow-upon-Humber and other parts of Lincolnshire, both held by Drogo de Beuvriere, Count of Aumale, possibly married to a niece of William. The Dee and Wirral coast east of north Wales, protecting against possible Norwegian or Danish invaders via Ireland, was covered by the northern Welsh march with Hugh d'Avranches as Earl of Chester, then there was the land between Ribble and Mersey with Roger of Poitou as tenant-in-chief. Similarly, facing Ireland and the south of Wales, Bishop Geoffrey of Coutances held grouped estates around Bristol and stretching into Somerset and Gloucestershire. Cornwall was with William's half-brother the Count of Mortain.

To the west of the Sussex Rapes, the Isle of Wight, which protected the two arms of the Solent and had often featured in potential invasion plans, was held in single ownership by William fitz Osbern, who was also Earl of Hereford, the southern Welsh march, then his son Roger until 1075, although they were physically based at Winchester. The sole ownership of the Isle of Wight did not persist as following Roger's revolt and imprisonment in 1075 it appears that William resumed direct overlordship of the Island. In the recent past it had acted as a springboard for invasions of central southern England by both Vikings and the Godwin family, and William was very aware of that fact.

In addition, Sussex was flanked further west by grouped single ownership manors granted to Robert de Mortain around Portland – protecting Dorset, Poole harbour and the River Frome, with further smaller groups or honours around Exeter and around Totnes, although William retained much direct overlordship in this area, probably following Exeter's earlier resistance. There were similar grouped holdings in Kent to the east, with Bishop Odo (also the Earl of Kent), holding Dover and extensive areas around Sandwich, Folkestone and north Kent, and with a smaller coastal zone around Hythe – 'the divisio' of Hugh of Montfort with a castle at Saltwood, not held directly from William, but from the Archbishop of Canterbury.

It has been estimated that in the 7th century Sussex consisted of about 70 Hundreds each containing 3200 or so hides, which were divided fairly equally between eastern and western Sussex – as divided by the River Adur, which runs north to south halfway through the Rape of Bramber. The Adur was later to be the ecclesiastical division between the archdeaconries of Chichester and Lewes. Larger groupings of Hundreds into district divisions evidently existed by the early tenth century, although they may not have been called Rapes, and the names and boundaries were not always the same. To complicate matters further, some of the imposed Norman Rape boundaries cut through the middle of Hundreds, particularly Easewrith, Windham and Fishergate

9 RAPES OF HASTINGS AND HUNDREDS OF THE RAPE OF HASTINGS

(aka Aldrington) and Hundred boundaries cut through villages. One-third of the town of Lewes lay in Pevensey Rape, but Lewes and South Malling manors were held as tenant-in-chief by the Archbishop of Canterbury. The names, borders and numbers of the internal divisions of Sussex were repeatedly adjusted, and Domesday reported how they were at one instant in time in 1086.

William's defensive zones:

Blue zones are earldoms,
N: Northumbria,
Ch: Chester,
Sh; Shrewsbury,
He: Hereford

Green 'divisios',

Purple 'warrior Bishops',
D: Durham

Red: Sussex Rapes:
A Arundel,
B Bramber,
L Lewes,
P Pevensey, H Hastings.

©BDHS Borders all indicative only

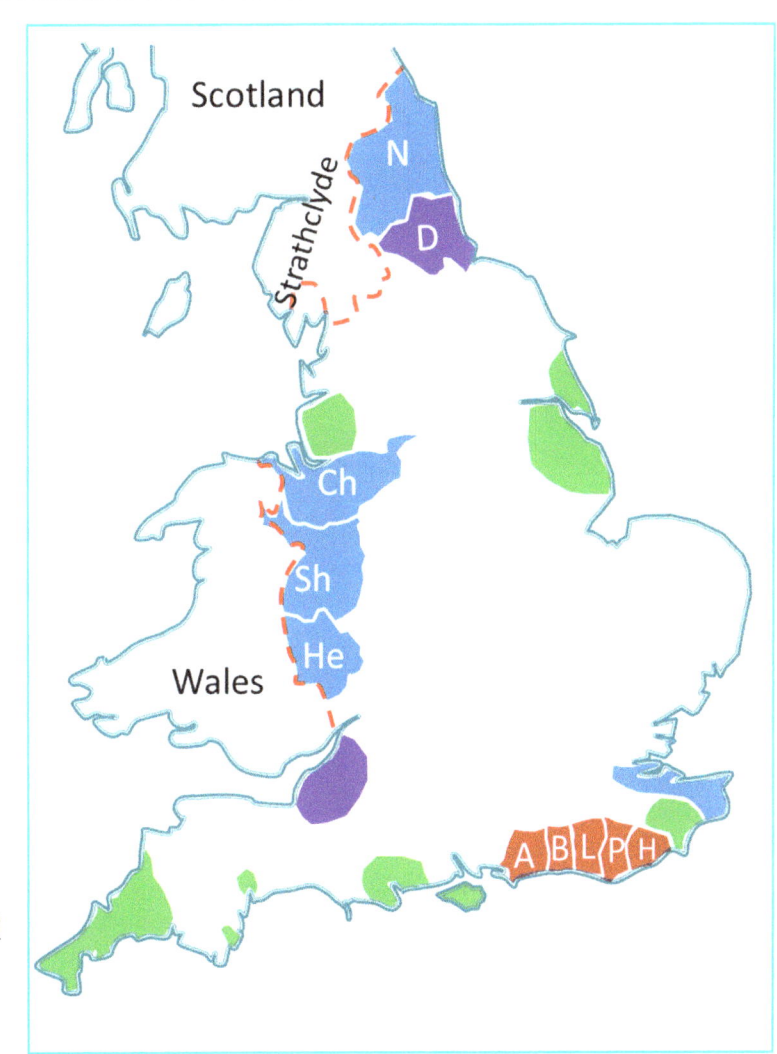

William I's initial Sussex Rapes were formed at an early stage after the Conquest, probably after his return from Normandy and landing at Winchelsea in December 1067 and certainly by 1071: Eu received Hastings by May 1070. Each was also a castelry centred on a castle, and held by a tenant-in-chief, all of whom were Normans and kin or trusted friends of William, each of whom appointed a non-royal sheriff.

This gives rise to the entirely logical conjecture initiated by Salzman and agreed

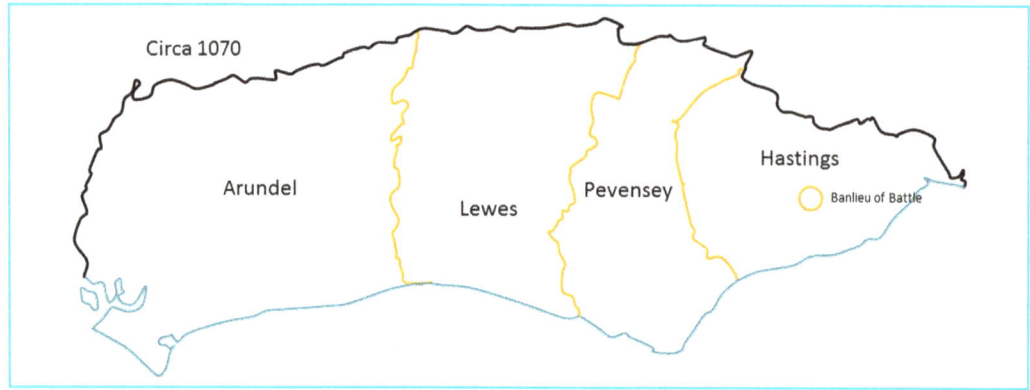

About 1070: The first of William's Rapes

The Banlieu of Battle was a Royal Peculiar, responsible directly to the crown with abbatial administration and justice and not part of Hastings Rape. The number of hides counted at Domesday west and east of the Adur was almost equal at around 1600 hides each. The modern coastline is shown. ©BDHS

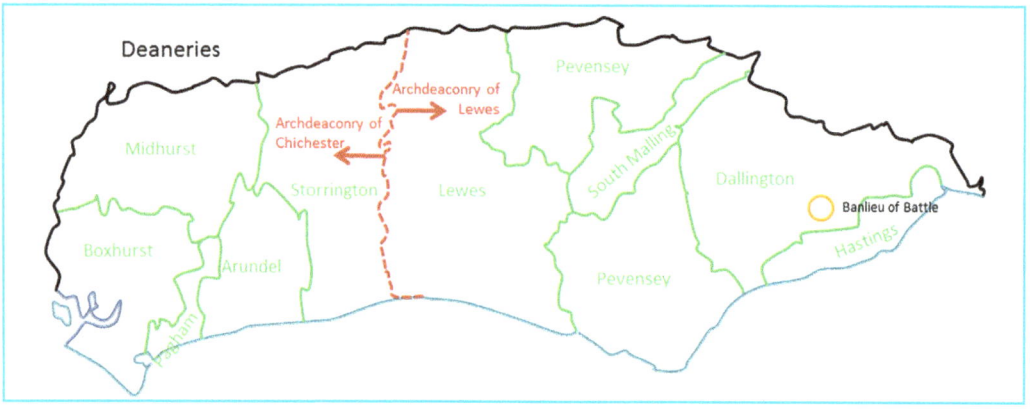

Deaneries: The old ecclesiastical deanery boundaries of the see of Chichester

There was some concordance with Rapes, particularly with the archdeaconry boundary being the river Adur, as was the initial Lewes/Arundel Rape boundary and the Dallington deanery boundary corresponded with the Hastings/Pevensey Rapes boundary. But William could happily ignore ecclesiastical boundaries. The Banlieu of Battle was free from the jurisdiction of the Bishop of Chichester

with by Mason that initially Sussex contained only four Rapes before 1073: Arundel to the west covering the whole of western Sussex to the Adur; the Rape of Lewes from the Adur to the Ouse; Pevensey, coincident with the ecclesiastical deaneries of Pevensey and the Archbishop of Canterbury's deanery of South Malling; and Hastings, coincident with the deaneries of Hastings and Dallington.

Possibly to reduce the burden on Earl Roger de Montgomery, who was well compensated by becoming earl of Shrewsbury, the middle Welsh march, and therefore receiving most of Shropshire on the Welsh border by 1072, a fifth rape, Bramber, was created out of the eastern end of Arundel and the western end of Lewes, leaving the ecclesiastical boundary stranded mid-Bramber. These and losses of further manors from north Lewes to Pevensey caused William to give to Earl de Warenne some manors in Norfolk, some of which are described in the Norfolk Domesday entries as of the exchange of Lewes in compensation for his Sussex manors.

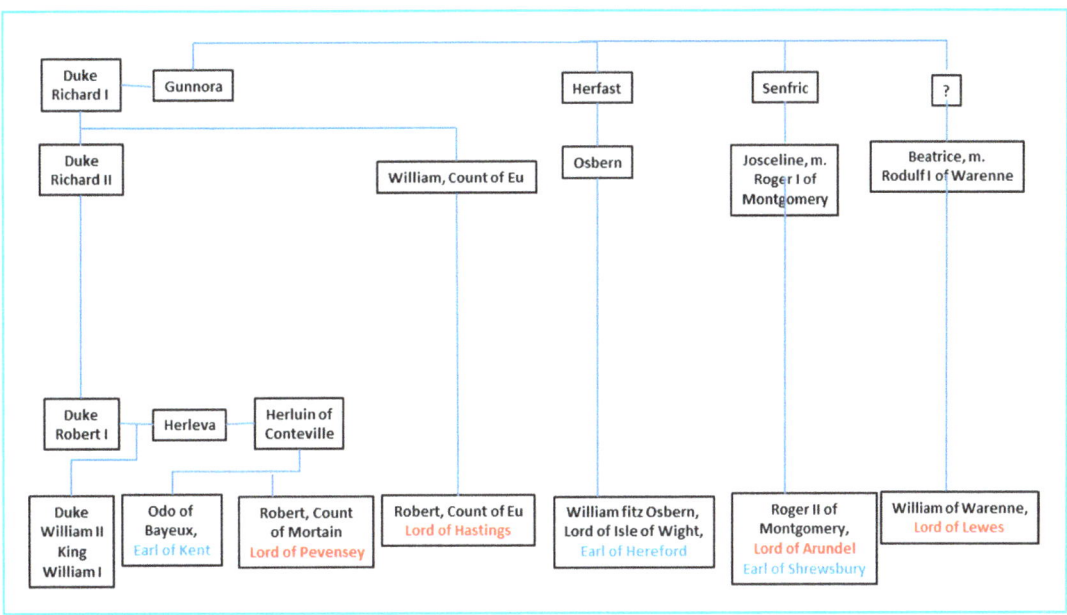

Many key castelry grants were made to supportive relatives of William I
Robert, Count of Eu was a cousin. Odo and Robert of Mortain were half-brothers. Some were related through his great-grandmother, Gunnora de Creppon, as shown above ©BDHS

So the initial Rapes, initially four in number, mainly corresponded with ecclesiastical deanery boundaries. The tenants-in-chief and their geographical extent were:

Earl Roger de Montgomery (The Rape of Earl Roger, later of Arundel and by 1275 to be divided into two called Rape of Arundel and Rape of Chichester. This covered western Sussex eastwards to the Adur)
William de Warenne (Rape of Lewes, from the Adur to the Ouse, plus the 28 or so manors north of the deanery of South Malling, the last later transferred to Pevensey, possibly at the same time as the creation of Bramber)
Robert, Count de Mortain (Rape of Pevensey, Ouse to the ecclesiastical boundary of the deanery of Dallington, later added to by the manors north of the deanery of South Malling)

Robert, Count of Eu (Rape of Hastings, from the ecclesiastical boundary of the deanery of Dallington to the Kent–Sussex border, but not including the banlieu, lowey or sometime Rape of Battle, given by William to the Abbey of St Martin at Battle, without compensation to local Norman land holders)

The next Rape to be formed only three years later in about 1073, with modifications to neighbouring Rapes, was held by William de Briouze or Braose. This Rape of William de Briouze, was initially centred on Steyning, later on Bramber Castle and only after 1187 called the Rape of Bramber. This creation entailed the transfer of about 17 valuable manors from Lewes and further manors from west of the Adur from Arundel. So in 1086 there were 49 Hundreds in Sussex and the number of Hundreds in each Rape was:

Arundel 14 plus ⅔ of Easewrith = 14⅔;
Bramber 6 plus ⅓ each of Aldrington and Easewrith and ⅔ of Wyndham = 7⅓;
Lewes 9 plus ⅓ each of Wyndham, Hartfield and Rushmonden and ⅔ each of Aldrington and East Grinstead = 11⅓;
Pevensey 12 plus ⅓ of East Grinstead and ⅔ each of Hartfield and Rushmonden = 13⅔;
Hastings 12 not including the banlieu of Battle.

The Rape structure is described in a fragmented way in the Sussex entries of the Domesday Book of 1086, but Mason valiantly untangled with some degree of certainty the major exchanges required to create Bramber – with reference to the manors gained in Norfolk by William of Warenne. Sometime after the creation of Bramber and by 1275 Arundel was divided into two: the Rape of Arundel (4⅔ Hundreds, all quite large), and the Rape of Chichester (10 Hundreds). In the introduction to Volume 4 of *VCH* covering the Rape of Chichester, it is commented that 'there is no trace of any castle at Chichester, the first known reference to one being in 1142' and that it seems 'that before 1250 there was no such entity as the Rape of Chichester'.

The Rapes then persisted after 1250, with minor changes and rationalisation of outlying manors as semi-administrative units until the 19th century. The sequence of the events is clarified in the maps above and below. A full coincidence of all deanery and administrative boundaries is unlikely given changes over the centuries and the maps are indicative only. Given the changes described above it is clear that the Rapes as then constituted to the west of Pevensey could not have been exactly the same as any pre-Conquest Rapes. But Hastings and Pevensey could have pre-existed as they were little changed except for enlargement of Pevensey, indeed Hastings may have been completely unaltered barring sorting out outlying manors. It is tempting to think that this may represent at least in part the semi-autonomous Hæstingas area, known since at least the eight century. This may also be why these two rapes retained for some centuries some Kentish local legal structures with Lathe (not Rape) courts to settle local matters, although these courts became more and more anomalous as their function gradually fell between those of the Hundred courts and the Justices' petty and quarter sessions. Lewes might also have existed as a Rape before 1066 as a comment is made in the pre-Conquest custumal of Lewes concerning buying slaves within the 'Rape'.

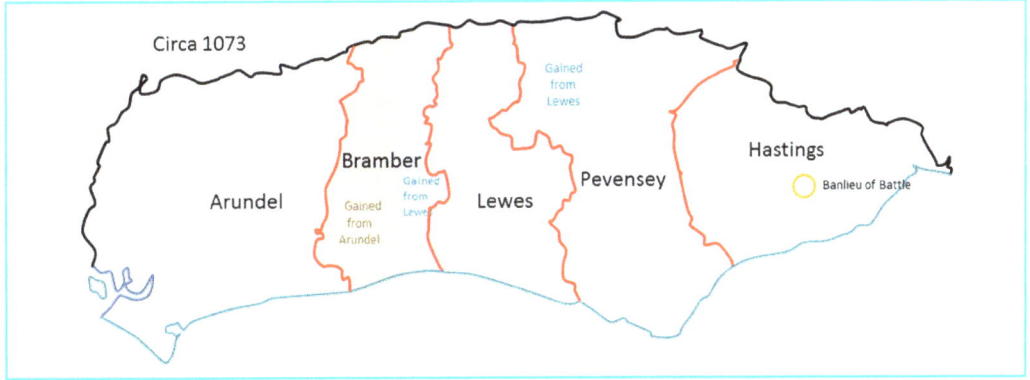

About 1073: The fifth Rape is added, with transfers of manors and Hundreds (not necessarily whole ones) from Arundel and Lewes to make up Bramber on either side of the Adur

Some manors also transferred to Pevensey from Lewes. Although the number and value of the Hundreds and manors 'donated' varied it appears that the total area from each neighbour may be roughly equivalent. William of Warenne was given manors in Norfolk to compensate for his losses. Earl Roger of Montgomery got most of Shropshire. Hastings Rape was unchanged. ©BDHS

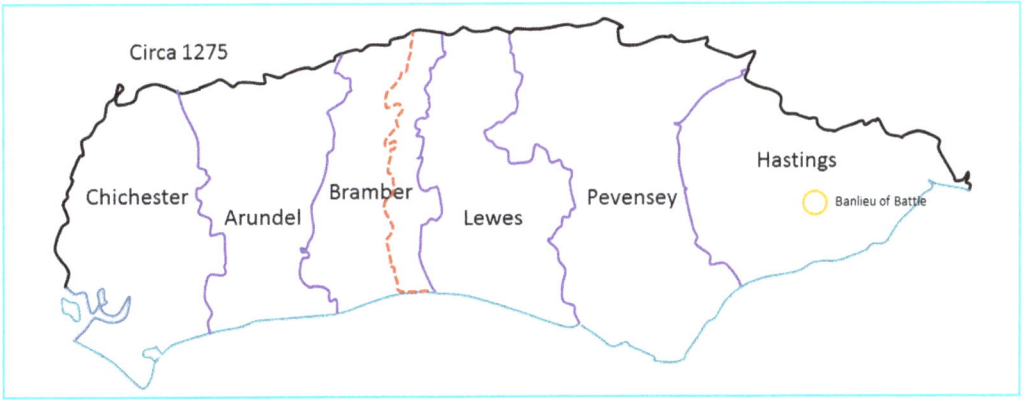

Before 1275: The later division of Arundel into two rapes, Arundel and Chichester

The old archdeaconry division (dashed line) is also shown for interest ©BDHS

Clearly the coastal castelries covered zones which controlled inlets, harbours, estuarine routes and landing beaches giving access to the littoral of Sussex. They also had hinterlands for some distance allowing defence in depth and a degree of control of westwards and eastward movements. By 1086 there were at least five stone castles in Sussex, one each in the Rapes of Hastings, Lewes, Bramber, Pevensey and Arundel (the first castle at Chichester is not noted until 1142). As Sir Henry Ellis asserted in 1833 the re-organisation/re-creation/establishment of the Sussex Rapes should be seen as creating defensive military districts or castelries rather than being seen as pre-Conquest administrative areas adapted for defence by William I. Although there was significant disregard of the manorial structure of Anglo-Saxon Sussex, the name Rape may also have just been conveniently absorbed as a local convention by William. As has been noted elsewhere place-name changes were rare.

Their original raison d'être of castelries as strong defensive lines disappeared quite quickly as the Norman–English state took full and firm control. North Sea neighbours thought long and hard before taking the Normans on. The last big scare to William I was in 1085, when he rapidly deployed an army from Normandy to counter a Danish threat. But Rapes continued to exist for a very long time, at first being used for local government and exchequer purposes in the collection of Subsidy Rolls, as judicial areas and for mustering and militia recruitment. They became mostly obsolete in 1889, following the Local Government Act 1888, when the three western Rapes became West Sussex and the three eastern ones East Sussex. By 1894 most administrative functions of the Rapes had ended, but it is noted that Hastings still had a franchise Coroner until 1960 under a rather complicated arrangement detailed in ESRO ref. SHE/2.

The six martlets (stylised birds similar to a house martin or swallow) on both East and West Sussex coats of arms are often said to represent the six Rapes, linking to the past. Another theory suggested that the emblem was linked to the Arundel family, but this idea did not take into account the Arundel family of Lanherne, Cornwall who bore arms that were black with six silver swallows and ignored the fact that the family associated with Arundel, Sussex, was d'Aubigny whose arms were red with a lion rampant! The most likely precursor is the arms of Sir John de Radynden, who from 1316 served as commissioner of array, who recruited men for military service. John de Radynden's daughter Alice married Sir Roger Dallingridge, whose son Edward married Elizabeth Wardedieu (Wardeux/Wardieu) who had inherited Bodiam Manor on the death of her father, Richard Wardedieu. Richard had married Margaret de Bodiam, heiress of William de Bodiam, thus gaining the Manor. Edward Dallingridge built Bodiam Castle in 1385 on whose gatehouse are seen the six martlets, as well as his own blazon and that of the Wardedieus'

Other recent administrative changes have continued to seriously confuse the historic structures. Originally Netherfield/Battle was one hundred of 'Hailsaltede',

9 RAPES OF HASTINGS AND HUNDREDS OF THE RAPE OF HASTINGS

Top: Photo of the blazons above the garehouse of Bodiam Castle.
L. to R.: Wardedieu, Dallingridge and Radynden/Sussex
Modern interpretations below. The colours of the Wardedieu blazon are unknown and therefore presented in black and white.

later split into Netherfield and Battle half-hundreds. Guestling incorporated Winchelsea and Rye plus the 'old town' area of Hastings. Baldslow incorporated the rest of Hastings. The superimposed dark blue boundaries on the diagram below show these differences from later boundaries.

The Hundreds of the Rape of Hastings

The Hundreds are described below by their modern name in table form, which shows some basic demographic information about each Hundred. Where necessary hidages etc. are added from numbers recorded in the Rape of Pevensey.

The number of households is as recorded in Domesday and the population density is calculated as four times the household density divided by the size of the Hundred in square kilometres, rounded to the nearest whole number. The value is rounded to the nearest £ and the areas of each are as stated in Brandon.

In terms of pre-Conquest value Bexhill, Baldslow and Guesting were the most valuable in terms of hidage, which represented a valuation of cultivated land. The valuation of Bexhill will reflect the previous ecclesiastical management of the area which has some good agricultural land. The value of Baldslow was probably due to the large holding by the king, and the presence within this Hundred of the pre-cursor of modern Hastings (Hæstingaceastre). Guestling also had a higher overall value in

The Hundreds of the Rape of Hastings and Pevensey Lowey

monetary terms probably because of the ownership and active management of the large Rameslie manor by Fécamp Abbey since the early part of the 11th century and the large number of valuable saltpans in their ownership.

The poorest areas include the area now around Battle which is hilly and at relatively high level with poor soils and some of the other poor areas contained either significant marshland or significant amounts of forest.

The population density is a better measurement of numbers of people on the ground. It is a slight surprise to note that Gostrow and Goldspur hundreds are slightly lower in population density that the more inland larger heavily forested zones, but they both include low-lying wetlands which may account for this.

Population density is calculated as number of households x4 divided by area in km2. The Hundreds are visually ranked for demographic value, size etc. by a colour key as below:

| Highest |
| High |
| Mid |
| Low |
| Lowest |

Modern Name	Domesday Name	TRE Hidage	No of Households	Population Density no/km²	Value £	Area Km²	Notes
Ninfield	Nerefelle	16.5 – of which 12 held by Harold Godwinson	100	13	38	32	71 households at Hooe. Ninfield and Catsfield small but both had churches. Good farmland.
Bexhill	Bexlelei	25	131	18	26	29	Bexhill and 'Bollington' (Pebsham +Sidley). Belonged to Bishop of Selsey, returned to Bishop of Chichester in 1148. Good land.
Baldslow	Baldeslei	36.5 – of which 15 at Filsham were held directly by King Edward	181	15	45	49	Included modern Hastings west of the Priory Valley, plus Hollington, Filsham, Wilting, Crowhurst, Ore and Westfield.
Guestling	Gestelinges	31.5 Of which 20 were in the manor of Rameslie	165 107 in Rameslie	13	74	49	Included Hastings east of the Priory valley, Fairlight, Pett, Icklesham, Winchelsea and Rye
Gostrow	Babinrerode	6.5	25	4	9	26	Brede and Udimore. Udimore had a church
Goldspur	Colespore	6	50	3	9	70	Beckley, Peasmarsh, Iden, Playden, East Guldeford. Beckley named in Alfred's will
Staple	Staple	12.5	115	9	25	52	Northiam, Ewhurst, Bodiam, Sedlescombe
Netherfield and Battle;	Hailsaltede *Later half-hundreds of Netherfield and Battle the latter being mainly the banlieu of the Abbey*	7	118	6	24	83	Mostly scattered smallholdings around a large area comprising present day Battle, Netherfield, Whatlington, Mountfield, Brightling and Dallington
Foxearle	Folsalre	15	147	11	37	55	Main foci of population Wartling and Herstmonceux. Small holdings around Ashburnham
Hawksborough	Hauches-berie	21 95% being managed by manors in the Rape of Pevensey	101	5	18	86	Burwash, Warbleton and part of Heathfield. The largest hundred by area

Modern Name	Domesday Name	TRE Hidage	No of Households	Population Density no/km²	Value £	Area Km²	Notes
Shoys-well	Shoes-welle	10.5 57% being managed by manors in the Rape of Pevensey	54	6	17	34	Ticehurst and area
Henhurst	Herhert	12.5 65% being managed by manors in the Rape of Pevens	101	10	21	42	Salehurst, Robertsbridge Etchingham

Table ©BDHS

10
Lords and People of the Rape of Hastings to 1538

'Think on Lord Hastings. Despair and die.'
Ghost of Lord Hastings to Richard III:
William Shakespeare, *Richard III*, Act V, Scene 3

After 1066, Sussex was governed and taxed through the lords of the Rapes and their sheriffs, previously known as viscounts in Normandy, and with the alternative name stewards. In Sussex the Lords of the Rapes appointed their sheriffs until about 1157, maybe until just after in Hastings, and we have some of their probable names and dates. There were also county sheriffs, whose role gradually changed and became more important after 1157, being responsible for justice and the enforcement of law. This is today an honorific role. As the post evolved there came into being a further local representative of the King dealing with the King's business in the shires. This office, much modified, also continues to this day as the Lord Lieutenant, the monarch's ceremonial representative in the county from after 1557.

This chapter covers the Rape of Hastings between 1070 and 1538 and tries to untangle the way in which the Rape evolved. The secondary sources for this are not numerous and are sometimes contradictory, and where possible cross checks have been made to primary information available via Pipe Rolls and elsewhere. If errors are perceived the author would be grateful to receive information including references and will make acknowledged corrections as necessary in any future edition. The text below tries to bring together that basic data to be found about the people of the Rape of Hastings before the Reformation. This encompasses the lords of the Rape, the sheriffs of the rape and the occasional glimpse through local taxation and military musters of the sub-tenants, knights and ordinary people of the Rape. With respect to the lords of the Rape these are grouped roughly in three phases:

> **The House of Eu (Ow):** This first phase encompasses the post-1066 founding House of Eu, from the appointment of Robert d'Eu in 1069–70 to Countess Alix d'Eu who voluntarily forfeited the Rape in 1243.

- **Entanglement with Richmond and Brittany**: In the second phase the Rape of Hastings became entwined with the Earldom of Richmond and the two Honours are used as bargaining chips between England and Brittany, until the Dukedom of Brittany had the Rape taken away and permanently forfeited its right to it.
- **Royal Favour**: In the last phase the Rape started to be granted as a result of service or favours given to a monarch and passed through a number of hands, including a couple of Pelhams (of buckle fame, subsequent to the story from 1356 at the Battle of Poitiers when a local knight, Sir John Pelham, together with Sir Roger de la Warr captured Jean the King of France, and because of this Sir John was given the King's belt buckle).

At the end of the period of interest it was in the hands of the Hastings family, who had their roots in the Midlands and no real connection to the area at all.

The holder of the Rape paid scutage tax, also known as knight's fees. The Rape was initially assessed for 60 knight's fees, but by 1148 the Bishop of Chichester had recovered his lands at Bexhill lost to Robert d'Eu in 1070 which accounted for the loss of four knight's fees and when the Abbey of Robertsbridge was founded that absorbed four more knight's fees, so the Rape was left to find 52.

The sections below follow the holders of the Rape in chronological order. The dates indicated are those between which the named person held the Lordship of the Rape, not their dates of birth and death although the latter may coincide.

Robert d'Eu (Lord of Hastings 1070–1089/93)

The blazon of Eu

The Lordship of Hastings Rape and Castelry was given by William I to Robert, Count of Eu in or before May 1070. The Hastings area and the building of a stone castle on the West Hill of Hastings had from October 1066 been under the supervision of the strong hands of Humphrey de Tilleul, son of Thurstan le Goz, viscount of Avranches.

Robert's father was William, Count of Eu, his mother Lesseline de Harcourt and his wife Beatrice de Falaise. His paternal grandmother was Gunnora of Creppon, also great-grandmother of William I. He was one of the chief counsellors of William, and had fought alongside William at the Battle of Mortemer in 1054. He was summoned to the Council of Lillebonne, when William asked his vassals for assistance to invade

England and Eu contributed or funded sixty ships towards William's invasion fleet. Not only did he fight at the Battle of Hastings, but he was a constant supporter of William throughout his subjugation of England. So the Rape of Hastings was in safe and trusted hands.

Robert of Eu rapidly seized the lands of the second most powerful lord in the Rape, the Bishop of Selsey, taking extensive lands at Bexhill and Bollington (Pebsham/Sidley). But he had to concede the banlieu of Battle, which had the same status as the Rape that it lay within, to his own overlord, William I. Robert was told by William to do right by the monks as you would do for myself, but there was still some discord amongst the Norman underlings who had already moved on to the lands to be occupied by the banlieu before it was established. More so, as apparently they were not compensated and were expected to give up the lands solely for love of William.

Much of the administration of the Rape of Hastings was in the hands of the sheriff, Reinbert, who was not only steward but also Robert's largest tenant, with lands at Wilting, Hollington, Whatlington, Bexhill, Udimore, a hide of land in Henhurst hundred that was probably Etchingham, Salehurst, Mountfield, land in Hooe and Boarzell in Ticehurst, from which his descendants were to form the core of the future Etchingham family estates. The seat of the Etchingham family from about 1300 was at Glottenham Castle, near Darvell. As he was so well embedded, with many manors and estates by 1086, it is likely that he had been appointed quite soon after Robert d'Eu was granted the Rape. He appears to have held the post until about 1101 or maybe as late as 1106 into Henry d'Eu's tenure of the Rape. Reinbert would hear cases brought before the Lathe court which met three-weekly and later in the 12th century alternated its venue between Netherfield and Sedlescombe. The Lathe court reflected the military needs of the 11th century, and continued until the 15th century when its functions were superseded. The jurisdiction was the count's but any profits from crown cases went to the king.

King William I at his death in 1087 bequeathed the Duchy of Normandy to one son, Robert Curthose and the Kingdom of England to another, William Rufus. This caused consternation amongst the barons who held lands in both Normandy and England and they began to take sides, many supporting the supposedly weaker Robert Curthose, which may have suited their own ambitions. Robert, Count of Eu, was still alive and is reported to have attended and listened to an early speech by Rufus at Winchester. He also seems to have played an active part in the early stage of the dispute between Rufus and Robert of Normandy. Owing fealty to both in respect of his English and Norman estates he, in common with the other nobles, found himself in a dilemma by reason of his dual allegiance. By 1090, Robert, Count of Eu, appears to have fully transferred his allegiance to Rufus.

Bishop Odo, Duke of Kent and half-brother of William the Conqueror, plotted against Rufus in 1088 and, according to some sources concerning the lords of the

Rapes of Sussex, only William de Warenne of Lewes was for William Rufus. Odo was joined by: Earl Robert of Mortain and Cornwall, Lord of Pevensey and Montacute; Earl Roger of Montgomery; and Bishop William of Durham (William of Calais). The following were also among the rebels: Robert, Earl of Northumberland; Roger, Earl of Shrewsbury; and Bishop Geoffrey of Coutances, assisted by Robert of Mobray and a William of Eu. This last person is puzzling as although there is some confusion concerning the date of the death of Robert of Eu which was between 1089–93, but more likely between 1091–93, he was alive and clearly still Lord of Eu and Hastings in 1088 and does appear to have supported Rufus. There is more about this William of Eu below.

The College of St Mary in the Castle at Hastings was founded in about 1090 by Count Robert. The college remained in the patronage of the founder's descendants until 1267, when, on the death of Alix, Countess of Eu, it became a royal chapel – until 1446 when it was granted, along with the Honour of the Rape of Hastings to Sir Thomas Hoo.

Rufus clearly used Hastings Castle as a base as in 1091, before sailing to Normandy, and at that time he summoned his nobles to Hastings to swear fealty. In 1093 his army was mustered again at Hastings expecting to cross the Channel but was detained by contrary winds for a whole month, during which the king lodged in the castle. In the following year 20,000 men were encamped around the area preparatory to a war with France, but Rufus, decided against this and dismissed them, first of all taking from them the ten shillings (50 p) a head travelling money they had received from their counties.

This account of using Hastings as a base is also rather against the proposition that the count of Eu was against Rufus in 1088 – although Rufus did need to take the next door Lord of the Honour of Pevensey, Robert de Mortain's, Pevensey Castle by siege. Unfortunately the Lord of Lewes, William de Warenne, was injured in this siege and died of his wounds. On his own death, Robert d'Eu was buried at Tréport Abbey.

William II d'Eu (Lord of Hastings 1089/93–1096)

Robert of Eu was succeeded by his son William II of Eu who only survived him by a few years, soon passing the lordship on to his own son Henry. But William was to support the third son of William I, Henry, on campaign in Brittany against Robert Curthose, and his own son Henry of Eu may have also taken part in this Brittany campaign.

Past authors including Dugdale, Stubbs, Freeman and those of *VCH* have counted a William of Eu as taking part in Earl Odo's 1088 conspiracy and have therefore presumed that the holder of the Rape of Hastings was part of it. However, this William of Eu should not be confounded with William, son of Robert, Count of Eu.

A William of Eu is separately referred to in Domesday of 1086 as holding manors in Gloucestershire and other parts of western England. He was a supporter of the Bishop of Coutances (Geoffrey de Mowbray) against Rufus, and he came to an unpleasant end in about 1097, accused of treason. Douglas realised the mis-identification, following the genealogical researches of Chester-Waters, and Searle and Dawson also concluded that different men were being referred to. While the West Country estates of the traitor William of Eu were confiscated by the Crown in 1095, the strategically important Rape of Hastings was left in the sounder hands of Robert, then William, Counts of Eu. Surely this would not have happened if William, Robert's son, had been the traitor to William Rufus.

William, or possibly yet another canonical namesake, was buried in the Collegiate Church of Hastings Castle. If this was the Count, he was unique as his Eu antecedents and descendants were all buried in Normandy.

Henry d'Eu (Lord of Hastings 1096–1140)

Henry Count of Eu married Marguerite, daughter of William of Sully who was the eldest son of Stephen, Count of Champagne, Brie and Blois, and the older brother of the Stephen who would become King of England after Henry I. Henry of Eu survived Henry I by two years.

After Rufus' death in 1100 and when Henry I became king, Henry of Eu sided with Rufus' brother Henry against Robert Curthose, Duke of Normandy in 1104–5. Henry had taken his campaign to Normandy with a view to repressing the anarchy of the time in the Duchy and re-uniting his father's dominions. This he achieved in 1106 at the Battle of Tinchebrai at which his brother Robert was captured and then imprisoned.

From about 1101, a man called Hugh, possibly Hugh Arbalistarius, who held lands at Hollington, Cortesley (in Hastings), Frankwell in Ashburnham and Welland in Ewhurst starts to attest charters and had probably taken over as sheriff from Reinbert or was acting as his deputy. A man called William, son of Wibart, is also mentioned around this time but as a county sheriff. His father held lands at Westfield, Herstmonceux, Warbleton, Bucksteep in Warbleton and in Ewhurst

Some years later, in 1119 Louis VI, King of France, invaded the Duchy of Normandy, but was defeated at the Battle of Brémule at which both Henry of Eu and William de Warenne were involved.

Between about 1107 and 1120, one Ingleram de Hastings/d'Eu who was mentioned in Domesday as holding lands at Wilting, Baldslow and Hooe is noted as sheriff. He was probably followed by Drogo of Pevensey from about 1120 to 1129. There is then a gap in knowledge of the names of possible sheriffs of the Rape until about 1153

Henry, Count of Eu, had several sons and daughters: 1. John, his successor; 2. Hugh, Archdeacon of Cornwall in 1135 and of Totnes in 1143, who may have been the Hugh, the Dean of Hastings College Church mentioned in the college's Confirmation Charter of Henry, Count of Eu; 3. William, Archdeacon of the Diocese of Exeter; 4. Beatrix; and possibly 5. Matilda.

John d'Eu (Lord of Hastings 1140–1170)

John became Count of Eu on his father's death in 1140. We are told that he was in favour with King Stephen and a frequent visitor to the English Court. The number of knight's fees to be paid was now 56.

In 1148 John gave the manor of Bexhill back to the See of Chichester, and the bishop may have been the first to start to build a house which would later become the manor house.

Among the Battle Abbey deeds are two charters of Stephen, the first of which is witnessed by Bishop Hilary of Chichester, who held the see from 1146 to 1149. The second was issued on behalf of the King from Hastings, but we have no evidence of a visit by Stephen to the Rape. From another charter we know that John d'Eu was in Normandy in 1151–2 and for some time after this was dealing with the affairs of his lands at Eu and in founding and improving religious establishments at Tréport, Foucarmont, and Eu.

A man called Gilbert is mentioned as sheriff or viscount in about 1153 when he witnesses a charter by John d'Eu. He is reckoned to be the son of one Gencelin whose lands at Sedlescombe were some time later granted to Robertsbridge Abbey.

John d'Eu issued a charter in 1167 responding to an order from Henry II, who wanted to know the number of knights fees in his realm so that he could more accurately extract the tax called 'scutage' from his tenants-in-chief according to the number of knights within their tenancy, and this gives us an early picture of his tenants and their relative wealth.

> Charter of John, Count of Eu (circa 1167): John, Count of Eu, to Henry, King of the English, Duke of Normandy, and Aquitaine and Earl of Anjou, 'Greeting. Know ye that I have of old enfeoffment in the rape of Hastings 56 knights' (fees), but my father in the time of King Henry, your grandfather, used to have 60 knights in the same rape, 4 knights whereof the Bishop of Chichester now has, whereof you have the service. Of these 56 knights, holding in the aforesaid rape of the old feoffment, the names are these:

Humphrey de Willecheres,	holding 7 knights' (fees).
William de Hekingham (Etchingham)	7 knights.
Matthew de Baelum	10 knights.

Roger de Bodiham	4 knights.
Hurste de Warbertone (Warbelton)	5 knights.
Gilbert de Balliol	4 (3 ?) knights.
Robert de Ricarville (Ricarwell)	10 knights.
Reginald de Oseburnham (Ashburham)	2 knights.
Walter Morlay (Morley)	1 knight.
William de Wikeshale (Wekeshall)	1 knight.
Hugh de Chekenora,	1 knight.

And besides these knights I have upon my lordship 6 knights and a half whereof the names are these:

Alured de St. Martin,	1 knight.
Robert Strabo,	1 knight.
Robert del Broc,	1 knight.
William de Bosco,	half a knight
William de Lancinges,	half a knight.
Daniel de Crevequer	
Roger de Freham (Trocham)	
Robert de Hastings,	half a knight.

Of the new feoffment I have no knight enfeoffed.

John, Count of Eu retired to the Abbey of Foucarmont and died there in 1170. He had married Alix d'Aubigny who was daughter of William d'Aubigny, Earl of Arundel and Alix de Louvain, Dowager Queen of England, the widow of Henry I. John had three sons, Henry, Robert (who witnessed a grant by his mother Alix to Robertsbridge Abbey in 1178, but died before Henry), John (Lord of Billington), and three daughters, Matilda, Margaret and Ida, the last of whom married a William de Hastings.

Henry II d'Eu (Lord of Hastings 1170–1183)

Henry became count of Eu in 1170, but was a minor under the wardship of the Earl of Arundel, who was his grandfather. He later married Matilda Plantagenet, widow of Osbert de Preaux, the daughter of Hamelin Plantagenet (*aka* Earl de Warrene and Surrey, who was a 'natural' brother of King Henry II) They had two sons, Raoul who died a minor in 1186 and Guy who also died a minor in 1185. Only one child grew of age to succeed him, a daughter, Alix.

The sheriff in 1175 may have been Alured de St. Martin, who was possibly related in some way to Ingleram a previous sheriff. Also an Ingelram de Monceux, a viscount, witnessed a grant to Battle Abbey from Henry II d'Eu, which must have been made towards the end of Henry's life.

After this date county sheriffs probably took over any residual sheriff duties within the Rape as King Richard II dismissed all sheriffs, putting the office up for sale and King John also interfered with appointments of sheriffs, undoubtedly for pecuniary gain. In the future the county sheriffs would be the prime law and order officers. A complete list of the sheriffs of Sussex since 1086 is given on the website of the Lord Lieutenant of West Sussex.

Temporary Resumption (Lordship of Hastings 1183–1191)

As Henry II of Eu died in March 1183, Alix (Alice) must have still been very young, but a husband was inevitably found for her by King Henry II, who will have resumed the Rape for a while, until sometime before 1190. Certainly he retained Hastings Castle in royal hands.

Ralph (Raoul) de Lusignan – Earl of Eu by marriage to Countess Alix d'Eu (Lord of Hastings 1191–1201/2)

This Ralph (Raoul) de Lusignan was distantly connected with the kings of both England and France. The Lusignan family also had wider and powerful connections in Europe and the Holy Land. By marriage he became 7th Count of Eu, Baron of Hastings. He and Alix had two sons, Raoul (or Ralph), 8th Count of Eu and Guarin, and two daughters, Maud and Joan.

Ralph became involved in crusades with Richard I, and after that king's death had severe difficulties with King John to survive. Interestingly, Ralph had made a specific oath of loyalty to John in January 1200, together with his brother Hugh, Count of March, but later in 1200 John had determined on marrying Isabella of Angouleme, possibly for strategic reasons. One difficulty of this was that she was already betrothed to Hugh, Ralph's brother. This made things very complicated as the Lusignan lands had provided a different key strategic route for John. John, unsurprisingly, handled this matter very badly and treated Hugh with contempt, from which followed a Lusignan insurgency that was then crushed by the English. John then suppressed Hugh's brother Ralph, both in the Eu lands of Normandy as well as by seizing the Rape of Hastings. John issued instructions in 1201 seizing the Rape and giving notice, that

> his lieutenants had permission to do what harm they could to Ralph, Count of Eu and we have commanded and willed to be taken to our use, the woods, stock, and all the chattels of the count of Eu in England.

Seizure of the Rape (in 1201/2–1214), when King John granted it to John of Eu, uncle of Alix

King John had seized the Rape of Hastings into his own hands, and then had granted it to John of Eu, uncle of the Countess Alix (Alice) of Eu. When John of Eu died in 1207 the Rape reverted to the crown until 1214.

Ralph de Lusignan, Earl of Eu, restored (1214–1219)

Blazon of the Lusignan Counts of Eu

Several years later, in 1214, King John had a change of heart after he had besieged Lusignan. Hugh IX de Lusignan had surrendered and after he had submitted and given homage to John we see:

> Witnessed at Parthenay, in the sixteenth year of our reign (23 May, Trinity Sunday, 1214): By this treaty John guaranteed to Ralph, Count of Eu, the whole inheritance which his wife (the Countess Alice) ever possessed or was entitled to possess in England

This, if true, gave Ralph more than he had lost in 1201–2; for he also obtained the Honour of Tickhill, near Sheffield, now in Derbyshire, as well as the Honour and Rape of Hastings. Then Ralph, Count of Eu, was appointed on 21 April 1216 as one of the commissioners to meet the King of France to make a truce. King John was always dangerously fickle and Lusignan skated on thin ice. Following King Henry III's accession in 1216 the Close Roll, 1 Henry III. 1217 says:

> The sheriffs of Nottingham and Sussex are commanded to take care that the Count of Eu have full and peaceable possession of all his estates (i.e. Tickhill, then in Nottinghamshire and Hastings) as he had before the war began between King John and the Barons.

Countess Alix d'Eu holds the Rape (1219–1243)

Ralph of Lusignan died at Melle in Poitou in 1219 and after this Alix, Countess of Eu, retained the Rape but lost the Castle and the College, which she ceded to King Henry III in 1225. The Castle was in poor condition and was already being lost to the sea but she retained her other property in the Rape of Hastings. As late as 1242 Henry III had by letters patent undertaken:

the protection and defence of the men, lands, goods, and all the other possessions of her the said Countess.

Only a year later in 1243 Henry III had a disastrous campaign in Poitou. After losing the Battle of Taillebourg he ordered all his vassals who had taken the side of King Louis IX of France to forfeit their lands. The Dauphin who had fruitlessly invaded England at the end of John's and beginning of Henry III's reign had become Louis IX of France.

House of Eu elects to forfeit the Rape (1243–4)

Alix elected to retain her possessions in France and the Eu ancestral estates in England were never again to be held by the house of Eu. Apparently the representatives of the Eu family tried in 1259 and 1290 to obtain a reversal of the decree of forfeiture of their estates, but without avail. The Rape reverted to the crown.

Rape held by the crown 1244–9 then passed to Peter II of Savoy (Lord of Hastings from 1249–1254 and Richmond from 1241–1268)

In 1249 Henry III granted the castle and honour of Hastings to Peter II of Savoy, uncle of his queen, Eleanor of Provence. This was with the instruction to refortify the castle and to fortify Rye. Peter had already been given the Honour (although apparently not earldom) of Richmond in 1241 and the Rape of Hastings now became associated with that earldom.

Henry had already given Pevensey Castle to Savoy in 1246 and in the 1250s he also repaired this Castle. He seems to have been very faithful to the king, and beyond some oppressive measures towards the church nothing much is recorded against him. He accompanied Henry III on his expedition to Gascony in August 1253. On capturing the Castles of La Reole and Bazas the king gave possession of them to Peter. In 1254 Peter released the Rape and Henry III granted it to his own son, Edward.

Prince Edward (also Lord of Eu, including the Rape of Hastings, 1254/5–1268)

It seems that, at this point, Henry III, as part of his long standing war with France, decided to bring the Rape of Hastings back in house and granted it and the French lands of Eu, over which he had regained control, to his son Edward. The lands were placed under the command of Geoffrey de Langley as Edward was busy elsewhere as we shall see below.

> 38th Henry III. 1254–5: Mandate of Lord Henry the King. Whereas the King has given to Edward, his son, the lands which formerly belonged to the Countess of Eu and other lands formerly belonging to the Normans, and the King is unwilling, on account of the danger which might threaten his crown in the course of time, if those lands should be returned to the right heirs, through peace or in any other manner, that any other liberties should be levied or used in the lands aforesaid than were accustomed in the said lands in the times of the lords thereof, command is given to Geoffrey de Langley that no other liberties shall be used in the lands aforesaid than were used in the same in the times of the lords aforesaid.

In May 1243 Langley had been appointed to the keeping of the Honour of Arundel for a year, following the death of the young Earl Hugh. According to Coss, Geoffrey de Langley was a servant of the crown, with a long and eventful if somewhat less than illustrious career. He was to achieve notoriety as a forest justice and as steward to Prince Edward when the Welsh rising of 1256 was precipitated.

Philips quotes that Geoffrey of Langley, possibly the above Langley's son, went on the crusade of Edward I of England in the Holy Land in the years 1270–71. Much more unusually he was later sent to the Mongol Il-Khanate court of Ghazan in 1291. Geoffrey left from Genoa, where he was joined by the Khan's ambassador to the West, Buscarel of Gisolfe, to go to the Mongol capital of Tabriz. The embassy is known in some detail because the financial accounts of it have remained.

Prince Edward must have severely irritated his father for he had to mortgage the Rape back to him to cover very large loans he had received from the King of France and from the Archbishop of Canterbury. In 1262 he restored the Rape back to the King who gave it to Peter of Savoy to look after once more.

Peter II of Savoy (Lord of Hastings [from 1262–1268] and Richmond [from 1241–1268])

Firstly Peter needed to retrieve the Honour of the Rape which had been seized by the barons, which he did by 1265. He was also regranted Pevensey castle at this time. He died in 1268 and by his will, he left Richmond to his niece, Eleanor, who promptly transferred it to the crown.

Thus began the involvement of the Dukedom of Brittany with the Rape of Hastings

Duke John I of Brittany (Duke of Brittany 1237–1286) receives the Honours and passes Richmond/Hastings to his son John of Dreux who later becomes John II of Brittany (Lord of the Rape of Hastings and Earl of Richmond, 1268–1305, & Duke of Brittany 1286–1305)

Blazon of John of Richmond (Duke John I of Brittany)
By Jimmy44   Image created for the Blazon Project of the French Wikipedia. [GFDL (http://www.gnu.org/copyleft/fdl.html)CC BY 3.0 (http://creativecommons.org/licenses/by/3.0)], via Wikimedia Commons

The dukes of Brittany had been the very first earls of Richmond from the time of the Conquest. But this was a restored second creation of the earldom. Hastings had been associated with the Earldom of Richmond since it was attached to that Honour for Peter of Savoy, so the Rape of Hastings now passed as a joint Honour together with the earldom.

The Honours, along with a couple of English princess's marriages, became bargaining chips between kings of England and the dukes of Brittany for or against France during the Hundred Years' War. The politics of the making and unmaking of the medieval Duchy of Brittany are far too complex to describe in this book. At the end of the section below, concerning Brittany after 1399, a chart attempts to clarify for the reader the positions of the dukes of Brittany with respect to the Earldom of Richmond and Rape of Hastings until 1399.

In 1268 Henry III granted the earldom to John I, Duke of Brittany (1217–1286), who additionally became Lord of the Rape of Hastings. But John I almost immediately resigned the earldom and passed it to his son, John I de Dreux, the future Duke John II of Brittany. So in 1268 John of Dreux, as he was then, became Earl of Richmond.

In 1260 John II of Dreux married Beatrice, Henry III's daughter. This marriage was meant to ally Brittany with England under the shield of England during the reign of Henry III whilst tensions rose with France. John and Beatrice had at least three sons, the eldest of which was Arthur. The second son was another John, II of Dreux. The third was Peter of Leon. Beatrice died in 1275 in London, before John I of Dreux became Duke John II of Brittany.

In both 1290 and 1295 the Rape was for a short time in the King's hands, firstly as Brittany had not fully supported England in Wales and, secondly and even worse, for briefly siding with the French.

In 1296 we get a glimpse of the people of the Rape through the Sussex Lay Subsidy Roll of 1296 and the entries for the Rape of Hastings. This can be viewed in the online appendices together with those of 1327 and 1332. The subsidy of 1296 was an eleventh; that in 1327 a twentieth, and that in 1332 a tenth and fifteenth of the value of moveables. The three Rolls are of value for their information of the names of contributors to this tax, which was the first form of general taxation.

Two years after the last one of them, in 1334 a fixed sum was assigned to each township, but then the names of the contributors are no longer recorded.

John II Duke of Brittany died in 1305.

Duke Arthur II of Brittany (Duke of Brittany 1305–1312) passes Richmond to his brother John II of Dreux, who becomes Earl of Richmond (1305/6–1334)

The first son of John II of Brittany and Beatrice of England was Arthur II (1261–1312), of the House of Dreux, who became Duke of Brittany from 1305 until his death in 1312.

Arthur was inconveniently campaigning against England and instead of claiming Hastings/Richmond in 1305, the Earldom of Richmond passed to his brother John who became Earl of Richmond in 1306 and also became active in King Edward I of England's service. He briefly lost his lands in 1325 after aligning himself during Edward II's reign with Edward's Queen Isabella as part of the move to force the abdication of her husband in favour of her son Edward III. The lands were subsequently restored by Edward III.

Although John married three times he failed to produce an heir. Towards the end of his life in 1333 he very briefly leased his English lands to his niece Mary, Countess of Pembroke, but he died in 1334.

The Earldom of Richmond and Rape of Hastings passed to his nephew, John III of Brittany, son of Arthur II by Mary of Limoges, his first wife. The offspring of Arthur II's second marriage to Yolande, Countess of Montfort, would later cause problems and spark the War of Breton succession, within the Hundred Years' War.

Duke John III of Brittany (Duke of Brittany 1312–1341 and Earl of Richmond 1334–1341)

Blazon adopted by John III
This blazon is still the arms of Brittany.

John III, son of Arthur II, was Duke of Brittany from 1312 and Earl of Richmond from 1334 to his death. In 1316 John III simplified his coat of arms to plain ermine.

Towards the end of his life, in 1339 we find a Muster Roll of the Rape of Hastings. This is particularly interesting; perhaps more than the Lay Subsidy Rolls, for it must list all the men of arms-bearing age from across every Hundred of the Rape, mostly with surnames. This can be seen in the online appendixes.

On John III's death, childless, in 1341 the inheritance of the Duchy of Brittany and the Earldom of Richmond became disputed. John III's niece, Joanna of Dreux, daughter of John III's eldest brother Guy and married to Charles de Blois, claimed the Duchy without apparently claiming to also be hereditary Countess of Richmond. John III's half-brother, Jean de Montfort, disputed Joanna's claim to the Duchy of Brittany. Their dispute was judged by the French king in a court of peers at Conflans, France. From that, Charles of Blois, Joanna's husband, became Duke of Brittany. This all unsurprisingly led to international complications. The adjudication raised the question of whether the Duke of Brittany and/or the Earl of Richmond, whether one and the same or not, owed homage to the French king. Amid the Hundred Years' War he was unlikely to get any homage from Richmond or Hastings.

Jean de Montfort fled Conflans and rejoined his troops, who occupied a number of castles from Nantes into Brittany. The French king then seized the county of Montfort from Jean de Montfort and caught and imprisoned him. He was freed in 1341, but died in 1345, leaving his son claiming the dukedom. During 1241–5 Jean de Montfort had used the title John IV of Brittany. But Joanna of Dreux and Charles de Blois, using his right of marriage continued as de facto Dukes of Brittany until his death in 1364, at the end of the Breton War of Succession which extended from 1341–64. After this the house of Montfort ruled again through John V, but with difficulty.

Titles of Earl of Richmond and Honour of the Rape of Hastings revert to King Edward III in 1341, who bestows them on Robert of Artois (1341)

In 1341 the title to Richmond reverted to Edward III and he bestowed it on Robert of Artois, who promptly lost his life less than a year later near Vannes during the Breton War of Succession.

John of Gaunt (Lord of the Rape of Hastings and Earl of Richmond, 1342–1372)

Before the start of the ownership by John of Gaunt, the fourth son of Edward III, his father caused a valuation of the Rape to be made in 1342. This included the names of some individuals and place names of local interest: This is to be found in the online appendices. John of Gaunt would have only been three years old when he received the Earldom of Richmond and Lordship of Hastings.

In 1350, when only ten, John was present at the naval Battle of Winchelsea. He was additionally created Duke of Lancaster in 1362. He campaigned with his elder brother the Black Prince, mortgaging the Rape of Hastings to cover his costs, and participated in many battles of the Hundred Years' War. He held the lands of Richmond and Hastings for 30 years and then for political reasons, again associated with Brittany, John of Gaunt surrendered the earldom and honours back to Edward III in 1372.

In that year he was granted Pevensey Castle, but did nothing to repair it and he was locally unpopular, with the Castle ransacked during the Peasants' Revolt. He died in 1399 and the custody of Pevensey Castle and the Rape of Pevensey passed to Sir John Pelham.

Duke John V of Brittany (Duke of Brittany 1364–1399, Earl of Richmond 1372–1381/2)

The earldom was then restored to the ducal house of Brittany and was given to John IV, Duke of Brittany, who had been forced into exile in England in 1373. But there were still difficulties between England, Brittany and France. Mary, Duchess of Brittany, who was Richard II's sister, was separated from the Duke by the king's Council and was refused permission to rejoin her husband, as the Duke had failed to support the English in Brittany.

In King Richard II's hands (1381/2–1387)

The Patent Rolls of March, October and November 1382, indicate that the King was in possession once more of the Duke of Brittany's earldom in England. This situation continued and Anne, Queen of Richard II, de facto held the Rape between 1384–1394 when she died and the titles resumed to the crown.

Restoration to Duke John V of Brittany (1387)

In March 1387–8 Richard restored John V, Duke of Brittany to the earldom of Richmond, but this was again not to last long.

Resumption to England and Final Forfeiture of the rights to the earldom of Richmond and Rape of Hastings by the Dukes of Brittany (1388–1399)

The lands were now briefly passed to Joan Basset, sister of the Duke of Brittany and widow of Lord Basset of Drayton, but then promptly resumed to the crown again in 1388. By 1390–1 we find:

> In the Parliament 14 Richard II. (1390–91), the Earldom and Lordship of Richmond, with the appurtenances thereof, were adjudged by the King and Lords as forfeit to the King, by reason of the adherence of John, Duke of Britanny, formerly Earl of Richmond, to the King's adversary of France.

On 20 July 1397 a safe-conduct was granted to John V, Duke of Brittany to come to England and soon afterwards by what appears a technical move, Richard II once more granted Richmond to Joan of Dreux, sister of John V of Brittany, and widow of Ralph, Lord Basset of Drayton.

> Richard, by the grace of God King of England and France, and Lord of Ireland, to his Archbishops, Bishops, Abbots, Priors, Dukes, Earls, Barons, Justices, Sheriffs, Reeves, Ministers, and all his bailiffs and faithful subjects, Greeting. Know ye that for certain reasonable causes us and our Council specially thereto moving, we do grant, and by this our present charter confirm, unto Joan, who was the wife of Ralph Basset, of Drayton, Knight … the earldom, castle, town, and honour of Richmond.

But the complicated story was not quite over. On Christmas Eve 1398, Richard II ordered his officers in the lordship of Richmond to return to the Duke of Brittany the rents which they had collected – but then on St. George's Day, 23April 1399, the Duke released to the King all sums of money due from the earldom of Richmond. Richard II was deposed on 30 September 1399 and died on 14 February 1400.

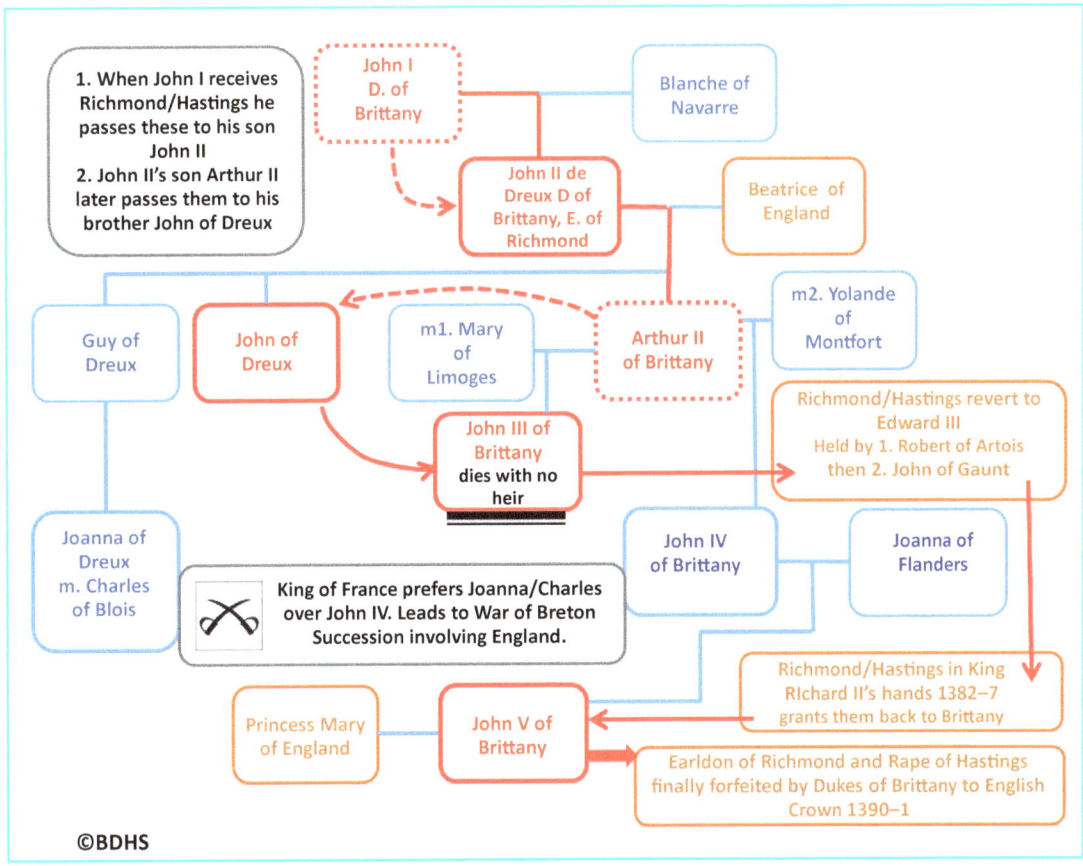

Henry Bolingbroke became King Henry IV of England and almost the first thing that Henry IV did on gaining the throne in September 1399 was to remove Richmond and Hastings from Joan Basset and to give the Honours to his new Earl Marshal. England would refuse to recognise the use of the title Earl of Richmond by the Dukes of Brittany ever again.

The chart above plots the involvement of the House of Brittany with respect to the earldom of Richmond and Honour of the Rape of Hastings. For dates and context see the text above.

Grant of the Rape to Ralph Nevill, Earl of Westmoreland (1399–1408)

The King had resumed the Honour of Richmond (but not the earldom) from Lady Joan Basset. He granted Richmond and Hastings to his new Earl Marshal the Earl of Westmoreland (Ralph Nevill) in the following terms:

> Henry, by the grace of God, King of England and France, and Lord of Ireland, to all to whom these present letters shall come, Greeting. Know ye that we,

inwardly considering the gratuitous care, labour, and expenses which our dearest brother, Ralph de Nevill, Earl of Westmoreland, Richmond, to have for the term of his life

Eight years later Ralph Nevill granted the Rape of Hastings to one John Norbury. This temporarily divorced Hastings Rape from association with the Earldom of Richmond for the first time, excepting some royal reversions, since 1243.

Rape granted to John of Norbury (1408–1412)

The Rape of Hastings was then granted to John of Norbury on 12 March 1408 by Ralph Nevill. John Norbury was a younger son of Thomas Norbury of Nantwich, of relatively lowly birth. He had a varied career, including military and diplomatic service in Brittany described in detail on the History of Parliament website. Although the text of this entry is extensive this does not mention his involvement with the Rape of Hastings

After Henry IV ascended the throne, Norbury achieved high office and was made Lord High Treasurer of England (1399–1401), Keeper of the Privy Wardrobe (1399–1405) and a member of the Privy Council. In 1406 he was acting as an ambassador to negotiate a further truce with the French. He retired in 1409 and died in 1414.

A Subsidy Roll of the Rape was taken in 1411 which shows valuations within the Rape and some valuations lying outside the Rape by landholders within the Rape, including Norbury's holdings elsewhere in Sussex. This is copied into the online appendices.

Henry IV grants the Rape of Hastings to Sir John Pelham (1412–1428)

Pelham coat of arms.
Azure three pelicans argent, quartering gules two buckles argent. By Wikimandia (Own work) [CC BY-SA 4.0 (https://creativecommons.org/licences/by-sa/4.0)], via Wikimedia Commons

When Ralph Nevill died in 1412 the gift of Hastings Rape must have reverted to the King as we find a grant of the Rape to Sir John Pelham, Constable of Pevensey Castle from 1399 to 1415 and lord of the Rape of Pevensey from 1409. At the same time he was granted many manors within the Rape of Pevensey, including Laughton, which was for many years the home of the Pelhams.

On 21 November 1412 (14 Henry IV), the King, in consideration of the acceptable services of his faithful servant Sir John Pelham, Knight, granted to him, on the death of Ralph, Earl of Westmoreland, the reversion of the Rape of Hastings, together with the manors of Crowhurst, Burwash, and Bivelham, with all profits and privileges appertaining thereto.

His father's smallholding at Warbleton and his mother's part of the manor of Gensing, in present day St Leonards-on-Sea, were the only properties he had inherited. In 1376 he was brought to trial for an alleged trespass on the land of a royal clerk at Brede and for assaulting a carpenter. So his origins were somewhat inauspicious, but he gradually gained very great influence as can be read in the History of Parliament website. He was a member of Henry V's council in England from about July 1417 to August 1422.

In 1412–13, the last year of Henry IV's reign, the remains of Hastings Castle were granted to Pelham, and in the same year he was involved in the removal of the Priory of the Holy Trinity from Hastings to Warbleton where he provided the land for a new priory. Was this his inherited smallholding? The new priory was dedicated in 1417.

> Whereas the church of the Holy Trinity of Hastyngs, and the dwelling of our beloved in Christ the Prior and Convent of the aforesaid church of Hastyngs, have been inundated and laid waste by the sea, so that they could no longer dwell there, as the said prior and Convent have given us to understand. For which reason our beloved and faithful knight Sir John Pelham, by our licence hath given and granted to the same prior and convent certain lands (at Warbleton, Sussex), etc., on which lands a new church and dwelling hath been begun, as it is said, etc.

He died on 8 February 1429 having requested to be buried at Robertsbridge Abbey.

Sir John Pelham grants the Rape of Hastings to his son, Sir John Pelham, junior (1428–1445)

In the sixth year of Henry VI (17 June 1428) Sir John Pelham, senior, just before he died, made a grant to his illegitimate son, Sir John Pelham, junior, of the Rape. Pelham's legitimate heirs, daughters of his two sisters, were seemingly ignored.

> To all the faithful in Christ to whom these present letters may come, John Pelham, senior, Knight, Greeting. Know ye me to have given, granted, and by this my present charter to have confirmed unto John Pelham, Knight, my (only) son, my lordship of the Rape of Hastings, with the manors of Crowherst, Burghersh, and Bivelham

This was a bit of a 'faux pas' on behalf of Sir John senior. It was done without the King's licence and it was deemed an 'intrusion', and the Rape reverted to the king. Pelham junior was compelled to pay a fine of 100 marks (£66.67) to release the Rape and he was pardoned for the intrusion, retaining the Rape.

7 Henry VI: April 1429 – it should be noted that Henry VI was only eight or nine at that time and the decision on this would have been taken by the Regency Council

> John Pelham, junior, that the aforesaid manors and Rape that he may again have and hold, to him and his heirs of us and our heirs by the services thence due and accustomed for ever, without let or impediment, etc. In witness, etc. Dated at Westminster, April 30th, 7 Henry VI.

John Pelham junior, in 1430, had to grant to Battle Abbey a general release from all rents, dues, and services owing to him from the monastery as lord of the same for their estates within that honour; a copy of which release was entered in the Abbey rental and is as follows :

> To all the faithful in Christ to whom this present writing may come. Sir John Pelham, Knight, Lord of the Rape of Hastings, sends greeting. Know ye that I, for the health of my soul and of the soul of Sir John Pelham, my father, and for the souls of all my ancestors, have remitted, released, and in all things quitted claim, and do hereby for myself and my heirs and all other in our names, for ever remit and release unto Thomas, Abbot of the Monastery of St. Martin of Battle, in the county of Sussex, all right, claim, and demand which I have in all lands and tenements held by the said Convent of me within the Rape of Hastings ; together with all rents and services issuing from the same, etc. In witness whereof I have to this present writing put my seal. Witness Robert Oxebregge, John Thamworth, Robert Arnod, William Arnod, John Penherste, and others. Dated at Battle aforesaid, the 24th of July, 8 Henry VI. (1430)

He had obviously transgressed against the Abbey's ancient charter and the Abbey made sure he knew it.

This episode is followed up by another interesting tale which may have been a result of Henry VI's known problems with decision-making and susceptibility to influence. In the early 1440s the Council had become concerned about how he distributed political favours. The king came of age in 1442, and in 1444 a truce had held with France for two years. A permanent peace was desired and on 22 April 1445 Henry VI was married to Margaret of Anjou, a girl of sixteen. Sir Thomas Hoo had been involved in arranging the marriage and, to the dismay of Sir John Pelham junior, Hoo suddenly received the Honour and Rape of Hastings.

The Rape is given to Sir Thomas Hoo (1445–1455): then held by his half-brother Thomas Hoo (1455–1461)

The arms of Sir Thomas Hoo

The grant to Sir Thomas Hoo, Knight of the Garter, in 1445 seems to have been awarded because of the King's wish to reward Sir Thomas for the services which he had rendered in his wars with France including fighting at Agincourt in his early years. A list of those from Sussex who fought alongside him is in the appendices. Also it was found that there was a defect in the original grant to Sir John Pelham, a grant which described the Rape as something that it was not at that time, i.e. 'parcel of the Honour of Richmond.' This error had caused the Rape never to have been officially out of the hands of the Crown. This opportune error gave the king (or more likely someone else of influence) the chance to remember the previous slight and to reward Sir Thomas Hoo, whose recent services superseded the memory of the services rendered by Sir John Pelham to Henry IV.

Sir John Pelham junior, feeling aggrieved by this grant to Hoo, presented a petition against it, quoting the grant by Henry IV to his father, Sir John Pelham, of the Manors of Crowhurst, Burwash, and Bivelham and the Rape of Hastings, after the death of Ralph, Earl of Westmoreland. The result of this petition is not recorded, but we can guess that it was ignored or turned down as Sir Thomas Hoo continued holding the Rape and was subsequently created Lord Hoo and Hastings, as in 1448 the King appointed Sir Thomas Hoo, Baron of Hoo in the County of Bedford, and of Hastings in the County of Sussex, to have the entailed title.

> Now we, of our special grace and certain knowledge and mere motion have erected, raised and created the aforesaid Thomas a Baron of our Kingdom of England …. give and grant unto the said Thomas the name, style, title, and honour of Baron of Hoo and of Hastings; and further we assign whatever of the Lordship of Hoo is within the County of Bedford and the Lordship of Hastings which is within the County of Sussex, to have and to hold, etc., to him and his heirs male for ever. Dated June 2nd, in the 26th year of the reign of Henry VI (1448)

In 1446 another Muster Roll of the Rape of Hastings was called, but this is less detailed than the previous example. A copy is in the online appendices.

Lord Hoo and Hastings was on the King's business in Normandy, in 1448 and

1449, and was governor of Mantes when the town fell to the French King Charles VII, although he was not actually present at the surrender. Following on from this Normandy was lost to England between the years 1449 and 1450. On 1 October 1449, Lord Hoo and Hastings returned to England and ceased to be Chancellor of France. He remained in England, and was repeatedly summoned to attend Parliament until his death.

Cade's Rebellion in 1450 took place during the lordship of Thomas Hoo. It was an uprising against the policies of Henry VI. Although led by property owners, most participants were peasants from Kent and eastern Sussex. No indication is found of any role by Hoo in this event.

From mid-1453 until the end of 1454 King Henry VI became mentally incapable and the Duke of York was appointed Protector during the King's illness. Lord Hoo and Hastings seems to have excluded himself from public affairs. On 24 May 1454 he pleaded that he was too sick and feeble to attend the Parliament. Nevertheless the Rape was confirmed to Lord Hoo and his half-brother also called Thomas, on 10 January 1455, just over five years after he returned from France. He died a month later on 13 February 1455 and was survived by this half-brother. Before he died he made provision for a chantry for himself and his ancestors at the altar of St Benignus at Battle Abbey His will was proved at Lambeth, on 11 December 1456.

> I, Thomas Hoo, Knyght, Lord of Hoo, and of Hastings, the Xllth daye of february, the yere of King Henry the sixt the xxxiij, beyng in good mynde, make this my wyll and ordenaunce etc .

The executors named in the will were his wife Eleanor and his half-brother Thomas Hoo; but they renounced this right, and letters of administration with the will were granted at Lambeth on 7 December 1455, to one Richard Lewknor. This was entered in the register of Archbishop Thomas Bourchier, but there is no copy of the will. He had died in possession of the Rape of Hastings, having a deed of conveyance from Sir John Pelham.

It has been suggested on the basis of the heraldry involved that the armoured effigies of the Dacre monument in the church of All Saints at Herstmonceux, said to be of Thomas, Lord Dacre (d. 1533) and his son, Thomas (d. 1528) are actually those of Thomas, Lord Hoo (d. 1455) and his half-brother, Thomas (d1486), whose family was linked to the Dacres. Ray proposed that they had been transferred from a tomb at Battle Abbey after the dissolution.

Thomas Hoo passes the Rape of Hastings to William, Lord Hastings (1461–1483)

Arms of the Hastings family, earls of Huntingdon: Argent, a maunch sable. A maunch is detachable lady's sleeve with a wide pendulous cuff. By Jimmy44. Image created for the Blazon Project of the French Wikipedia. [GFDL (http://www.gnu.org/copyleft/fdl.html) CC BY 3.0 via Wikimedia Commons

Nearly seven years after the death of his brother, Thomas the half-brother of Thomas, Lord Hoo and Hastings, passed the Rape of Hastings to Lord Hastings on 11 November 1461. William, Lord Hastings had married Katherine Nevill of the powerful Nevill family. There is no indication of why the Rape was granted to William Hastings as his base was in the Midlands, and he was already wealthy, but it may be that he just wished to become Baron Hastings of Hastings. There is little indication that either he or his two sons who succeeded to the title showed any interest in Hastings at all.

> To all the Faithful in Christ to whom this present writing may come, Thomas Hoo, Esquire, Nicholas Husee Esq., Thomas Hanwell clerk, William Gaynesford, Henry Pole citizen and goldsmith of London, Thomas Hertley clerk, and John Wodye, Greeting in God everlasting. Know ye us to have made, constituted, and in our place to have put our beloved in Christ Bartholomew Bolney, and William our true and lawful attorneys conjointly and separately to deliver for us and in our names, unto William Hastynges Lord de Hastynges, Knight, full and peaceable possession of and in the Lordship, Barony, Honour and Rape of Hastynges with their appurtenances in the county of Sussex, according to the true form and effect oi a certain Charter to the said William Hastynges thereof made ; hereby ratifying and confirming all and whatsoever they our aforesaid attorneys, or any of them, shall do or cause to be done in the premises. Witness, etc. Dated 16 November, 1 Edward IV.

The manors of Crowhurst, Burwash, and Bivelham, the hundreds of Baldslow, Hawkesburgh, and Shoeswell, and the other premises excepted in the grant from Sir John Pelham junior to Thomas Hoo, with the Castle and Rape in the preceding grant from Edward IV to Lord Hastings, were included in the above grant. As might be expected this caused dispute. So a release was executed by Lord Hastings to Sir John Pelham.

> 5 Edward IV. "This Indenture made the 28th day of Marche the fifth yere of the reigne of King Edward the IV. (1465) betweene William Ld. Hastynges Knyght, on that one partie, and John Pelham Knyght, on that other partie witnesseth that whereas divers variaunces have ben between the said parties,

for the title and possession of the Mannoires of Crowherst, Burgherst, and Thomas Hoo Grants the Rape to Lord Hastings

There was a letter of attorney from Thomas Hoo to Lord Hastings delivering:

> unto William Hastynges Lord de Hastynges, Knight, full and peaceable possession of and in the Lordship, Barony, Honour and Rape of Hastynges with their appurtenances in the county of Sussex, according to the true form and effect oi a certain Charter to the said William Hastynges thereof made; hereby ratifying and confirming all and whatsoever they our aforesaid attorneys, or any of them, shall do or cause to be done in the premises. November 18th, I Edward IV

And then final confirmation from Edward IV, which also returned the Collegiate Church of St Mary in the Castle from the crown. The extract below was preceded by a long preamble which clarified the confusing issue of Richmond mentioned above. Within the same Patent Roll is the grant of the previous possessions of Fécamp Abbey, within the Rape to Syon Abbey.

> Dated 6 February 1462 Pat. Roll Edward IV Part 5. The king confirms in fee simple to the said William Hastynges the castle, lordship, barony and honour of Hastynges, the manors of Crowehurst, Burwaysshe and Bevylham, the hundreds of Balslowe, Haukesbergh and Shosewell, and further grats to him the advowsons of the denaery and prebends of the college or free chapel within the said castle and the churches of St Clement and All Saints, Hastynges and St George, Brede, and of the churches of St Thomas the Martyr, St Giles and St Leonard at and within the town of Wynchelsee, sheriifs turns held yearly at Derfold, return of writs, wreck of sea and other specific rights. By p.s.

So who was Lord Hastings? The following is a very brief and incomplete summary collated from numbers of sources. His story is complex. William Hastings, 1st Baron Hastings, (*c.* 1431–13 June 1483) was an English nobleman who succeeded to the family estates in Leicestershire and Warwickshire and was sheriff of both counties. He supported the House of York and fought alongside Edward at the Battle of Mortimer's Cross. He was present at the proclamation of Edward as King Edward IV in London on 4 March 1461 and also when Edward secured the crown at the Battle of Towton. He became a key figure in the realm, notably as Master of the Mint and Lord Chamberlain. Whilst Master of the Mint he introduced the coinage of gold nobles worth 100d, and two other gold pieces worth 50d and 20d, which appears like an early attempt at decimalisation. He also undertook some ambassadorial duties in France, Brittany and Burgundy. When Warwick drove Edward IV into exile in 1470 and Henry VI was briefly restored Hastings went with Edward, and accompanied him back in the following spring. He raised troops for Edward and served as one of the captains of the Yorkist forces at both Barnet and Tewkesbury. In 1475 Hastings was sent to France with an invading force. A treaty of peace followed, the Treaty of Pecquigny. Hastings became even more important during the second half of Edward IV's reign. He continued to serve as Chamberlain and was also appointed Lieutenant of Calais.

Lord Hastings swore loyalty to King Edward's eldest son, but he was apparently not on good terms with Queen Elizabeth Woodville. When Richard of Gloucester tried to obtain Hastings support, Hastings seemed to be about to support the Queen's party, but eventually supported Richard's formal installation as Lord Protector and collaborated with him in the royal council. Suddenly on 13 June 1483 during a council meeting at the Tower of London, Richard of Gloucester supported by the Duke of Buckingham, accused Hastings and other council members of having conspired against his life with the Woodvilles, with Hastings's mistress Jane Shore, formerly also a mistress to Edward IV, acting as a go-between. Hastings was immediately beheaded in the Tower courtyard without any formal trial. Gloucester acceded and reigned from 26 June, being crowned Richard III on 6 July 1483.

Richard had not issued an attainder against Hastings and his family, so his wife and sons were eventually allowed to inherit his lands and properties. The death of Lord Hastings is covered by Shakespeare in his *Richard III*; he has a moderate sized part in the play, but the denouement is at the end of Act 3 Scene 4 with his final words:

> "O bloody Richard! Miserable England! I prophesy the fearful'st time to thee
> that ever wretched age hath looked upon. Come, lead me to the block; bear
> him my head. They smile at me who shortly shall be dead."

Hastings also appears in Shakespeare's *Henry VI*, Part 3.

Rape held by default by King Richard III and the Crown (1483–1486)

Richard III's rule lasted only two years, until his defeat and death at Bosworth Field on 22 August 1485. During that time the Castle and Rape of Hastings remained, by default, in the hands of the crown.

Edward, Lord Hastings resumes the Rape (1486/7–1506)

Edward was born in November 1466.

One of Henry VII's earliest measures was to pass an Act of Resumption, with a view amongst other things of reversing the ruination inflicted on adherents of the cause of Lancaster. This might be seen as just but in fact he held much of the property himself – but a fortunate 107 attainders of Lancastrians were reversed. In this Act of Resumption a particular note was made by Henry VII in favour of his faithful follower, Edward, the son and heir of Lord Hastings, to resume the Castle and Rape of Hastings, etc. It was noted:

> That William Hastings of Hastings, Knight, held at his death the Castle, Lordship, and Rape of Hastings, in the county of Sussex, and that he died on June 13th, in the first year of the reign of King Edward the Bastard " (Edward V), and that Edward Hastings, Knight, Lord Hastings, was the son and heir of the said William, and was aged seventeen years and upwards.

Edward appears to have kept his nose clean and was High Steward of Leicester and constable of Leicester Castle in 1485. He was appointed a Privy Councillor in 1504. He died in November 1506.

George, Lord Hastings, Earl of Huntingdon, holds the Rape (1506–1544)

George, Lord Hastings, Earl of Huntingdon, born in 1486/7 succeeded his father Edward, and seven years afterwards we find the following documents from the reign of King Henry VIII relative to the Rape, Castle, etc.

> 5 Henry VIII. (February 24th). A grant from John Heron and others to Richard Sacheverell and others, to the use of George, Lord Hastings, of the Manor, Rape, Castle, etc., of Hastings, with a Letter of Attorney for the possession of the same, as follows :
> (1513–14, 5 Henry VIII.}
> Henry, by the Grace of God, King of England and France, and Lord of Ireland, to all to whom these present letters shall come, Greeting. We have seen the letters patent of Confirmation of our Lord Henry the Seventh, late King of England, our father, in these words: Henry, &c. (Here follows a verbatim recital of the Charters of Henry VII. and Edward IV.).
> Now We, the said Letters and Charters, and all and singular contained in them, have ratified, and of our grace for us and our heirs as far as in us lies, do accept and approve and the same do confirm and ratify unto our beloved George Hastinges, Knight, Lord Hastinges, and his heirs, according to the tenour of the same presents, and as in such letters and charters aforesaid is reasonably witnessed. In testimony whereof we have caused these our letters to be made patent. Witness the King at Westminster, the 21st day of November in the 7th year of his reign.   For forty shillings paid into the Hanaper.

He served with Henry VIII's army in France during 1513, including when both

Therouanne and Tournai, near the present French–Belgium border, were besieged and taken. He was created Earl of Huntingdon on 8 December 1529.

In 1533 Katherine of Aragon's marriage to Henry VIII was declared null and void by Archbishop Cranmer. Henry created Anne Boleyn Marchioness of Pembroke, and on 10 October took her with him to Calais with many followers, including Lord Hastings, the new Earl of Huntingdon. She was crowned on the following Whitsunday. Two days before the coronation Lord Hastings, Earl of Huntingdon, received the order of Knight of the Bath.

George, Earl of Huntingdon, 3rd Baron Hastings, 5th Baron Hungerford, 6th Baron Botreaux and 4th Baron de Moleyns died in 1544.

11
The Lowey or Liberty of Pevensey to 1538

A marsh is a whole world within a world,
a different world, with a life of its own...
                    Guy de Maupassant (1850–1893)

The name Pevensey probably derives from an OE personal name, Pefen with the suffix ey or eye as seen applied to the many islets of the old Pevensey embayment. A less likely alternative might be *Poefn eig* (Poefn's river). In Norman times it was sometimes called Pevenesel, the similar word Peunesel was used pre-Conquest in old Latin land charters. It was never part of the Rape of Hastings, and was the seat of the castelry of the Rape of Pevensey. But it was within the Cinque Ports Confederation.

It is clearly a significant part of 1066 Country. The Lowey of Pevensey was part of the Hundred of Pevensey and comprised the parishes of Westham and Pevensey. They were entirely within the Levels and later the Lowey was regarded administratively as constituting part of the port of Hastings, as a Limb, entitled to all the privileges and immunities enjoyed by the Cinque Ports.

Some general information about Pevensey in early mediaeval times has already been described in this book, for example that it was a late Saxon foundation and that there were many salterns, and that it featured in the adventures of a number of kings. After 1066 it was also the administrative centre for the Rape named after it. We also know that Domesday recorded that Pevensey before 1066 had 52 burgesses, 28 of whom where tenants of the Bishop of Chichester or the priests Edmer, Ordmer or Doda, plus market tolls of 20 shillings and port dues of 35 shillings. By 1086 it had 110 burgesses, tolls of £4 and a small mint. The last was established in 1077 although it closed in the 1150s. The growth must have been in part due to some efforts by the first lord of the Rape, Robert de Mortain, to promote his new fiefdom. Pre-Conquest a priest called Eadmer also held the church at nearby Herste (to become Herstmonceux), this may been the same priest named above.

In 1207 the town was granted a royal charter by King John, became linked to the

Cinque Ports, and received permission to remove to a site nearer the sea, which was already blocking up the entrance to the haven. After that it was governed by Pevensey Corporation but there is no record that the township ever moved. We can note that although in the early 13th century it remained a useful port, by the end of that century the number of burgesses had more than halved to 46 and it was struggling. The focus of main activity had moved to the newly reclaimed lands on the marsh

The *Chronicle of Battle Abbey* describes Battle Abbey's long term capital investment with the purchase of land and reclaimed marsh at Barnhorne on the eastern fringe of Pevensey marshes, and their reclamation work and building of a tide mill. At first good cereal crops were produced from the newly recovered farmland. Indeed, during the 14th century the Levels generally appear to have had good new arable land, supporting an increasing rural population. The burgesses of Pevensey petitioned for a bridge over the Pevensey Haven in about 1300, to replace a ferry, to deal with increased travel from and to new farms and places like Bexhill and Wartling over the inned marshland. By 1320–6 the bridge was built.

Commissioners of Sewers (Drainage) were appointed in 1289 by Edward I to direct the work to combat flooding of the low-lying coastal areas of Sussex and they soon set to work. As soon as they started, Battle and Bayham Abbeys, large landowners at the margins of the marsh, complained that a bank was being constructed across the levels and predicted, from the knowledge that they had gained, that this would lead to flooding. The Abbeys were correct. The land started to experience more and more freshwater flooding and by 1402 much of the Levels were under water, and the outlet from the Levels to the sea via sluices was deviated further and further eastwards. Battle Abbey recorded in its Barnhorn accounts that of its 450 acres (180 ha) some 150 acres (60 ha) were sown, mainly for cereals, by 1325 but that by 1430 this had reduced to only 60 acres (24 ha), the rest being moved over to cattle and horse, the land also having become too wet for sheep. The adjacent parishes of Ninfield and Hooe also reported the loss of hundreds of acres of reclaimed marshland to fresh-water and sea-water flooding. There had been severe floods in 1401, 1402 and 1409 but a devastating flood called the 'St Elizabeth's Day' flood of 19 November 1421, killing many in the Netherlands, caused arable farming on the Levels virtually to cease. The so-called reclamation work also caused Pevensey Haven to silt up and continue to do so, and the size of vessels able to enter the port went down year on year, until finally there was only a beach-based fleet. The town may not have moved, but access to the sea certainly had. By 1337 Pevensey could only provide one ship to the Cinque Ports fleet.

To cure the freshwater flooding, a new cut was made to an outfall via a sluice at Normans Bay. This reduced freshwater flooding but then the power of the sea began to cause problems. The Commissioners were not responsible for the maintenance of the sea walls since they were the responsibility of the landowners, including the Abbeys, and it appears that because of the damage to their previously reclaimed land that farming became uneconomic and they were neglecting the walls. By the mid-1400s it was hard to find tenants for the remaining burgesses of Pevensey, and by 1538 there were only about 20 houses paying rents. Clearly, although the conversion of the Levels to farmland had bought some temporary benefits to those who owned the new land, it had had a detrimental effect on the prosperity of Pevensey Lowey. The underlying problem was that as soon as the marsh was dammed off at high tide to prevent the sea coming in, the accumulated freshwater level rose and this could only be discharged to the sea through the sluices as the tide fell. So particularly at times of high rainfall the land behind the sea wall was always at risk of flooding.

After 1538 and the dissolution of the monasteries the sea walls were neglected even further and drifting shingle blocked the tidal channels resulting in much of the Levels between Pevensey and Bexhill to return to salt marsh.

It took another 158 years beyond the scope of this book until 1696 to declare that the Inning of the Pevensey Levels had been completed, and a map showing the final situation is reproduced overleaf. Salzman and Dulley's papers describe the Inning (reclamation) of the Levels and the port and Levels in the middle ages in some detail, and Sacret's collected papers summarise much of this history. Turner has described and copied the statutes of the marshes of Pevensey dated 1402.

We know from previous chapters that Pevensey Castle played a role of some military significance during the reigns of William II Rufus, Henry I, Stephen, Henry II, Henry III, Richard II and Henry IV. Rufus had found Bishop Odo hiding there but perhaps its most famous and long siege took place in 1264–65 when the supporters of Henry III, fleeing from their defeat by the Barons at Lewes, took refuge in the Castle. By 1300, the sea had started to recede from around the Castle and its military importance declined.

William, Count of Mortain, son of Robert the first lord of Pevensey, had forfeited Pevensey in 1104 after siding with Robert Curthose against Henry I. The Castle later passed into the hands of the Laigle family, whose heirs had a hand in the foundations of the hospital at Westham and Otford/Bayham Abbeys to which they gifted properties. After this the Castle passed though many hands by various royal gift. Early in 1399 it was in the possession of Richard II, but Sir John Pelham took the Castle on behalf of Henry Bolingbroke, later Henry IV. Pelham was elected to the parliament which deposed Richard II. In 1400 he was made Constable of the Castle itself, later in 1409 he was granted the lordship of Pevensey.

Whilst Pelham held the Castle it was used as a royal prison for a while – amongst the prisoners perhaps the most important was King James I of Scotland. He had been captured as Prince James of Scotland by English pirates led by Hugh atte Fen of Great Yarmouth whilst en route to France in 1406 when still only twelve years old. The pirates were rewarded by Henry IV who already held the Earl of Douglas and Murdac Stewart, the oldest son of the Duke of Albany, after the English had defeated a Scots

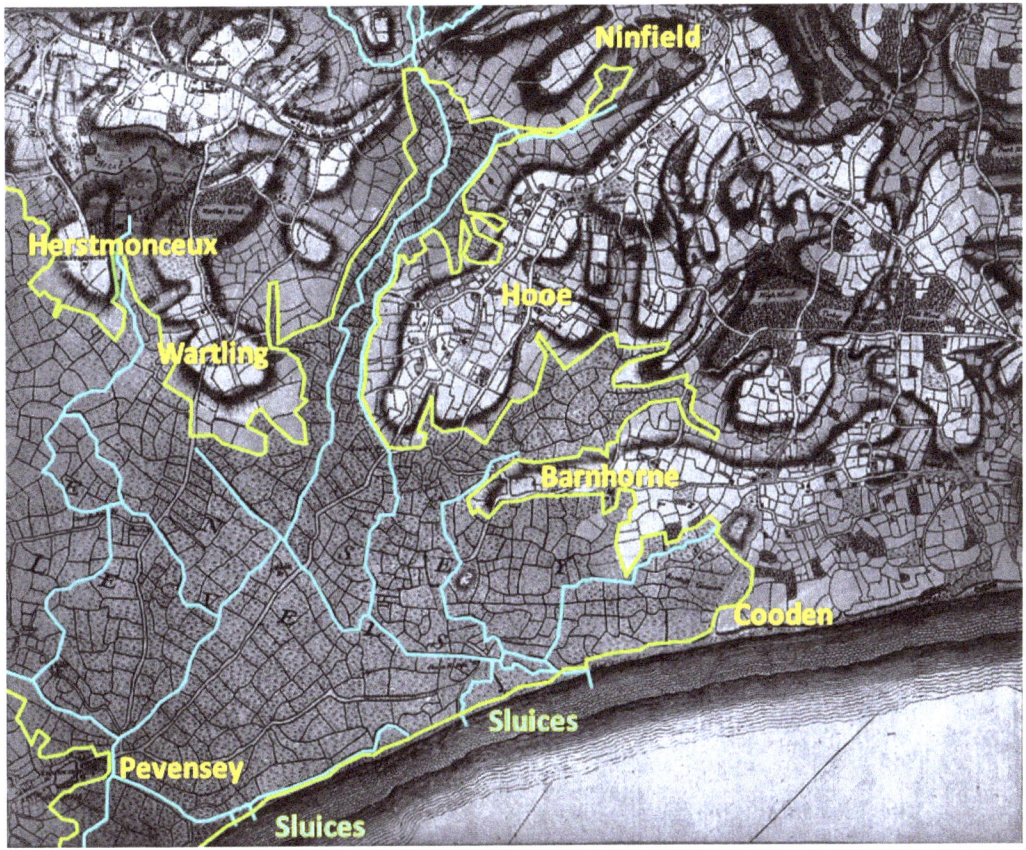

The 'end' point of the Innings after 1696. Overlays on the Yeakell and Gardner map of 1778 showing the central and eastern part of the Pevensey Levels.

The green line outlines the land recovered from marshland and the pale blue lines the major waterways and sluice positions as in the late 1700s. Other smaller dykes criss-cross the whole area. New roads cross the marsh, but all at that time converge on the bridge at Pevensey. From 1696 until today major works have been and still have to be undertaken from time to time to balance the risks of freshwater and tidal flooding. It is an area which would be at risk if there was to be a significant rise in sea level in the future.

The area is in 2019 under the management of the Environment Agency.

Overlays by Keith Foord after the concept of Salzman. ©BDHS

invading force at the Battle of Homildon Hill in 1402. Two weeks after his capture James' father King Robert III of Scotland died and James became King of Scotland, thus a very valuable hostage indeed. Henry IV took an interest in James and he was treated and educated well, and had a small Scots household. But he was moved around and was lodged not just at Pevensey, but also at Windsor, Nottingham and Kenilworth with trusted servants of the English king. On Henry IV's death in 1213 Henry V moved his Scots hostages to the Tower of London. Murdac Stewart was released in 1215 and it was probably at this time that James was moved to Pevensey, for Sir John Pelham was his custodian and for this received the sum of £70 for expenses in that year – although on his return from Agincourt Henry moved James back to the Tower of London along with his more valuable French hostages. He was moved to Kenilworth in 1418 and started regular communications with Scotland. After 1419–20 James became more closely involved with Henry V, particularly in French campaigns against the French and their Scottish allies and was clearly being used as a pawn against the French–Scots alliance. When Henry V died in 1422 his son was a minor and the regency council moved to release James, although by now given his support of Henry V against Scots in France there was some reluctance in Scotland. He eventually married Lady Joan Beaufort, a grand-daughter of John of Gaunt, in 1423 and was released in 1424 after payment of a 60,000 marks (£40,000) ransom, returning to Scotland to be belatedly crowned, with a shaky truce with England.

Other prisoners were Joan of Navarre (accused of witchcraft by her stepson, Henry V); Edward, 2nd Duke of York; and Sir John Mortimer were all held at some time between 1405 and 1423. The Castle had also functioned as a common prison after 1178. But by 1500 the Castle was unoccupied and was decaying.

The Castle, port and marshes (the Levels), with particular references to the Castle and management of the marshes have rightly received much historical attention. Harris commented in his paper on Pevensey for the Sussex Extensive Urban Survey that a scholarly study of the medieval town itself was somewhat lacking, and accurate information about the township is indeed difficult to find, although Larking has described and copied the custumal of Pevensey.

The church of St Nicholas, which is Grade I listed, is dated from about 1200 (the church dates its anniversary from 1216), when it replaced an early two-cell church, the foundations of which have been found within the inner ward of the Castle. Allan (the author of the excellent online resource about Sussex parish churches) and Rudling suggest that this may be of pre-Conquest date. Therefore it could have been the base for the priests mentioned in Domesday. St Nicholas itself was moderately large for the time it was first built, probably reflecting the town prosperity at that time and contains two fine 13th century Purbeck marble tomb slabs. It appears that the church was not enlarged much after the mid-13th century, as Pevensey township started to decline as discussed above. Post-1538 a first restoration was carried out in 1587.

The Great Seal of the Corporation of Pevensey, made of iron in about 1230, can be seen in Pevensey Court House Museum. It bears an abbreviated Latin inscription on its reverse, SCE NICOLAE, DUC, NOS, SPONTE, TRAHE, PEV which might be translated to read 'St Nicholas, lead us willingly and bring us to Pevensey', but there would undoubtedly be other possible translations.

12
Members of Parliament representing Sussex, Hastings, Rye and Winchelsea 1334 until 1538

Representatives appeared only by royal command and they treated upon those matters in which the king was interested
George L. Haskins in 'Parliament in the Later Middle Ages'
The American Historical Review, Vol. 52, No. 4 (July 1947)

The parliamentary constituencies of interest in eastern Sussex in this period are those of Sussex county and of the three tightly knit Cinque Ports boroughs or liberties of Hastings, Rye and Winchelsea, but there was of course little resemblance to the boundaries of present day constituencies. The members sent to the various parliaments from the county and the boroughs differed considerably in their backgrounds and a review of some of those who became MPs, particularly of the Cinque Ports boroughs, helps to give a flavour of life in the middle levels of society at this time

The first Parliaments of England, and subsequently of the House of Commons of England, of Great Britain and then of the United Kingdom, were composed of two members from each constituency. Indeed, a small number of these two-member seats survived until the 1950 general election, which was the first that returned members for only single-member seats.

Before the Reform Act of 1832, the electorates were not only small but boroughs varied in composition. Unlike some small towns of the same size or even smaller, Battle and its rural area never had an MP of its own under the old régime. Only the counties, and boroughs in possession of a royal charter, could boast such a privilege. Until the reform of 1832, the county of Sussex elected two MPs, as did each of the boroughs of Arundel, Bramber, Chichester, East Grinstead, Hastings, Horsham, Lewes, Midhurst, New Shoreham, Rye, Seaford, Steyning and Winchelsea. Voting was open, not secret.

It will therefore be seen that up to 1538 and indeed beyond that to 1832, the few electors for Sussex would have included all males who lived in the rural areas of eastern Sussex, including Battle, and were qualified by wealth. It is unclear as to the electoral status of the freemen of the liberty of Pevensey, which was a limb of Hastings, as their electors may have voted in the early years with Hastings. The History of Parliament website has no entry for Pevensey.

Being elected an MP for Sussex was seen as one of the duties of the local landed gentry, along with being high-sheriff or lord lieutenant or holding some other post of local or even national significance. The residences of these men can usually be identified, though some would have held land in many different places. Beyond that it is not always easy to see the areas with which the locally elected members were associated in their non-parliamentary lives, particularly at times of sectarian strife, given the present anonymity of some of their names and the wide application of some of the others. Each former MP is briefly considered where there is some local or other interesting information about him. In those days there were no hers.

The MPs selected below were for the county of Sussex, or for one of the boroughs of Hastings, Rye and Winchelsea. It should be noted that although all of Hastings, Rye and Winchelsea returned two MPs each at that that time, property owners from each borough could also vote in the Sussex elections if they held property outside the borough, but not usually vice-versa. The full lists of MPs are given in the online appendices where a blank means that the returns are missing or no information is available. Where more than two members are listed after an election, it means that the later one was returned at a by-election. Dates are given where known, but it should be noted that until 1918, general elections were held within a given period rather than on a single day.

The information about all the Sussex county MPs has been drawn from various sources by Kiloh, and he notes that in some cases sources differed and a choice had to be made. The information for Hastings, Rye and Winchelsea MPs has additionally been drawn by the author from a number of other sources which are noted below.

There were no party allegiances in the early days. In Hastings, Rye and Winchelsea the MPs were normally from the leading citizens: Cinque Port bailiffs, mayors and jurats. All had to be 'portsmen'. Comparison of the lists of leading citizens for all these towns and their MPs shows many similarities, as would be expected.

The very first parliament to invite representatives of the major towns was de Montfort's Parliament in 1265, which summoned not only the supporting barons but also shire knights, abbots, bishops and burgesses from the larger towns. Invited were two knights from each county and two citizens from each town, but no less than four men from each of the Cinque Ports. The writs sent out to summon representative to that parliament can be seen in the Close Roll of Henry III, 1264–68, 84–87 held at the National Archives. There is an excellent review of that parliament and the inspeximus of Magna Carta by Ambler.

Once Henry III resumed the throne of England, he continued to summon parliaments, sometimes inviting county knights, but on only one occasion some burgesses until his death in 1272. From Edward I's Model Parliament of 1295 onwards, representatives of the boroughs, including towns and cities, were admitted. After this, each county sent two knights of the shire and each borough sent two burgesses. The right to representation of each county was accepted, but the monarch could disfranchise boroughs at will and burgesses were almost powerless, as any independence shown by burgesses could lead to their towns being excluded. The county representatives were in a stronger position, but still less powerful than the lords and bishops in what was still a single house of Parliament. It should be noted that whilst at Udimore in November 1298 Edward I called a parliament, but it met in London in his absence, otherwise it would have been the first and only parliament to have sat in Sussex.

It was not until Edward III became King in 1327 that the Commons – representatives of the counties (knights of the shire) and of the towns (burgesses – but 'barons' from the Cinque Ports) – became a permanent part of Parliament. After 1332 the Lords and Commons sat together in one chamber, but only nine years later in 1341 the Commons were discussing matters separately from the lords, in two houses – the Commons and the Lords. Initially the Commons did not have a recognised meeting place, but in 1352 it started to meet in the chapter house of Westminster Abbey, and in 1397 it moved from there to the Abbey refectory. In 1547 Edward VI gave the Commons the use of St Stephen's royal chapel in the Palace of Westminster after the dismissal of the canons of St Stephen's at the Reformation. They met there until it burned down in 1834.

Sussex MPs 1334–1538

The gentry and knights of Sussex lived close enough to Westminster not to need long absences from their residences to attend the Commons, but Sussex was far enough away, particularly given the parlous state of its roads, to prevent the county from being dominated by London. Clearly, as a frontline coastal county, Sussex needed efficient government and adequate defence, which was organised before 1538 by its combination of resident lords, Battle Abbey and the bailiffs and more wealthy commoners of the Cinque Ports, who became jurats, and of owners of country manors, such as Bodiam. The majority of the county MPs at this time belonged to a close-knit group of Sussex families and many at some time had been engaged in royal service in Surrey and/or Sussex as commissioners or as holders of the posts of sheriff or escheator.

Sussex during a significant period was clearly under the influence of the Fitzalan family, Earls of Arundel, in particular Richard (d.1397) and Thomas (d.1415), lords of Arundel and Lewes, who held positions of supremacy in Sussex during the reigns of Richard II and Henry IV. 75% of Sussex MPs who sat in the ten Parliaments summoned between 1386 and Earl Richard's arrest for treason in the summer of 1397 were attached or somehow linked to the Earls.

There seems to have been a convention that one MP should come from the west and the other from the east, but the Sussex election results were certainly tallied and announced at Chichester. The larger places, including Battle, were where people voted.

Before 1407 the names of those chosen were generally sent to Chancery in the returns attached to the parliamentary writs. The names of Sussex-wide MPs in the appendices are as presented by Kiloh after extensive research. Some had his comments attached to their names and some are given as mini-biographies below, to give a flavour of the types of individual elected to these early parliaments.

Selected Sussex members

1378 Sir Edmund Fitzherbert (1338–93) was a Dorset man, knighted in 1372, who came to Ewhurst in about 1378. As with all landed men, he held a number of senior local offices in Dorset, Somerset and Sussex. He inherited large properties in Sussex in 1375. He served in the navy against the French in 1377 and later.

1386 Sir Edward Dallingridge (*c.* 1346–1393) held many offices in Sussex and elsewhere, including membership of Richard II's Council and, briefly, ambassador to France. He was involved in the defence of Sussex against French attacks. The Dallingridge family appears to have had a rapid rise to wealth, due to advantageous marriages; it was Edward's wife who brought Bodiam into the family. Few men could avoid involvement in the difficult politics of the time and he fell out with John of Gaunt, then the most powerful man in England. He served time briefly in prison but was released to fortify Rye and Winchelsea against the French in 1385; this led to his being licensed to crenelate Bodiam Castle.

1394–5 Sir Thomas Sackville (the second) bore a name that is rich in history, and it is well-remembered in Sussex though now best known in connection with Knole near Sevenoaks in Kent. According to one source, the Sackville family first came to Withyham in 1068, not 1066 – as William the Conqueror had left a number of supporters, including Herbrand de Sauqueville, in Normandy to keep order. They were granted the manor at Buckhurst following a marriage to the heiress of Buckhurst, Ela de Dene. Buckhurst is at Withyham, just north of Crowborough. The family lived there until the time of Elizabeth I, who was a cousin of Thomas Sackville through her mother's family, the Boleyns of Hever. Such a connection at court allowed Thomas to amass a considerable fortune, making him able to draw up plans for a new, far more elaborate mansion on the Buckhurst estate than the then existing house. The site that was chosen for the project was formerly used as a hunting box for the popular sport of deer coursing and despite being granted the vast palace at Knole by the Queen, Sir Thomas continued with his plans for Buckhurst. He also found himself being elevated to Lord Buckhurst and then to Earl of Dorset, although his descendants were to outrank him by becoming dukes.

Clearly Sir Thomas the Second, an MP at the end of the fourteenth century, was a scion of this Herbrand. He was in fact an illegitimate son of Sir Andrew Sackville (about 1306–1360), who may have been MP for Sussex, and he married Margaret, daughter of Sir Edward Dallingridge of Bodiam. The use of the suffix the second refers to a distant cousin, of Fawley in Hampshire, who may have had a better claim to the Sackville estates than had the MP. Thomas seems not to have suffered under the stigma of bastardy, which may have been lifted by the knowledge that he was indeed his father Andrew's son and had inherited a very considerable estate.

He played a minor part in the difficulties attending the end of Richard II and the accession by conquest of Henry IV, but managed to keep his lands and position. He died in 1432. His best-known descendants lived at Knole but the family had a large Sussex property.

1397 (January and September) John Ashburnham (d. 1417) was of the family that occupied Ashburnham Place, not without some gaps, up to the 1950s. His father was an improvident man who had to lease out the property, and his great-uncle had been executed for treason, which was far from unusual in families of the time. Nevertheless the future MP Ashburnham was a loyal supporter of Richard II and could wield influence at court. This did not halt his progress under Henry IV, when he was again Sheriff of Sussex. Unfortunately his accounts were not well kept and posthumous lawsuits followed in respect of his properties and his debts.

1402 Sir John Dallingridge (died 1408) was a son of Sir Edward, of Bodiam. He served with his father in naval expeditions against France and even fought in what is now Lithuania; he was then knighted. However, his father's various difficulties were visited upon him and he was suspected of disloyalty to Richard II. He was indeed associated with Richard's rival, Henry Bolingbroke, and on the latter's accession as Henry IV in 1399 became close to the crown. He was brother-in-law to Sir Thomas Sackville the Second.

The Cinque Ports Confederation and MPs

By the 13th century, the Cinque Ports Confederation was made up of the five head ports of Dover, Hastings, Hythe, New Romney and Sandwich, and the two ancient towns of Rye and Winchelsea. They had many rights and privileges and as independent boroughs elected MPs. To these head towns were attached other ports known as limbs or members stretching from Seaford in Sussex to Brightlingsea in Essex. The ports consulted together, and from the reign of Henry III they sent representatives to a Brotherhood which met twice a year at New Romney. Originally a limb of Hastings, the town of Seaford later returned its own MPs but somewhat sporadically. Pevensey was a limb of Hastings, and its portsmen living in the liberty of Pevensey may have assisted in electing Hastings MPs.

The Lord Warden of the Cinque Ports was answerable to the crown and responsible, amongst other duties, for the return of parliamentary writs. He could also appoint MPs where there was a vacancy, and otherwise had a considerable influence on who was elected. Freemen of the Cinque Ports were called portsmen, and their MPs barons. The latter honorary title reflected the similarity of their position to that of the county tenants-in-chief. Parliamentary writs of summons were delivered to the Lord Warden at Dover Castle, or in his absence to the Lieutenant of the Castle. The clerk of the Castle then issued precepts addressed to each of the ports and borne by a messenger called a boderer whom the ports paid on delivery.

The results of the elections were sent to Dover, where the clerk made a schedule of the names for despatch to Chancery, while himself keeping the indentures from the ports. An ordinance passed by the Brotherhood in 1451 that only men with municipal experience should be MPs was normally adhered to during the period to 1538, with occasional defaults and minimal external interference until towards the end, when both Archbishop Cranmer and Thomas Cromwell made nominations.

Hastings MPs 1366–1538

Little is known about many of the MPs for Hastings. Many barons were elected to two or more parliaments, but some multiple times. Richard Huntingdon stands out, being elected to nine of the parliaments called between 1413 and 1429. Most of the parliamentary barons resided in the town, and the majority owned some land in the surrounding countryside. Most must have obtained the majority of their income from trade or fishing, and a few are recorded as masters of ships. Some had held the office of Bailiff of Hastings.

In the pre-1538 period Hastings was governed by a bailiff and 12 unelected jurats chosen by him. As in other ports, the bailiff was appointed by the crown but only in Hastings was he also the head of the town government. Even though formally a crown nominee, he was normally elected annually by the freemen, known as portsmen in the Cinque Ports, meeting at the Hundred place on the second or third Sunday after Easter.

Since no election indentures (declarations of elected members) and almost no town records have survived for the period, it is impossible to know exactly how parliamentary elections were carried out at this time, but elections were normally held at a general assembly of the bailiff, jurats and portsmen in the Hundred place.

Despite being greatly decayed as a port, Hastings was still able to pay its MPs and at least one of its limbs, Pevensey, agreed on at least one occasion, to pay 20s (£1) towards parliamentary expenses in each session. This suggests that the portsmen of the liberty of Pevensey may have been part of the Hastings electorate, but this is uncertain and they may only have had representation though Sussex county. It appears that as a limb of the Cinque Port of Hastings that the liberty of Pevensey was not levied for the Lay Subsidy taxes of the late 13th century and early 14th century.

The names of Hastings' recorded MPs to 1538 are given in the online appendices. The full list has been compiled using a combination of data from: Baines' *Historic Hastings*, Thornton's *Hastings: A Living History* and the History of Parliament website. The notes below about selected members are modified from these sources.

Selected Hastings members

1383 (February) John Salerne was four times MP for Hastings 1378–83 and also for Rye in 1372–3 and 1391. He held positions for the county of Sussex a number of times including as Sheriff of Surrey and Sussex 1397–8. He became a landowner in both Kent and Sussex and was often involved in large scale financial affairs.

1410 Edward Martham attended six parliaments between 1384 and 1410. He may have been related to Batholomew Martham the Hastings Bailiff of 1316–7 and to two of the MPs who sat for Rye. He held the office of bailiff himself 1402–4. He was a wine importer and master of a ship supplied as a Cinque Port contribution to Henry V's fleet before Agincourt.

15 October 1429 Richard Hunthyngdon or Huntington was MP for Hastings no less that nine times between 1413–1429. He may have only acquired the rights of a portsman after 1410 by purchase of property as before that he is recorded as holding lands at Catsfield, Hooe and Wilting. It is suspected that he had some legal training and was involved in others' land settlements as well as in the direct employ of the Cinque Ports in conjunction with writs and legal proceedings at Westminster.

10 October 1435 John Parker was six times the MP, the Cinque Ports bailiff at Yarmouth in 1436 and 1443 and bailiff of Hastings 1439–41. He attended seven Brotherhood meetings.

Rye MPs 1366–1538

Henry II granted Rye and Winchelsea the privileges enjoyed by the Cinque Ports. After this, they stopped being limbs of Hastings, acquiring the status of ancient towns of equal status to the founding ports. Rye's bailiffship remained in royal hands and until 1358 this office had been combined with Winchelsea. From 1386 the office of bailiff was granted to royal servants as a sinecure, often for life, the profits going to provide their pay or pensions, but the duties in the town were generally delegated to deputies. However the bailiff could not take office until he had taken an oath before the mayor to observe the liberties and customs of the town.

The mayor was chosen annually by the jurats (usually twelve in number) and the commonalty of freemen (portsmen) who met annually at the Hundred place on the Sunday after St Bartholomew's day to elect a mayor. The same group appears to have carried out parliamentary elections. Re-election to successive parliaments occurred infrequently, but all the MPs identified held property in Rye and the majority lived there. Nearly all of Rye's MPs also had land in the surrounding countryside, and a few became landowners of substance, although after doing so they often lost interest in the affairs of Rye and did not stand as an MP again.

The full data is from Vidler's *A New History of Rye* and the History of Parliament website and the mini-biographies of selected members are derived from these.

Selected Rye members

16 September 1381 Simon Lonseforde was a vintner and in 1364 was licenced to buy wine from Gascony. Mayor in 1375 and 1379–80, he was joint bailiff of Rye in about 1382 with John Baddyng, and the pair ran into problems concerning financing the fortification of Rye. Lonseford left Rye and moved to New Romney for which he was MP in 1386 and he was also employed by that town to act for them in various disputes.

3 February 1388 Stephen Elyot was MP six times in 1377–88. He was mayor of Rye in 1380–2. Another vintner, he was licenced to buy wine at Bordeaux. He was outlawed in 1393 for failing to appear in court for debt, but died soon afterwards.

3 November 1391 Laurence Lonseforde was probably a brother of Simon above. He was himself three times MP in 1383–1391. He was mayor of Rye in 1387–8, 1389–90 and 1392–3. In 1393 he was accused of falsely imprisoning and nearly killing a man from Hooe.

20 October 1407 John Baddyng was probably a son of Richard Badding. John Badding was MP for Rye six times, was joint bailiff in about 1382 and acting bailiff in 1390, mayor in 1390–1, 1393–4 and 1395–7.

2 December 1420 William Longe was MP for Rye five times in 1410–20. A wine and wool merchant, he owned a ship called *Mariebote* of Winchelsea. He became one of the more notorious pirates of the time, sailing the English Channel and causing mayhem on both sides and on the high seas. This extended to events involving his crony Sir John Prendergast which threatened to break diplomatic truces. This fascinating story is beyond this chapter to cover but can be read about on the History of Parliament website and elsewhere. He died in 1426.

2 May 1421 Robert Onewyn was four times MP between 1413–1421. Onewyn was also acting mayor in 1409, mayor in 1415–17, and in1426–7 twice a jurat and deputy bailiff in 1413. He was a land acquirer but also had shipping interests and owned a ship, which on occasion was involved in piracy. He was appointed to administer the goods of the above William Longe who had died intestate, paying off Longe's debts and distributing alms for his soul.

9 November 1422 John Shelly was MP for Rye three times, 1420–22. Afterwards he went on to be MP for Sandwich three times in 1426–35. He was mayor of Rye twice and a jurat, and went on to be a Sandwich jurat, their mayor in 1426–7 and deputy mayor in 1434. Acting for the Cinque Ports he petitioned in 1417–8 against supplying an extra five ships for Henry V and was later involved in other petitions to court.

12 January 1431 William Thirlewale was MP seven times 1421–31. In 1429 the Brotherhood chose him plus a member from New Romney to plead a case for the Cinque Ports to be exonerated from a new tax.

21 January 1437 Thomas Longe, senior was MP for Rye four times in 1407–1437. A wine importer, he was an occasional pirate with his brother William (see above). He was master of the *Jesus* of Winchelsea, one of the ships sent to assist Henry V. He clearly led an interesting life being accused at Winchelsea concerning crimes committed at Portsmouth amongst other dubious adventures and related to financial dealings.

Winchelsea MPs 1369–1536

Winchelsea shares its early history with its neighbour Rye: both were originally held by Fécamp Abbey and developed together from being limbs of Hastings into ancient towns enjoying equal status with Hastings and the other Cinque Ports. In its heyday Winchelsea was a very important port in the defence of England, along with a thriving commercial trade in wool, wood and wines and many other products.

Winchelsea was held of the crown from its surrender by Fécamp in the first half of the 13th century and after this was governed largely by a crown bailiff, as noted above shared with Rye until 1358. In 1506 the bailiwick and the manor of Higham or Iham, in which the liberty of the town lay, were granted by the crown to Sir Richard Guildford and they remained in Guildford family hands until 1663.

The town has charters dating back at least to the reign of Henry II and there was an elected governing body headed by a mayor and about 12 jurats. Parliamentary elections were carried out by the portsmen in the Hundred court after 1368–9. Most of the time MP appointments were shared fairly equally among the leading townsmen and there was a greater chance of becoming an MP than there was of being made mayor.

By the 16th century, the silting up of its harbour had ruined Winchelsea's trade and from being a leading Cinque Port in its heyday, it became the least important – and had become in essence a so-called rotten borough with a handful of electors. Strangers were admitted to its freedom for the purposes of becoming an MP and the

Lord Warden of the Cinque Ports claimed the right to nominate one of the members.

The full list of members is in the online appendices and is a combination of lists from Wikipedia, the History of Parliament website and Cooper's *The History of Winchelsea: One of the Ancient Towns added to the Cinque Ports*. The mini-biographies of some of Winchelsea's MPs are given below, using these sources.

Selected Members for Winchelsea

1407 John Salerne II was the son of Simon Salerne, merchant of Winchelsea, and was related to John Salerne the entrepreneurial former MP for both Rye and Hastings (see above). He had previously in 1386 and 1388 been the MP for New Romney, probably through marriage to a New Romney property-holding widow and was active in civil duties there. He was active in the landholding market and also in trading using his mother's ship *Lythenard* of Winchelsea. He built windmills at Iham and Hastings. He died in 1411 but his line had failed and much of his wealth went to third parties; some paid for Salerne's chantry in St Clement's church, Hastings, 40 years later, an event which involved William Courthope who had been an MP for Hastings

1427 Roger atte Gate went to parliament eight times between 1399 and 1427. He was also four times mayor, in 1409–11, 1415–6, 1418–9 and 1430–1, deputy mayor in 1434 and a jurat in 1431–43. He was active in the affairs of Winchelsea and the Cinque Ports for 40 years. He probably flirted with piracy and land deals, some joint with Robert Onewyn of Rye.

Also 1427 John Tamworth sat for Winchelsea three times and was mayor 1421–2. He was a shipping merchant and land acquirer and obtained a house called Stonehall in Battle. A kinsman called Hugh Tamworth was almoner at Battle Abbey between 1438–1450. In 1435 he agreed that the Abbey could access a piece of land called Federeslond to repair a conduit and he sold this land to the Abbey in 1438.

His interests moved to the Hastings area after about 1430 and this led to his attending Brotherhood meetings on behalf of Hastings no fewer than ten times. He was also elected bailiff for Hastings at least three times as well as being Hastings' MP in 1435 and 1445.

1444 William Alard was perhaps the last of his family to live in Winchelsea. His forebear Gervase Alard was made captain and admiral of the Cinque Ports fleet in 1303 by Edward I, being elevated in 1306 to captain and admiral of the Cinque Ports. A superb chantry on the south side of St Thomas' church was installed by his son Stephen in 1312. The arch above has carved heads of Edward I and his second queen Margaret on either side, with centrally a green man.

A final word about the MPs

The full lists online and the above sketch biographies cannot be seen as the final word; much information is missing. Nevertheles, it is clear that the county was dominated by the wealthy landlords and the boroughs largely by trade and local associations. The influence of the Lord Warden of the Cinque Ports is not greatly evident from the above, except in early 16th century Winchelsea, but from the supporting evidence it is clear that it was considerable, and it became much more visible after 1538.

The electorates for the boroughs were tiny, and one may easily imagine the dealings, often corrupt, between those involved and the motives for supporting one or other of the possible candidates.

The MPs for the Cinque Ports outnumbered those of Sussex county 3:1. Some of the Cinque Ports barons were 'cultivated' by Sussex county members, sometimes as feoffees – for the portsmen could be used to avoid normal taxations. In early times, a feoffee was a trustee invested with a freehold estate to hold in possession to be transferred later either back to the holder or a third party, heir or charity. Some therefore became richer, and men such as John Salerne even obtained county appointments through their contacts.

The close relationships between Hastings, Rye and Winchelsea are obvious, not just because they were all Cinque Ports but because of the intermingling of families. One can also imagine the similar, dealings between the landowners and aristocracy who wished to represent the county as a whole, who had close social and family relationships and intermarriages.

There is no real ending. It's just the place where you stop…

Frank Herbert (1920–1996)

13
An End Piece

Eastern Sussex is a most interesting area. Even as we look at it today it remains to a degree a slightly cut off part of south-east England. Communications with the outside world remain constrained with relatively poor road and rail links. The coastal route has never been strategically utilised in the modern era for road or rail traffic from the near European mainland to the counties to the west and to Wales, a major strategic error for the nation, but something that has preserved a feeling that this is a place to belong to and which in its quirkiness has attracted artists, writers and musicians.

This is partly due to its geography: at the eastern end of Sussex, it is separated by the flat lands of Dungeness from south Kent; the marshes of Pevensey from the Vale of Sussex; and from mid-Sussex, mid Kent and Surrey by the steep sandstone hills and clay valleys of the Weald. The cross-country routes through the Weald are beautiful, but winding and narrow. In the period covered by this book, they were so poor that they could be impassable in winter.

To the south, the English Channel is ever present, reminding the coastal towns that they have no hinterland to the south and that England stops here. The sea is still exploited for fish and shellfish but on no large scale, for the fairly good harbours that existed 1000 to 600 years ago have been lost to significant coastal changes. The remaining harbour at Rye is small and tidal. Fishing is now mainly from beach launched boats, as with the famous and picturesque small fleet at Hastings, which practises ecologically sound inshore fishing. Although the coastal zones benefitted from fishing, with fish sent to market in London, and at times imports or exports in wines, lace and wool, this faded too. In its wake came piracy and smuggling, desperate trades for desperate folk.

Eastern Sussex's military history is tightly bound to its position. It was ever a possible route for invasion, and the histories in the previous chapters of this book have shown time and time again that, although all seems peaceful, many lives have been changed, influenced or lost by eastern Sussex being frontier country. It was particularly hard pressed in mediaeval times. Although there were privileges and some tax exemptions for the Cinque Ports for being the first line of national defence, there was little strength in depth. The local population was supposed to defend not only the realm but also its own towns and pastureland with the same manpower. The human and financial costs of doing so were not fully shared by the crown and the rest of England, a situation which led to deep despair, unrest, and sometimes unjust punishments if seen to fail.

It has never been a particularly rich area economically. There was early commercial exploitation for iron in Roman and early modern times, but this rapidly faded when coal started to be mined in more northern counties and the Wealden forests were no longer raped for wood to make vast quantities of charcoal. Its farmland is also mainly poor, with heavy clays hard to work, with lower crop yields than in more fortunate areas.

This volume covers the area from 1067 until 1538, as the latter date saw local critical changes. The dissolution of the abbeys and other religious houses which had multi-functional roles, as employers, as local social-welfare providers, and as extensive land-holders with many tenant farmers and creators of secondary wealth, meant great dislocation of established functional linkages. They had been a significant presence as the religious arm of firstly Norman feudal and later royal governments for 458 years and their sudden departure was to say the least a culture shock.

In this book you will have seen how the area evolved down the years, from the earliest periods when the coastline was remarkably different. The sea was an ever-present influence and economic friend, and sometimes a destroyer in great storms. It was also a cultural hazard as it provided a route for colonisers and invaders. The associated acculturations, particularly in the early days when influenced from Kent, shaped the area and left it with somewhat different outlooks from the rest of Sussex.

The Norman invasion of 1066 had led on to a period when coastal life became somewhat more dangerous. It also created major changes in land ownership. The Normanisation of an established English church, which was originally embedded in Anglo-Saxon society, changed it into a dominant force with large manorial land holdings. The church also sometimes had a military role, as seen at Battle Abbey.

The role of piety in those times cannot be overemphasised; it was one of the main features of life. There was true fear of being stuck in purgatory or going to hell in the afterlife. This led to huge financial support of the church and the establishment of some well-endowed religious houses, which became even bigger landlords through their wide landholdings. These houses were supported by gifts to pay monks to pray for forgiveness of the sins of the donors and their families and for the souls of the departed. This was expressed in the wills of even lowly folk and by extravagant bequests from the wealthy.

Life for the peasants could be grim, with life expectancies on average being 32–35 years, although it was not impossible with luck to live to old age. But all – rich or poor

13 AN END PIECE

– lived in fear of injury and illness – all could die of the complications of small infected wounds and minor illnesses. Serious injury could lead to a family losing a breadwinner and suffering extreme poverty. And of course childbearing was a time of great danger to women from complications of childbirth and from post-partum infections. If their children survived infancy child mortality was high.

This book has explored many changes across eastern Sussex, and as far as possible the results of them on the common people. This last objective is always difficult as the history is that of those who wrote it, but the effects on common folk can often be inferred. It is like writing about the tip of an iceberg, from scraps of information about royal visits, wars and quarrels in the church. Often, as I searched for a source for information which I thought might be misleading or just plain wrong, I thought of how hard to it is to look for a black cat in a dark room, particularly if there is no cat at all.

Fortunately the lists of muster rolls, poll taxes, MPs etc. can give an idea of the names of many ordinary folk, as well as an idea of their occupations or their forebears' occupations and places of origin. Some of these names are given above in the text, but in much greater numbers in the online appendices. These will be of interest genealogically, although to establish any linkages to these people is almost impossible.

The last seals of Battle Abbey were attached to the document surrendering the Abbey to the commissioners.
Left, was in red wax, the common seal of the Abbey.
Right which was in white wax is the seal of John Hammond, the last Abbot of Battle.
Images from Lower.

Appendices via BDHS websites

The decision has been made by BDHS to place all the appendices for this book on-line. These comprise illustrations, spreadsheets and tables, some of which are very large. In some cases the data can be much better appreciated on-line than formatted to fit the constraints of page size which would display them sub-optimally.

To view an appendix go to:

https//battlehistorysociety.com//CollectaneaOurVirtualLibrary and locate by its number, **or**

http://bdhsarchives.com and search using the COL code below

Paper No.	COL Code	
A3.6	COL00118	The surrender document of Battle Abbey
H1.2	COL00121	Members of Parliament for eastern Sussex 1344-1538
R4.2b	COL00101	Data for an analysis of the Rolls of Battle Abbey, otherwise known as the 'Companion Rolls to William the Conqueror' (transcribed and edited by the author from old sources freely available on line but never collated in this analytical way. This appendix is a large Excel workbook)
X2.1	COL00122	Names from Rentals of Battle Abbey: c. 1102-1115
X2.2	COL00123	Seals of the Counts of Eu and Hastings College
X2.3	COL00124	Taxation of Pope Nicholas IV within Hastings Rape: 1288
X2.4	COL00125	Lay Subsidy Rolls of the Rape of Hastings: 1296
X2.5	COL00126	Lay Subsidy Rolls of the Rape of Hastings: 1327
X2.6	COL00127	Lay Subsidy Rolls of the Rape of Hastings: 1332
X2.7	COL00128	Subsidy Rolls of the Rape of Hastings: 1411
X2.8	COL00129	Names of Sussex Men at Agincourt: 1415
X2.9	COL00130	Muster Roll of the Rape of Hastings: 1339
X2.10	COL00131	Muster Roll of the Rape of Hastings: 1446
X2.11	COL00132	Supporters of Cade Rebellion in the Rape of Hastings:1450
X2.12	COL00133	Major Tenants in the Rape of Hastings: 1475
X2.13	COL00134	Lay Subsidy Rolls of the Rape of Hastings: 1524-5

Bibliography

Al-Idrisi, M. *The Book of Roger* [*Kitab Ruyar*], 1154
Ambler, S.T. 'Magna Carta: Its Confirmation at Simon de Montfort's Parliament of 1265', *English Historical Review*, Vol. 130, August 2015: 801–830
Anon. (ascribed to Vidler, J.) *Gleanings Respecting Battel and its Abbey*, 1841
Anon. 'The Temporary Museum at Hastings', *Sussex Archaeological Collections* (*SAC*), 14. xiii, 1862
Ashley, M. *The Mammoth Book of British Kings and Queens*, 1999
Austen, E. *Brede, the story of a Sussex Parish* 1946
Bain, J. ed. *Calendar of Documents Relating to Scotland Vol.5 1108–1516* 1881. Re-edited and revised by Simpson, G.G. and Galbraith J.D. for the Scottish Record Office, 1986
Baines, J.M. *Historic Hastings* ,1955
Baines, J.M. *Sussex Notes and Queries* 11 1946
Baker, A.R.H. 'Some evidence of a reduction in the acreage of cultivated lands in Sussex during the early fourteeth century', *SAC*, 104, 1966
Balfour-Melville, E.W.M. 'The Later Captivity and Release of James I', *Scottish Historical Review* Vol. XXI, No. 82, 1924
Ballard, A. *The Domesday Boroughs*, 1904
Barber, R. *The Devil's Crown*, 1978
Baring, F.H. 'Hastings Castle 1050–1100, and the Chapel of St. Mary', *SAC*, 57, 1915
Barlow, F. *The Carmen de Hastingae Proelio of Guy, Bishop of Amiens*, 1999
Bartley, L.J. *The Story of Bexhill*, 1971
Bates, D. *William the Conqueror*, 2018
Bates, D. *Normandy before 1066*, 1982
Bates, D. *The Normans and Empire*, 2013
Blaauw, W.H. *The Barons War*, 2nd edn, 1871
Bleach, J. and Gardiner, M. 'Medieval Markets and Ports', in Leslie, K and Short, B., *An Historical Atlas of Sussex*, 1999
Bliss, A.J. 'The Companions of the Conqueror', *Litera*, vol. III, 1956
Brandon, P. Ed. *The South Saxons*, 1978
Brandon, P. and Short, B. *The South East from AD1000*, 1990
Brooks, R, *Lewes and Evesham 1264-65: Simon de Montfort and the Barons' War*, 2015
Brown, M. *James I*, 1994
Burchall, M.J. *The Medieval Sheriffs of Surrey, Sussex and Sussex Rapes 1086–1400*, CD, 2008
Burke, J.B. *The Roll of Battle Abbey, Annotated*, 1848

Burke, J.B. *Vicissitudes of Families,* 1863, Appendix has the Dives list
Burnley D. and Wiggins A. Eds. *The Auchinleck Manuscript. National Library of Scotland Advocates MS 19.2.1* https://auchinleck.nls.uk/
Calendars of Charter Rolls, Close Rolls, Fine Rolls and Patent Rolls for the reign of Edward I
Camp, A. J. 'My Ancestors Came with the Conqueror: those who did and some of those who probably did not', *Society of Genealogists,* 1988
Carpenter, D. and Gillingham, J. 'Two Kings and Battle Abbey', *Journal of Battle and District Historical Society,* 2016
Carpenter, D. *The Battles of Lewes and Evesham* ,1987
Carpenter, D. *The Minority of Henry III,* 1990.
Carpenter, D. *The Reign of Henry III,* 1996
Castor, H. *She Wolves,* 2010
Chambers, C.E, 'The French Bastides and the town plan of Winchelsea', *Archaeological Journal,* 94, 1938
Cheney, C.R. *King John and the Papal Interdict,* 1948. Text of a lecture given at Manchester University.
Church, S. *King John: England, Magna Carta and the Making of a Tyrant,* 2015
Clark, G. 'A Thousand Years of Social Mobility in England: New evidence by tracing surnames from the Domesday Book to today', *Economic History Society Annual Conference,* 2011
Cleveland, Duchess of: *The Battle Abbey Roll with some Account of the Norman Lineages,* 1889.
Cokayne, G.E. *The Complete Peerage of England, Scotland, Ireland, Great Britain, and the United Kingdom Extant, Extinct, or Dormant,* 1st Edn, 1887–1898
Cole, T.H. *The Antiquities of Hastings,* 2nd Edn, 1886
Cooper, G.M. 'Notices of Robertsbridge Abbey', *SAC,* 8, 1856
Cooper, G.M. 'The Premonstratensian Abbey of Bayham', *SAC,* 9, 1857
Cooper, W.D. 'Notes on Sussex Castles', *SAC,* 18, 1866
Cooper, W.D. *The History of Winchelsea one of the Ancient Towns added to the Cinque Ports,* 1850
Cooper, W.D and Ross, T. 'Notices of Hastings and its Municipal Rights', *SAC* ,14: 69–118, 1862
Coss, P.R. *Lordship, Knighthood and Locality: A Study in English Society, c.1180–1280,* 2004
Court roll of the Lathe court of the rape of Hastings, ESRO, AMS6281
Courthope E.J. and Fermoy B.E.R. 'Lathe Court Rolls and Views of Frankpledge in the Rape of Hastings', *Sussex Record Society,* Vol. 37, 1934
Cousins, H. *Hastings of Bygone Days and the Present,* 1920
Cowdrey, H.E.J. 'Bishop Ermenfrid of Sion and the penitential ordinances following the Battle of Hastings', *Journal of Ecclesiastical History,* 20: 225–42, 1969
Crispin, M.J., Macary, L. *Falaise Roll Recording Prominent Companions of William Duke of Normandy at the Conquest of England,* 1935
Cronne H.A. and Davis R.H.C. *Regesta Regum Anglo-Normannorum 1066–1154,* Vol. 3 1135–1154, 1968

Cushing, G. *Edward III and the War at Sea: The English Navy 1327–1377,* 2011
Davis, H.W.C. *Regesta Regum Anglo-Normannorum 1066–1154.* Vol.1. 1066–1100, 1913
Dawson, C. *History of Hastings Castle – The Castelry, Rape and Battle of Hastings, to which is added a History of the Collegiate Church within the Castle, and its Prebends,* Vols 1&2, 1909
Denton, J.H. *Robert Winchelsey and the Crown 1294–1313,* 2000
Douglas, C.H. *William the Conqueror: The Norman Impact Upon England,* 1964
Douglas, D.C. and Greenaway, G.W., Eds. *English Historical Documents,* Vol. 2 1042–1189, 1968
Douglas, D.C. *William the Conqueror,* 1964
Douglas, D.C. 'Companions of the Conqueror' *History,* vol. 28: 130–147, 1943
Douglas, D.C. 'The Ancestors of William Fitz Osborn', *English Historical Review,* 59: 62–79, 1944
Doherty, G. 'Analysis of a Document setting out the Liberties of Battle and the inhabitants of Battle, dated 1493', *Collectanea paper A3.4 from the BDHS website.* http://battlehistory.btck.co.uk/Collectanea-OurVirtualLibrary/ABlack 2018
Draper, G. *Rye: A History of a Sussex Cinque Port to 1660,* 2009
Duchesne, A. *Historiae Normannorum Scriptores Antiqui,* 1619
Dugdale, Sir W, *Monasticon Anglicanum,* 1693
Dulley, A.J.F. 'The Level and Port of Pevensey in the Middle Ages', *SAC,* 104, 1966
Eden, F.S. 'The arms of Battle Abbey', *The Connoisseur,* 86, 349, 174–5, 1930
Eyton, W. *History of King Henry II,* 1878
Farrer, W. *An Outline History of Henry I,* 1919
Foord, K and Clephane-Cameron, N. *1066 and the Battle of Hastings, Preludes, Events and Postscripts,* 2015 rptd 2016; rvsd 2018
Foord, K. *Battle Abbey and Battle Churches since 1066,* 2011
Ford, Maddox F. *The Cinque Ports,* 1900
Forester, T., Ed. & Trans. *The Chronicle of Henry of Huntingdon – The History of England,* 1853
Forester, T., Trans. *The Ecclesiastical History of England and Normandy by Ordericus Vitalis,* Vol. 1, 1853
Freeman, A.E. *The History of the Norman Conquest of England,* 1876
Fuller, T. and Brewer, J.S., Ed. *The Church History of Britain, from the Birth of Jesus Christ until the Year MDCXLVIII,* 1845
Fulton, T.W. *The Sovereignty of the Sea,* 1911
Gardiner, M. 'Shipping and Trade between England and the Continent', *Anglo-Norman Studies,* XXII: 71–93, 1999
Gardiner, M. 'Economy and Landscape Change in Post-Roman and early Medieval Sussex 450–1175', in Rudling D., Ed. *The Archaeology of Sussex to AD2000.*
Gardiner, M. *Medieval Settlements and Society in the Eastern Sussex Weald before 1420,* Ph.D. Thesis, University of London, 1995
Gardiner, M. 'Saxo-Norman Hastings, Reflections on its Development', *HAARG Journal,* New Series 8, 1999

Gardiner, M. 'Some Lost Anglo-Saxon Charters and the endowment of Hastings College', *SAC,* 127, 1989

Gelling, M. *Place-Names in the Landscape,* 1985

Gervers, M., Ed. *Dating Undated Medieval Charters,* 2002

Gibbs, V., Ed. *The Complete Peerage of England, Scotland, Ireland, Great Britain, and the United Kingdom,* Vol. 5, 1910

Giles, J.A., Ed. [Gildas] 'The Works of Gildas' in *Six Old English Chronicles,* 1866

Giles, J.A., Ed. [Nennius] 'History of the Britons' in *Six Old English Chronicles,* 1866

Giles, J.A., Ed. 'Chronicle of Æthelweard' in *Old English Chronicles,* 1906

Giles, J.A., Trans. *Roger of Wendover's Flowers of History,* 1858

Giles, J.A., *Matthew Paris's English History 1235–1278* Vol. 1, 1889

Giles, J.A., *Matthew Paris's English History 1235–1278* Vol. 2 ,1853

Giles, J.A., *William of Malmesbury's Chronicle of the Kings of England,* 1847

Gillingham, J. 'Richard I and the Science of War in the Middle Ages' in Strickland, M., Ed.. *Anglo-Norman Warfare,* 1992

Gillingham, J. *Richard I,* 2002

Gillingham, J. *William II* ,2005

Gordon, E. 'The site of Eynsham Abbey: a Historical Note' in Grey, M and Clayton N. 'Excavations on the site of Eynsham Abbey, 1971' *Oxoniensia,* XIII, 1978

Gough, H. *Itinerary of King Edward I,* Vol.1 1272–1285, 1900

Gough, H. *Itinerary of King Edward I,* Vol.2 1286–1307, 1900

Graham, R. *English Ecclesiastical Studies,* 1929

Greenway, D., Ed.. *Henry of Huntingdon, Archdeacon of Huntingdon: Historia Anglorum: The History of the English,* 1996

Hamilton, J. *The Plantagenets: History of a Dynasty,* 2010

Hardy, T.D. *A Description of the Patent Rolls, to which is added an itinerary of King John,* 1835

Hare, J.N. *Battle Abbey: The Eastern Range and Excavations of 1978–1980,* 1985

Harris, R.B. *Pevensey: Historic Character Assessment Report,* 2008

Harris, R.B. *Robertsbridge: Historic Character Assessment Report,* 2009

Haskins, C.H. *Norman Institutions,* 1918

Hearne. T., Ed. *Liber Niger Scaccarii,* 1771

Henry III Close Rolls 1216–1225

Henry III Close Rolls 1261–1264

Henry III Close Rolls 1264–1268

Henry III Patent Rolls 1216–1225

Hey, D. *Family Names and Family History,* 2000

HMSO. *Calendar of charters and documents relating to the Abbey of Robertsbridge co: Sussex : reserved at Penshurst among the muniments of lord De Lisle and Dudley,* 1873

Hodgkinson, J. *The Wealden Iron Industry,* 2008

Holinshed, R. *Chronicles of England, Scotland and Ireland* ,1577

Homan, W.M. 'The founding of New Winchelsea', *SAC,* 88, 1949

Howell, M. *Eleanor of Provence: Queenship in Thirteenth-Century England,* 1998.

Hudson, W., Ed. 'Introduction', in 'The Three Earliest Subsidies For the County of Sussex

1296, 1327, 1335', *Sussex Record Society,* Vol. 10: 15–28, 1910

Hudson, W. 'The Ancient Deaneries of the Diocese of Chichester' *SAC* , l 55, 1912

Ashdown-Hill, J. *The Private Life of Edward IV,* 2016

Jeakes, S. *Charter of the Cinque Ports,* 1728. Written in 1678 and published posthumously

Jenkins, J.C. 'Monasteries and the Defence of the South Coast in the Hundred Years War', *Southern History,* 34: 1–23, 2012

Johnson, C. and Cronne, H.A. *Regesta Regum Anglo-Normannorum 1066-1154,* Vol. 2 1100–1135, 1954

Joliffe, J.E.A. 'The Domesday Hidation of Sussex and the Rapes', *The English Historical Review,* Vol. XLV, Issue CLXXIX: 427–435, 1 July 1930

Jones, M. 'War and Diplomacy in the Making and Unmaking of the Medieval Duchy of Brittany, *c.* 1286–1491', *XXXI Semana de Guerra y diplomacia en la Europa occidental,* 2005

Keats-Rohan, K.S.B. *Domesday Descendants: Pipe Rolls to Cartae Baronum v.2: A Prosopography of Persons Occurring in English Documents 1066–1166,*2002

Kiloh, G. 'Members of Parliament who have covered Battle and District' in *Collectanea paper H1.1 from the BDHS website* http://battlehistory.btck.co.uk/Collectanea-OurVirtualLibrary/HPalegreen, 2018

Knowles, D, Brooke C.N.L. & London V.C.M., Eds. *Heads of Religious Houses England and Wales,* Vol.1 940–1216, 2001

Lappenberg, J.M. & Thorpe, B., Trans. *A History of England under the Norman Kings,* 1857

Larkin, LB. 'The Custumal of Pevensey' *SAC* 4 1851

Leland, J. [*c.* 1503–1552] *De Rebus Britannicis Collectanea,* 6 vols., Ed. Thomas Hearne, 1716

Leslie K. & Short, B., Eds, *An Historical Atlas of Sussex,* 1999

Lilley, K., Lloyd, C. and Trick, S. *Mapping the Medieval Townscape: a digital atlas of the new towns of Edward I,* York: Archaeology Data Service, 2005 Includes: Early history of Winchelsea and Design and Plan of the Town

Lower, M.A. *The Chronicle of Battel Abbey,* 1851

Lower, M.A. 'On Pevensey Castle and the recent excavations there', *SAC,* 6, 1853

Loyd, L.C. [author]; Clay C.T. & Douglas D.C., Eds.: *The Origins of Some Anglo-Norman Families,* 1951 rptd 1975

Lucy, B. *Twenty Centuries in Sedlescombe,* 1978

MacKay, A. and Ditchburn, D. *Atlas of Medieval Europe,* 1997

Maddicott, J. *Simon de Montfort,* 1994

Maitland, F.W. *Domesday Book and Beyond,* 1896

Martin, A.R. *Franciscan Architecture in England,* 1937

Martin, D. *Bexhill – The Manor House,* Rape of Hastings Architectural Survey Report 0183, 1975

Martin, D. Martin, B. and Whittick, C. *Building Battle Town, an Architectural History 1066–1750,* 2016

Martin, D. and Martin, B. 'An Architectural History of Robertsbridge' *Hastings Area Archaeological Papers,* no. 5: 88, 1975

Martin, D. and Martin, B. *New Winchelsea Sussex: a Medieval Port Town,* 2004
Martin, D. and Martin, B. *Rape of Hastings Architectural Survey,* unpublished report 0792, 1982
Martin, D. 'HAARG – Investigation of Hastings Priory site', *Sussex Archaeological Society Newsletter,* May 1973
Mason, J.F.A. 'The Companions of the Conqueror: An Additional Name', *English Historical Review,* vol. 71, no. 278: 61–69, 1956
Mason, J.F.A. 'The Rapes of Sussex and the Norman Conquest', *SAC,* 102, 1964
Mason, J.F.A. 'William the First and the Sussex Rapes', pp. 37–58, in Coakley, W.P., Ed., *1066 Commemoration Lectures,*1966
Mawer, A and Stenton, F.M. *The Place Names of Sussex* ,1969
Mawer, A. *Problems of Place Name Study,*1929
Mayhew, G. *Tudor Rye,* 1987
Moore, D. *The Welsh Wars of Independence,* 2007
Moriarty, G.A. 'The Companions of The Conqueror', *The American Genealogist,* Vol 21, No 2: 111–113, October 1944
Morris, J Ed. and Mothersill, J., Trans. *Domesday Book – Sussex,* 1976
Morris, M. *A Great and Terrible King: Edward I and the Forging of Britain,* 2008
Morris, M. *King John,* 2015
Moss, W.G. *The History and Antiquities of the Town and Port of Hastings,* 1824
Murray, K.M.E. *The Constitutional History of the Cinque Ports,* 1935
Ogbidge, B.B. *Jack Cade's Rebellion,*1869
Page, W., Ed. *A History of the County of Sussex,* Vol. 2, 1973
Page, W., Ed. 'Collegiate Churches: Hastings', *A History of the County of Sussex,* Vol. 2: 112–117, Ed. William Page, 1973
Page, W. *Victoria County History of Sussex,* Vol. 1, 1905
Paton, Sir J.N. 'Note on the Sword of Battle Abbey', *Proc. Soc. Antiquaries of Scotland,* Vol X: 463–75 plus Plates XV, XVI, 1874
Piper, J.J. *History of Robertsbridge, Salehurst Parish Church and Neighbourhood,* 1906
Planché, J.R. *The Conqueror and His Companions,* 1874
Platt, C. *Medieval England – A Social History and Archaeology from the Conquest to 1600AD,* 1994
Powlett, C. *History of Battle Abbey,* 1877
Pratt, M. *Winchelsea, a Port of Stranded Pride,* 2005
Pratt, M. *Winchelsea, the Tale of a Medieval Town,* 2005
Prestwich, M. 'The royal itinerary and roads in England under Edward I' in Allen, V and Evans, R., Eds. *Roadworks: Medieval Britain, Medieval Roads,* 2016
Prestwich, M. *Edward I,* 1997
Ramsay, J.H. *The Foundations of England,* Vol. 2, 1898
Ray, J.E. 'The Church of St Peter and St Paul at Bexhill', *SAC,* 53, 1910
Ray, J.E. 'The Parish Church of All Saints, Herstmonceux and the Dacre Tomb', *SAC,* 58, 1916
Ridgeway, H. 'Foreign Favourites and Henry III's Problems of Patronage 1247–1258,'

English Historical Review, 104: 590-610, 1989

Rigold, S.E. *Bayham Abbey* 1974, revised by Coad, J., 2016

Rose, S. *England's Medieval Navy 1066–1509,* 2013

Rotuli Chartarum. 7 February 1205

Rotuli Litterarum Patentium. 9 April 1206

Round, J.H. 'The Companions of the Conqueror' *Monthly Review,* , iii: 91–111, 1901

Rudling D., Ed. *The Archaeology of Sussex to AD2000,* 2003

Sacret, G.C. and Slater, R., Ed. *Pevensey, the Port and the Levels,* 1982, edited 2017

Salzman, L.F. *The History of the Parish of Hailsham, The Abbey of Otham and the Priory of Michelham,* 1901

Salzman, L.F. 'Political History' in Page, W., Ed. *The Victoria History of the County of Sussex,* Vol.1, 1905

Salzman, L.F. 'Documents relating to Pevensey Castle', *SAC,* 49, 1906

Salzman, L.F 'The Inning of Pevensey Levels', *SAC,* 53, 1910

Salzman, L.F. 'The Rapes of Sussex', *SAC,* 72, 1931

Salzman, L.F., Ed., *Victoria County History of Sussex,* Vol 9 ,1937, rptd 1973

Searle, E., Ed.& Trans. *The Chronicle of Battle Abbey,* 1980

Searle, E and Burghart, R. 'The Defense of England and the Peasants Revolt', *Viator.* Vol.3: 365–377, 1972

Searle, E. and Ross, B. *Accounts of the Cellarers of Battle Abbey 1275–1513,* 1967

Searle, E. *Lordship and Community – Battle Abbey and its Banlieu 1066-1538* 1974

Searle, E. 'Inter amicos: the abbey, town and early charters of Battle', *Anglo-Norman Studies XIII*: Proceedings of the Battle Conference 1990, 1–14

Shakespeare, W., *The Tragedy of Richard the Third* in Bate, J and Rusmussen, E., *William Shakespeare Complete Works,* pp. 1299–1381, 2007

Sharpe, J., Trans. and Giles, J.A., Ed. *William of Malmesbury, Chronicle of the Kings of England,* 1904

Sherley-Price, L., Trans. *Bede: A history of the English Church and People,* 1955

Smith, D., Ed. *Heads of Religious Houses England and Wales,* Vol.3 1377–1540, 2008

Smyser, H.M. 'The List of Norman Names in the Auchinleck MS', in Holmes, U.T. and Denomy, A.J., Eds., *Mediaeval Studies in Honor of J. D. M. Ford,* pp. 257–87, 1948

Stacey, R. *Politics, Policy, and Finance Under Henry III 1216–1245,* 1987.

Starr, A.J. *Making History in Pevensey,* 2017

Stevenson, J., Ed. *Simon of Durham – The Church Historians of England,* 1855.

Stevenson, J., Trans. 'Chronicle of Chronicles', published as *Florence of Worcester: A History of the Kings of England from the Invasion of Julius Cæsar to the Accession of Henry II,* 1988

Stowe, J. and Howes, E. *Annales or Generall Chronicle of England,*1615, contains le Talleurs list

Tanner, T. *Notitia Monastica,* 1744

Taylor, A.J. 'Evidence for a pre-Conquest origin for the chapels in Hastings and Pevensey castles', *Studies in Castles and Castle-building,* 1986

Temperley, G. *Henry VII,* 1917

Thornton, D. *Hastings: A Living History,* 1987

Thorpe, L., Trans. *Geoffrey of Monmouth –History of the Kings of Britain*, 1973
Thorpe, T. *Muniments of Battle Abbey,* 1835
Turner, E. 'The Statutes of the Marshes of Pevensey and Romney and the Custumal of the Town, Port and Leege of Pevensey' *SAC,* 18, 1866
Tweddle, D. *The Corpus of Anglo-Saxon Stone Sculpture:* Vol. 4 South-East England, 1996
Twiss, Sir T. *The Black Book of the Admiralty,* Vol.1, 1871
Vidler, LA. *A New History of Rye,* 1971
Walcott, M.F.C. *Battle Abbey and Notices of the Church and Town,* 1870
Weir, A. *Eleanor of Aquitaine,* 1999
West, F.J. *The Justiciarship of England 1066–1215,* 1966
Whistler, R.F. 'Penhurst: Being some account of its Ironworks, Manor House, Church, etc.' *SAC,* 36, 1888
White, G.H. 'Companions of the Conqueror' *Genealogist Magazine,* Vol VI: 51–53, 1932
White, G.H. 'Companions of the Conqueror' in *Cokayne's Complete Peerage,* rvsd edn, vol. 12, postscript to Appendix L, 47–48:
Williams, A. and Martin G.H., Eds. *Domesday Book – A Complete Translation,* 1992
Williamson, J.A. *The Evolution of England,* 1931
Willis, B. *Mitred Abbeys* Vol. 1 [1718], Vol. 2 [1719], copied in Leland, J *Antiquarii de rebus britannicis collectanea,* Volume 6, 1770

Web Bibliography

Auchinleck Manuscript: https://auchinleck.nls.uk
BDHS Collectanea papers: http://battlehistory.btck.co.uk/Collectanea-OurVirtualLibrary/
BDHS Archives: http://bdhsarchives.com/
Bishop Adam de Moleyns: http://historyinportsmouth.co.uk/events/adam-moleyns.htm
Cade's Rising – Sussex: http://www.archive.org/stream/sussexarchaeolo23socigoog#page/n46/mode/2up
Bexhill Manor House: http://www.bexhilloldtown.org/origins-of-the-manor
Charters of the Cinque Ports: http://www.ccsenet.org/journal/index.php/res/article/view/27830
Cheron, Henry (French senator): https://www.senat.fr/senateur-3eme-republique/cheron_henry0337r3.html
Dives Notre Dame Church: http://william-the-conqueror.co.uk/dives-sur-mer-the-church-of-notre-dame/
Dives Roll: http://www.robertsewell.ca/dives.html
Domesday Explorer: http://www.domesdaybook.net/domesday-explorer/domesday-explorer
Environment Agency: https://environment.data.gov.uk/catchment-planning/OperationalCatchment/3361/Summary
Falaise Roll: http://www.robertsewell.ca/falaise.html
Henry III Fine Rolls Project: http://www.finerollshenry3.org.uk/home.html
High Sheriffs of Sussex: http://www.westsussexlieutenancy.org.uk/west-sussex-lieutenancy-1540-high-sheriff-1086-1974.html
History of Parliament: https://www.historyofparliamentonline.org/
Itinerary of King John project: http://neolography.com/timelines/JohnItinerary.html
Magna Carta Project: http://magnacartaresearch.org/read/feature_of_the_month/Mar_2014
Norbury, John MP: http://www.historyofparliamentonline.org/volume/1386-1421/member/norbury-john-1414
Order of St Benedict: http://www.osb.org
Patent Rolls 1 Edward IV: https://archive.org/details/calendarpatentr14offigoog
Pelham, John MP: http://www.historyofparliamentonline.org/volume/1386-1421/member/pelham-john-1429
Percy, Lord Eustace MP: https://api.parliament.uk/historic-hansard/people/lord-eustace-percy/index.html
Robertsbridge: http://www.aboutrobertsbridge.org.uk/index.htm

Robertsbridge Abbey: http://www.scooterman.co.uk/areas/web09/founding.htm also see https://www.dhi.ac.uk/cistercians/abbeys/robertsbridge.php, https://historicengland.org.uk/listing/the-list/list-entry/1221354 and https://www.sussexrecordsociety.org/dbs/biblio/places/R/Robertsbridge/
Survey of Hastings Priory site: http://sasnews.pastfinder.org.uk/pdf/newsletter_010.pdf
Sussex Parish Churches (John Allen): https://sussexparishchurches.org/
Sussex, its Rapes and the Hundreds history: https://hydra.hull.ac.uk/resources/hull:522
Victoria County History of Sussex: https://www.british-history.ac.uk/vch/sussex/
When the French invaded England: http://britishlibrary.typepad.co.uk/digitisedmanuscripts/2015/05/when-the-french-invaded-england.html
William's Knights: http://www.hrfhs.org.uk/wp-content/uploads/2016/05/Williams-Knights.pdf
Winchelsea Excavations 1974–2000: http://www.winchelsea.net/images/WinchelseaExcavations.pdf
Winchelsea, Sussex: A medieval port town: http://www.winchelsea.net/images/WinchelseaTownMartins.pdf

Other recent books by members of the Battle and District Historical Society

Neil Clephane-Cameron and J Lawrence, *1066 Malfosse Walk*, 2000[a]
Keith Foord, *Battle Abbey and Battle Churches since 1066*, 2011[b]
Keith Foord, *The Methodist Road to Battle*, 2013[b]
Keith Foord, *Winchelsea Methodist Chapel*, 2013[b]
George Kiloh, *The Brave Remembered*, 2015[a]
Adrian and Sarah Hall, *Edmund Langdon and His World*, 2017[a]
Keith Foord and Neil Clephane Cameron, *1066 and the Battle of Hastings – Preludes, Events and Postscripts*, 2015, revised 2018[a]
Adrian and Sarah Hall (Eds), *Battle at War 1939–45*, 2019[c]

[a]Published and available from Battle and District Historical Society,
c/o 16 Upper Lake, Battle TN33 0AN or see
http://www.battlehistory.btck.co.uk/BooksandArts/HowtobuyBDHSbooks for an order form. Also available from some booksellers to order

[b]Available from Battle Methodist Church, Emmanuel Centre,
Harrier Lane, Battle TN33 0FL – see http://bmc.btck.co.uk/History.
Also available from some booksellers to order

[c]Available from Battle Museum of Local History, High Street, Battle TN33 0EA – see http://www.battlelocalhistory.com/battle-museum.html

Index

Abbeys – see under place names. There is no indexing of Battle Abbey (St Martin's Abbey) due to its frequency of appearance.
Abbots of Battle – see under personal names
Abernon, John d' 32
Adrian IV, pope x, 20, 52
Alan de Retlyng, abbot of Battle xiv, 40, 63, 66, 129–30
Alard, Gervase 119, 194
Alard, William 194
Aldingbourne, bishop's palace 25
Alexander III, pope 57, 58, 62
Al-Idrisi map x, 4
All Saints church, Hastings xv, 89, 98, 176
All Saints church, Herstmonceux 174
Alton, Hampshire 15
Amiens, mise of 30
Amulets 11
Andreadsweald 2
Anjou, Geoffrey Plantagenet count of 20, 52
Anselm, archbishop of Canterbury 12, 13, 14, 38, 47–49, 105
Apocryphal Statute (De Officio Coronatis) 116
Appledram, West Sussex 16
Arthur, son of Prince Geoffrey 23, 26, 36
Arthur II, duke of Brittany 165–6, 169
Ashburn stream 1
Atte Fen, Hugh 182
Atte Gate, Roger 194
Aubigny, Alix d' 108, 159
Aubigny, Philip d' 28
Aubigny, William d', earl of Arundel 108, 159
Auchinleck manuscript and Roll xiv, 75, 77–80, 84
Augustinian order 89
Augustinian friary, Rye xv, 90–1, 103
Baddyng, John 192
Baldwin, bishop of Worcester, archbishop of Canterbury 59
Balliol, Gilbert de 55, 159
Baranton, Drogo de 32
Barnhorn/Barnhorne 93, 181
Barons 1st War 113
Barons 2nd War xiii, 113, 121–2
Batan, Edward 105
Battle Abbey, Rolls of 73, 77, 79
Battle of Agincourt xv, 134–5, 173, 184, 191
Battle of Alnwick 108
Battle of Bosworth Field xvi, 138, 177
Battle of Brémule 157
Battle of Castillon xvi, 127, 136
Battle of Edgecote Moor 138
Battle of Hastings ix, 1, 2, 20, 43, 73, 75, 77, 84, 87, 102, 155,
Battle of Lincoln (first) 19
Battle of Lincoln (second) 28
Battle of Losecote Field (Empingham) 138
Battle of Mortemer 154
Battle of Sandwich 28
Battle of Taillebourg 162
Battle of Tewkesbury 138, 177
Battle of Tinchebrai x, 16, 50, 77, 95, 157
Battle of Towton 136, 176
Battle of Wakefield 136

INDEX

Battle of Winchelsea xiv, 130, 167
Battle of Zwin 25, 61
Bayham (Begham, Beigham, Begenham) Abbey 90–1, 106–108, 140
Beatrice of Falaise 154
Beatrice, princess, daughter of Henry III 164–5, 169
Beaufort, lady Joan 184
Beaumont, Roger de 74, 87
Beche, Hugh de 39, 56
Beche, Reinbald de 59
Becket, Thomas à x, 19, 45, 53–8
Beket, William 68
Bells of Battle Abbey church, names 71–2
Berkeley castle 124
Berwick upon Tweed, blockade 119
Bexhill x, 1, 2, 3, 5, 55, 94, 109, 149, 151, 154–5, 181–2
Bexhill, manor of 94, 158
Bexhill minster 89, 91, 93–5
Black Book of the Admiralty 24, 79, 114
Black Death vii, xiv, 5, 40, 63, 66, 91, 100, 104, 118, 128–30
Blancard, Robert ix, 38, 43–47
Blanche, niece of King John xii, 25, 36
Blanche of Navarre 169
Bodiam castle xv, 133, 148, 187–9
Bodiam, Margaret de 148
Bodiam, William de 148
Bolognia, Robert de 43
Boniface VIII, pope 122
Bourne valley, Hastings 5
Boxley, abbot of xi, 22, 109
Boyes, William 139
Brabazon, Sir Roger 120
Braose/Briouze, William de 31, 146
Brecon (Brecknock), priory of, cell of Battle 50, 64, 66, 72
Brede xi, xiv, 5, 119, 140, 171, 176
Brede manor xii, xiv, xv, 5, 29, 125, 134, 139, 151,
Brede river 2, 118
Bretigny, treaty of xiv, 129–30

Bricet, Sir Walter 22, 100
Brihtwin, beadle of Battle town 59
Brittany, dukes and dukedom xiii, xv, 154, 163–9
Brompton, Joannes, abbot of Jervaulx 84
Brompton's *Chronicle* 78, 84
Browne, Sir Anthony ii, 73, 106, 139
Buckingham, duke of 177
Bulverhythe 1, 91, 94, 106, 124
Burrell Collections – stained glass 41–2, 67
Cade Rebellion xvi, 40, 69, 111, 133, 135–6, 174, 200
Caen 75, 83
Caen, Abbaye aux Hommes 10
Cardiff castle 16
Carileph (Calais), Gausfrid de 38, 48–9
Carlisle 123
Carlisle, bishop of 39
Carmarthen 16
Castelries 141, 148
Castle, see under castle name
Catherine de Valois 134
Châlus castle 22
Chichester, See of 6, 12, 19, 55, 63, 94, 106, 144, 158
Chilham castle 25
Chinon xi, 21, 59
Chowte, Philip 104
Churches, see under name
Clare, Gilbert de, earl of Gloucester x, 19, 31, 33
Clare, Robert fitzRichard de 19, 51
Clement V, pope 122
Cleveland, duchess of 71, 76–7, 79–80
Coche, William 43
Codex, the Robertsbridge xiv, 109–10
Collegiate Church of St Mary, Hastings 89, 94, 97, 105–6
Combe Haven, river 1
Combwell affray, near Ticehurst 31
Commissioners of Sewers 181
Cordelay, William, constable of Battle 68
Corfe castle 25, 61

Cornhill, Reginald de, sheriff of Kent 61
Council of Lillebonne 154
Coutances, bishop of, Geoffrey: Also see Geoffrey de Montbray 74, 142, 156–7
Coutances, bishop of, Roger 12
Cowdray House 73
Criel, Peter de 39, 56
Dacre, lord Thomas 174
Dallingridge, Sir Edward xv, 133–4, 148–9, 188–9
Dallingridge, Sir John 189
Dallingridge, Sir Roger 148
Dawson, Henry 98
de Montfort's parliament 186
Delisle, Leopold 82
Dene, Ela de 188
Dene, Ralph de 107
Denis, abbot of Robertsbridge xi, 22, 108–9
Dering collection 70
Dieppe 25
Dives Rolls 75, 78–9, 82–3, 87
Dives sur Mer 75, 82
Doda, a priest 180
Dominican friary, Winchelsea xiv, 90, 92, 105, 124
Douglas, earl of 182
Dover 3–4, 25–6, 61, 114, 142, 189–90
Dover, bishop of 104–5
Dover castle 28, 32–4, 113, 190
Dover, Richard of, archbishop of Canterbury 56–7
Drogo de Beuvriere, count of Aumale 142
Drogo of Baraton 32
Drogo of Pevensey 157
Duchesne's Roll 75–6, 79–80
Dungeness 2, 197
Dunninc, moneyer 10
Eadmer/Edmer, a priest 180
Eadwine, moneyer 10
Ecclesiastical boundaries of Sussex 142, 144–6
Edemer, Tomas, constable of Battle 68
Edgar Atheling 14

Edith of Scotland, princess (Queen Matilda of England) 14
Edward I's Model Parliament 187
Edward, Lord Hastings 177
Eleanor of Aquitaine 20–1, 36
Eleanor of Provence 29, 36, 63, 162
Elyot, Stephen 192
Emperor Henry V 18, 20
Emperor Henry VI 22
Ermenfrid, cardinal bishop of Sion 43
Etchingham 152, 155
Etchingham family xiv, 155
Etchingham, William of 30
Eu, Alix countess of xiii, 106, 108, 153, 156, 159–62
Eu, Henry d', lord of Hastings 157
Eu, Henry II d', lord of Hastings 159
Eu, John d', lord of Hastings 158
Eu, Robert d' count of, lord of Hastings 154
Eu, William II d', lord of Hastings 156
Eu, William of, traitor 156–7
Eustace, son of King Stephen x, 19–20, 36
Evesham, battle of xiii, 33, 113
Exeter St Nicholas, priory of 39–40, 47, 49, 51, 68
Falaise Roll 75, 79, 83–4, 87
Falaise, Beatrice de 154
Falaise, treaty of 22, 108
Fécamp 25
Fécamp, Abbey of ix, xi–v, 5–6, 10, 29, 43, 89–92, 95–7, 99, 118, 125, 134, 139, 150, 176, 193
Feoffees 195
Feretory 11, 48, 50
Field of the Cloth of Gold xvi, 139–40
Fiennes, John de 121
Fiennes, Roger de xv, xvi, 135
Finch family, Winchelsea 92, 103
Fitz-Alan, John 31
Fontevrault Abbey 21–2
Foucarmont Abbey 159
Franciscan order 90
Franciscan Priory of Winchelsea xii, xiii, 29,

90, 103–4, 118
Friary of the Sack, Rye xii, 90, 92, 102
Gaunt, John of ii, 132, 134, 167, 169, 184, 188
Gausbert, abbot of Battle ix, 13, 16, 38, 46–8, 52–4, 56
George, Lord Hastings, earl of Huntingdon xvi, 138, 153 175–7
Gilbert, bishop of London 57
Gloucester, earl of 31, 33
Glottenham castle xiv, 155
Godwin, Earl 6
Godwinson, Harold ix, 10, 48, 151
Goz, Thurstan le 154
Great Park of Battle Abbey 44
Gregory IX, pope 62,
Gundalf, bishop of Rochester 12
Gunnora of Creppon 145, 154
Hammond, John, abbot of Battle 38, 40, 64, 72, 199
Hamo de Offynton, abbot of Battle 40, 42, 67
Harcourt, Lesseline de 154
Harrying of the North 43
Hæstingaceastre xiii
Hastingas 2
Hastings castle 4–5, 12–13, 15, 19, 29, 105, 120, 128, 156, 171
Hastings College of St Mary in the Castle ix, xiii, xvi, 11, 89, 94, 97, 105, 139, 157, 176
Hastings mint 6, 10, 19
Hastings peninsula 2
Hastings, lord William Hastings of 138, 175–7
Hastings, lord William Hastings of, execution 177
Hastings, Matthew de 33
Haye, John de la 31, 33
Henry VI, Part III, by William Shakespeare 177
Henry de Aylesford, abbot of Battle xiii, 39, 65, 117

Henry of Bec, abbot of Battle 38, 48
Heraldic arms of abbots of Battle 41–2
Heringod family 121
Herste – in Battle Abbey's manor 43–4
Herstmonceux – previously Herste xiii, xv, xvi, 32, 120, 135, 151, 157, 174, 180
Herstmonceux castle xvi, 121
Herstmonceux, manor of 120
High Weald 1–2
Hilary, bishop of Chichester 20, 51–2, 54, 62, 158,
Holinshed's Roll 75, 79–81
Holy Trinity priory, Hastings xi, 4, 22, 100–1, 171
Honorious III, pope 62
Hoo, Sir Thomas, Lord Hoo and Hastings 106, 156, 172–4
Hoo, Thomas (half-brother of Sir Thomas Hoo) 174–5
Hospital of St Bartholomew, Playden nr. Rye xii, 96
Hospital of St Bartholomew, Winchelsea xiii, 92, 99, 105
Hospital of St John the Baptist, Westham xiv, 92, 98–9
Hospital of St John, Winchelsea xiii, 92, 99–100
Hospital of St Mary Magdalene, Hastings xiii, 5, 89, 91, 97, 101
Hospital of the Holy Cross, Winchelsea xi, xiii, 92, 99, 105
Hospital of Thomas the Martyr, Battle 89
Hundred Years War 64, 66, 69, 127, 133–6, 164–7
Hundreds of Sussex 127, 142, 146–7
Hundreds of the Rape of Hastings 130, 132, 141, 149–52, 175–6,
Hunthyngdon, Richard 191
Iham xiii, 34, 105, 117–8, 193–4,
Ingleram de Hastings 157
Innocent III, pope 60, 62
Innocent VI, pope 66
Isabella of Angoulême 21, 23, 36, 160

Isabella of France xiv, 124–5, 127, 165
Isabella of Gloucester 36
John Crane, abbot of Battle 40
John de Dubra (Dover), abbot of Battle 39, 60–1
John de Nortburne, abbot of Battle 39,
John de Pevense, abbot of Battle, 39
John de Taneto (Thanet), abbot of Battle 39, 65, 117
John Lydbury, abbot of Battle 40
John Newton, abbot of Battle xvi, 40, 138,
John of Whatlington, abbot of Battle 39, 64–6, 117
John, bishop of Bath 12
Jordan, abbot of Otham then Bayham 107
Juliana, dowager countess of Norfolk 107
Kenilworth 183-4
Kenilworth, dictum of xiii, 33
King Æthelred II 14, 19
King Alexander II of Scotland 26
King Charles VI of France 134
King Charles VII of France 135, 137, 174
King Cnut 29
King David I of Scotland 19
King Edgar of Scotland 14
King Edward the Confessor ix, 3, 35, 105,
King Edward I xiii-iv, 24, 64–5, 90, 97, 99, 102, 107, 109, 112-124, 130, 163, 165, 181, 187, 194
King Edward I, itinerary in Sussex 102, 121-2
King Edward II xiv, 3, 64-7, 90, 92, 105, 107, 124-5
King Edward III xiv, 3, 67, 97, 123, 127, 130, 132, 136, 165, 167, 169, 187
King Edward IV xvi, 4, 136-9, 175
King George III 27
King Henry I 48-52, 95, 108, 124
King Henry II 52-3, 56, 58-9, 108
King Henry III 27-36, 39, 63-4, 77, 79, 102, 109, 113, 117, 121, 124
King Henry IV xv, 134, 136, 169–71, 173, 182–3, 187, 189

King Henry V xv, 100, 134–5, 137, 171, 183–4, 191, 193
King Henry VI xvi, 106, 111, 114, 127, 135, 137–8, 171–7
King Henry VII xvi, 4, 69, 138–9, 177–8
King Henry VIII xvi, 4, 72, 78, 106, 137, 139–40, 178–9
King James I of Scotland 182
King John xi, x, 21, 23–4, 27, 30, 39, 59–62, 98, 106–7, 113, 116–7, 121, 160–1, 180
King John, galley named 'Deulabeneie' 25
King John, itinerary 26,
King Louis VI of France 157
King Louis VIII of France 29 (also see Louis, dauphin of France)
King Louis IX of France 29–30, 63, 162
King Louis XI of France 137
King Malcolm III of Scotland 14
King Philip I of France 10
King Philip II of France 23–4
King Philip VI of France 127
King Richard I 21–2, 24, 36
King Richard I, ransom 22, 109
King Richard II xv, 4, 68, 105, 132–4, 136, 160, 167–9, 182, 187–9
King Richard III xvi, 137–8, 153, 177
King Robert III of Scotland 183
King Roger of Sicily 4
King Stephen x, 36, 51–2, 54, 157–8, 182
King William I of Scotland 22, 108
King William II Rufus ix, x, 4, 10–14, 36, 38, 47–8, 53, 105, 155–7, 182
Kingdom of Kent 2
Kingdom of Sussex 2
Knights fees for Rape of Hastings 158
Laigle, Engenulf de 102
Laigle, Gilbert de x, 22, 100, 102
Laigle, Richer 19
Laigle family ii, 182
Lambeth, treaty of 28
Lanfranc, archbishop of Canterbury 13, 46, 49, 52–3

Langley, Geoffrey de 162–3
Langton, Stephen, archbishop of Canterbury 60–2
Lathe courts 141, 147, 155
Lathes of Kent 141
Lawrence Champion, abbot of Battle 40–2, 71
Lay Subsidy Rolls 165–6, 191
Leland, John 78
Leland's Rolls 75, 78–9
Lesseline de Harcourt 154
Lewes, archdeacon of 120
Lewes castle 31–2
Lewes Priory 19, 51, 62, 69, 90, 111, 136
Lewes, battle of xiii, 32, 39, 64, 109, 113, 182
Lewes, mise of 32
Lewes, song of 112
Lillebonne, council of 154
Lincoln castle 19
Longe, Thomas 193
Longe, William 192–3
Lonseforde, Laurence 192
Lonseforde, Simon 192
Louis, dauphin of France xii, 25–9, 36, 162 – also see King Louis VIII
Louvain, Alix de, dowager queen of England 159
Luci, Richard de ii, x, xi, 19–20, 39, 51–4, 56, 58–9
Lusignan, Hugh de 23, 161
Lusignan, Ralph (Raoul) de, earl of Eu ii, 160–1
Lyons, second Council of 102
Magna Carta xi, xii, 23, 25, 27–8, 30, 33–4, 39, 62, 119, 186,
Magny, compte Edouard de 75, 82
Malling, manor of (Deanery of South Malling) 23, 58, 121, 143–6
Margaret of Anjou 135, 138, 172
Margaret de Bodiam 148
Margaret, queen of Scotland 14
Marlborough, statute of 34

Marmoutier, monastery/abbey/abbot of 38, 43, 45–6, 48
Marshall, William xii, 27–8,
Martham, Edward 191
Mary, duchesse of Brittany 167
Matilda, empress x, 18–9, 36, 52,
Maurice, bishop of London 14
Members of Parliament for Hastings 190–1
Members of Parliament for Rye 191–193
Members of Parliament for Sussex 187–9
Members of Parliament for Winchelsea 193–4
Michelham 22, 100, 102, 120
Michelham Priory xii, 4, 91, 102
Minster church, Bexhill 5, 91, 93–4
Mitred abbeys/abbots 41, 45
Monceaux, John of 121
Monceaux, Maud 121
Monceaux, Waleran de 33
Monceux, Ingelram de 159
Montbray/Mowbray, Geoffrey de 74, 157 – also see bishop of Coutances
Montfort, Eleanor de, countess of Leicester 33
Montfort, Henry de 32, 113
Montfort, Richard 33
Montfort, Simon de, earl of Leicester ii, xiii, 30–4, 64, 186
Montfort, Simon de, junior 32–3
Montgomery, Roger de 87, 144–5, 147, 156, 180
Mortain, Count Robert of ix, 10, 142, 156,
Mortain, Count William of x, 15, 95
Mortimer, Roger xiv, 125, 127
Mortimer, Sir John 184
Navarre, Joan of 184
Nevill, Katherine 175
Neville, Ralph 22, 100
Neville, Ralph, earl of Westmoreland 169–70,
New Winchelsea, freehold granted xiii, 117
Nicholas IV, pope, papal returns, 4
Noble coin 176

Norbury, John 170
Nottingham, 183
Odo of Canterbury, abbot of Battle xi, 39, 57, 59, 89
Odo, Bishop of Bayeux and Earl of Kent ix, 10, 11, 73–4, 142, 145, 155–6
Old Romney 2
Old Winchelsea ix, xi, xii, xiii, xvi, 2, 4, 7, 9, 15, 21, 25, 29, 34, 89–90, 99, 103, 114, 117–8
Oléron, sea laws of 24
Onewyn, Robert 192, 194
Ordinance of the Sea 24,
Ordmer, a priest 180
Osmund, bishop of Salisbury 12
Otham (Hottenham, Oldham) abbey xi, 90–1, 106–8,
Oxford, provisions of xii, 30, 32, 34
Papal Interdiction on England 60–3
Paris, treaty of 30
Parker, John 191
Payn, Alan 89
Peasants' Revolt 129
Peasmarsh, minster 89–91, 93–4
Pecquigny, treaty of 177
Pelham, Sir John xv, 4, 101, 134, 154, 167, 170–1, 173, 182, 184,
Pelham, Sir John, junior 171–4
Pencester, Stephen de 118
Penitential Ordinance 43
Pett Level 1
Pevensey ix–xi, xiii, xv, xvi, 2–11, 15, 25, 31–2, 82, 87, 90–1, 95–6, 98–9, 102, 106, 122, 141, 144–50, 156, 170, 180–4, 186, 189–91, 197
Pevensey castle x, xii, xiii, xv, 11, 17, 19, 21, 26, 29, 32–3, 92, 98, 102, 122, 132, 136, 162–3, 167, 170, 182
Pevensey castle church 95
Pevensey haven, river 6, 181
Pevensey islets or 'eyes' 95, 180
Pevensey Levels 182–4
Pevensey mint 6

Phillipa of Hainault 127
Pilgrims Rest 68
Plantagent, Hamelin 159
Plantagenet, Matilda 159
Poll Tax 132–3
Popes, see under pontifical name
Portsmouth x, 15, 25, 32, 61, 93–4
Preaux, Osbert de 159
Premonstratensian Order 90
Prémontré, abbey of 90
Prince Edward xiii, 31–4, 113, 162–3 – also see King Edward I
Priory valley, Hastings xiii, 4, 5, 100, 151
Queen Elizabeth II 27
Queen Elizabeth Woodville 177
Queen Matilda 43–4
Queen Victoria 27
Radynden, Alice de 148
Radynden, John de 148
Ralph de Covintre (Coventry), abbot of Battle xii, 29, 39, 63
Ralph of Caen, abbot of Battle x, 16, 38–9, 49
Ralph, bishop of Chichester 50–3
Rameslie, manor of 5, 29, 89, 150–1
Rape of Arundel xiii, 145–6
Rape of Chichester 145–6
Rape of Hastings 146, 149–50, 153–79
Rape of Lewes 144–5
Rape of Pevensey ix, xv, 2, 6, 10, 15, 145, 149, 152, 167, 170, 180,
Rape of William de Briouze (Bramber) ix, 142, 146
Reading, land at 16–8, 49
Reginald of Brecon(Brecknock), abbot of Battle xii, 31, 39, 64, 66, 117
Reginald, abbot of Bayham 107
Reginald, bishop of Chichester 48
Reinbert, sheriff of the Rape of Hastings 155, 157
Richard III by William Shakespeare 153, 177
Richard Dertmouth, abbot of Battle xvi, 40,

69, 133, 136
Richard of Gloucester 177 – also see Richard III,
Richard of Horwode, abbot of Battle xi, 39, 62
Richard Tovy, abbot of Battle 40, 70
Richard, duke of York 136
Richmond, earldom of xiii, 154, 162–70, 173, 176
Rivallis, Peter de 29
Robert Curthose ix, x, 10–1, 13–6, 19, 36, 87, 155–7, 182,
Robert de Bello, abbot of Battle xiv, 40, 66, 130,
Robert of Gloucester 19,
Robertsbridge xii, xiii, 2–3, 6, 21, 28, 108–9, 111, 118–9, 121, 152
Robertsbridge abbey xi, xii, xiv, xvi, xvii, 6, 31, 62, 90–1, 106, 108–11, 135, 139, 154, 158–9, 171
Robertsbridge Codex xiv, 109
Robertsbridge market 7, 30
Robertsbridge, hundred of 109
Roches, Peter des, bishop of Winchester 29, 63
Rochester castle 11, 31, 34
Roger, bishop of Coutances 12
Rokesle, Gregory de 118
Roman de Rou 75, 77–9, 86
Romans 2
Romeney, John de 99
Rouen xv, 10,
Rowghton, Thomas of Rowghton 114
Rye Camber xvi, 2, 5, 114, 119, 138–9,
Sackville, Ela de 107
Salehurst xi, xii, 6, 21, 90–1, 108–9, 111, 152, 155
Salehurst market 7, 30
Salehurst, prebend 106
Salerne, John 191, 195
Salerne, John II 194
Salerne, Simon 194
Sandwich, battle of 28

Saumur castle x, 52
Savoy, Peter of xii, xiii, 26, 29, 31, 120, 162–4
Scotney, Walter de 22, 100
Seffrid, bishop of Chichester 50–1
Selsey, bishop of 93, 95, 151, 155
Shakespeare and Lord Hastings of Hastings 153, 177
Shakespeare, William 79
Shareshell, Stephen, beadle of Battle town 68
Sheffield, manor of (nr. Fletching) 31
Shelly, John 193
Sidney, Sir William 111, 140
Siege of Meaux 134
Slyhand, William 98
Somerset, earl of 136
St Andrew sub Castro church, Hastings 4
St Clement's church, Hastings xiii, xv, 89, 98, 132, 176, 194
St George's church, Brede 5, 176
St Giles church, Winchelsea 90, 105, 118, 176
St James church, Northeye 93
St Katherine of Rouen, abbey of 5
St Leonard's church, Winchelsea 118, 176
St Leonard's church, Hastings xvi, 5
St Leonards on Sea 1, 171
St Margaret's church, Hastings xi, xvi, 5, 97
St Martin, Alured de 108, 159,
St Martin, Geoffrey de 108
St Martin, Robert de 108
St Mary Magdalene parish 5, 97, 101,
St Mary's church, Battle vii, x, 5, 49, 63, 72
St Mary's church, Battle, chapel of St Katherine 72
St Mary's church, Rye 5
St Mary's church, Udimore 122–3
St Mary in the Castle – see Hastings College
St Michael's church, Hastings xi, xvi, 4, 5, 100–1,
St Nicholas at Exeter, priory of 39, 40, 49, 51, 68

St Nicholas church, Pevensey 184
St Peter's church, Bexhill 6, 91, 93–5
St Peter's church, Hastings xii, xvi, 5
St Peter and St Paula church, Peasmarsh 91
St Pierre en Porte 132
St Thomas church, Winchelsea 90, 118, 176, 194
St Valery sur Somme 73, 82
Statute of Labourers 128
Stewart, Murdac 182
Steyning 146
Stigand, bishop of Chichester 46, 52–4
Sucton, Henry 105
Sussex blazon/coats of arms 148–9
Sword of Battle Abbey 40–2, 68–9
Syon Abbey xv, 91, 97, 106, 134, 139, 176
Talleur, Guillaume de's Roll 75, 78
Tamworth, John 194
Taxatio Ecclesiastica 107
The Devil's Crown 21,
The Lion in Winter 20
Theobald, archbishop of Canterbury 52, 56
Theodred, moneyer 11
Thirlewale, William 193
Thomas Ludlowe, abbot of Battle then Shrewsbury 40–1, 68–9,
Thomas Taylor, last abbot of Robertsbridge 139
Thorney, abbot of, former prior of Rochester Priory 38–9, 49
Tickhill, near Sheffield (Yorks.) 161
Tilleul, Humphrey de 74, 154
Tonbridge castle 11, 31,
Tréport 15
Tréport abbey 95, 109, 156, 158
Troyes, treaty of 134
Turnham, Michael 107
Turnham, Sir Robert de 107
Turonis, Stephen de 21
Udimore xiv, 109, 118–9, 121–3, 151, 155, 187
Vetulum, Theobald 43
Veulettes 132

Vivian, king's chaplain 38, 48
Walchelin, bishop of Winchester 12
Waldegrave, Sir Richard 133
Waleys, Henry le 118
Wallers Haven river 1
Walter de Luci, abbot of Battle x, 20, 39, 51–2, 55, 62
Wardedieu (Wardeux/Wardieu), Elizabeth 148
Wardedieu (Wardeux/Wardieu), Richard 148
Warden of the Cinque Ports 120, 190, 194–5
Warenne, countess of 21
Warenne, John de 31
Warenne, William de (earl of Lewes) ix, 145–7, 156–7
Warner, abbot of Battle x, 17, 19, 39, 50–1
Warre, John la 33
Wartling x, 15, 106, 127–8, 151, 181,
Welsh campaigns of Edward I 116
West Dean 121
Westminster abbey 14, 30, 35, 91, 97, 123, 127, 187
Westminster, palace of 35, 113, 187
Westminster, provisions of 34
Weston, Richard, prior of Hastings 102
William de Blois, earl Warenne 21
William Merssh, abbot of Battle 40, 68
William Waller, abbot of Battle 40
William Westfield, abbot of Battle 40
William, abbot of Fécamp 5
William, bishop of Durham 12
William, son of King Stephen – see William de Blois
Winchelsea, battle of xiv, 130, 167
Winchester 14, 15, 28, 41, 43–4, 142, 155
Winchester, rout of 19
Winchester, treaty of 20
Winchilsey, Robert, archbishop of Canterbury 118–9, 121–2
Wolsey, cardinal 107–8, 140
Woodstock 14, 17

Worcester cathedral 26
Wrothe, Robert 99
Wye, manor of 46, 48, 56, 59, 66, 130
Yolande, countess of Montfort 165, 169
York, Edward duke of 184
York, Richard duke of 136
Zwin 25, 61

www.ingramcontent.com/pod-product-compliance
Ingram Content Group UK Ltd.
Pitfield, Milton Keynes, MK11 3LW, UK
UKHW062045180426
11947UKWH00030B/2051